COMPARATIVE RELIGIOUS ETHICS

COMPARATIVE RELIGIOUS ETHICS

Everyday Decisions
for Our Everyday Lives

Christine E. Gudorf

Fortress Press
Minneapolis

COMPARATIVE RELIGIOUS ETHICS
Everyday Decisions for Our Everyday Lives

Cover image: Indian woman with newborn child © iStockphoto.com/Bartosz Hadyniak; Military uniform soliders row © iStockphoto.com/Ilya Andriyanov; Homeless woman crying © iStockphoto.com/ PhotoTalk; Mosque and church © iStockphoto.com/ Joel Carillet; Depressed kid © iStockphoto.com/ Imgorthand; Begging | Portrait © iStockphoto.com/ Shaun Lombard; Dancing couple © iStockphoto.com/ Oleg Filipchuk; Minks © iStockphoto.com/ Charles Taylor; Burma Novice & nuns alms collecting © iStockphoto.com/ Marcus Brown; Homeless Woman © iStockphoto.com/ Carol Thacker
Cover design: Alisha Lofgren
Book design: PerfecType, Nashville, TN

Library of Congress Cataloging-in-Publication Data
Gudorf, Christine E.
  Comparative religious ethics : everyday decisions for our everyday lives / by Christine E. Gudorf.
    p. cm.
  Includes bibliographical references and index.
  ISBN 978-0-8006-9861-4 (pbk. : alk. paper) — ISBN 978-1-4514-2621-2 (ebook)
1. Religious ethics—Comparative studies. I. Title.
  BJ1188.G83 2013
  205—dc23
                      2012035090

The paper used in this publication meets the minimum requirements of American National Standard for Information Sciences—Permanence of Paper for Printed Library Materials, ANSI Z329.48-1984.

Manufactured in the U.S.A.

18   17   16   15   14   13   1   2   3   4   5   6   7   8   9   10

CONTENTS

PHOTO ACKNOWLEDGMENTS

Fig. 1.1. Photo: Reuvenk / GNU Free Documentation License.

Fig. 1.2. Huriye Akinci Iriyari / istockphoto.

Fig. 1.3. Photo: Christine Gudorf.

Fig. 1.4. Daniel C. Maguire, *Ethics: A Complete Method for Moral Choice* (Fortress Press, 2010), p. 71.

Fig. 2.1. Photo: Andres Balcazar / istockphoto.

Fig. 2.2. Photo: Matthias Kabel / GNU Free Documentation License.

Fig. 2.3. Photo: Lisa F. Young / istockphoto.

Fig. 2.4. Photo: Magdalena Kucova / istockphoto.

Fig. 2.6. Photo: Joan Vicent Cantó Roig / istockphoto.

Fig. 3.1. Photo: John Atherton / CC-BY-SA 2.0.

Fig. 3.3. Photo: Kristian Sekulic / istockphoto.

Fig. 3.5. Photo: Maurizio Costanzo / Creative Commons 2.0 Attribution license.

Fig. 3.6. Photo: Julien Harneis / CC-BY-SA 2.0.

Fig. 3.7. Photo: Zudin / istockphoto.

Fig. 4.1. Photo: Tanuki Photography / istockphoto.

Fig. 4.2. Photo: Darren on the Road / Creative Commons Attribution 2.0 Generic license.

Fig. 4.3. Photo: Ilya Terentyev / istockphoto.

Fig. 4.4. Photo: Bernard Gagnon / CC-BY-SA 3.0.

Fig. 4.6. Photo: bravobravo / istockphoto.

Fig. 4.7. Photo: Andrey Nekrasov / istockphoto.

Fig. 5.1. Photo: Giovanni Dall'Orto. Used by permission (Wikimedia Commons).

Fig. 5.2. Photo: Boris Katsman / istockphoto.

Fig. 5.3. Photo: Christine Gudorf.

Fig. 5.4. Photo: "Niabot, with the reason in mind, that prudery shall not take over the world." / CC-BY-SA 3.0.

Fig. 5.5. Photo: Terry Lawrence / istockphoto.

Fig. 6.3. Photo: Naomi Bassitt /istockphoto.

Fig. 6.5. Photo: craftvision / istockphoto.

Fig. 7.1. Photo: 1MoreCreative / istockphoto.

Fig. 7.2. Photo: Sujit Kumar / CC-BY-SA 3.0 license.

Fig. 7.3. Photo: Luca Galuzzi / Creative Commons Attribution 2.0 Generic license.

Fig. 7.4. Photo: Wesley VanDinter / istockphoto.

Fig. 7.5. Photo: pixiduc / Creative Commons Attribution 2.0 Generic license.

Fig. 8.1. Photo: Peter Brutsch / istockphoto.

Fig. 8.2. Photo: Pattanaik / Creative Commons Attribution 3.0.

Fig. 8.3. Photo © Jorge Royan (www.royan.com.ar) / CC-BY-SA-3.0.

INTRODUCTION

Comparative Religious Ethics and the Contemporary Search for Meaning

Comparative study of religions, and by extension, comparative religious ethics, began as ways for persons from one religion, confronted by persons of differing beliefs and practices, to learn about one or more other religions and their ethical practices and beliefs. In the many decades since comparative study of religions began, we have learned a great deal. One of our most striking findings is how difficult it is to be "objective" in a study of the religions and cultures of others. This is not just a matter of prejudice, or assumed superiority of one's own religious culture, though that has certainly been a prominent problem as well. Even well-intentioned persons have encountered pitfalls in attempting to learn other religious cultures.

Perhaps the most basic problem is that we inevitably approach another religious culture limited by our own culture and experience. Limited to experiences of our own religion, we take it as the norm, though in some areas our own may be the most idiosyncratic of world religions, and not typical at all. All the concepts that we know are limited by our language; just as there are some sounds that are peculiar to some languages and not to others,

there are also many concepts that are specific to some religious cultures and not found in any form in others. Thus when we approach another religious culture, in our ignorance of the range of religious cultures we may apply inappropriate norms based on our experience of our own religion. However, it would be wrong to assume that it is those without any religion at all who are most objective in approaching any religion. For persons without any religious training at all often lack, or have already rejected, some of the most basic concepts in all religions, such as the idea that humans can experience ultimate reality and that there is a goal and purpose to human life. Without openness to such concepts, understanding religions is virtually impossible.

As in language study, once we have learned one religious culture outside our own, we not only understand our own religion more clearly and objectively, but we are better prepared to learn another and yet another more easily, because our sense of the structure of religious culture is better informed, based on our having access to more and more examples.

This pattern—the adequacy of understanding increasing with growth in knowledge of successive religious cultures—is not only true for individuals. It is also true for the discipline of comparative religion as a whole. Because there are many more scholars today who have been exposed to more religions in more depth than in the past, scholarly capacity to compare religions without distortion, while still difficult, is constantly deepening. While comparative study of religion and of religious ethics has not been in the past and is still not today totally free of religious and cultural bias, the situation has greatly improved over that of a century or two ago. Three of the factors that have facilitated that improvement are modern communications media, modern modes of travel, and migration. More and more data are available about more and more religions not only through increased publication, but also through digital means. At the same time, travel is so much faster than in the past that international conferences at which scholars from different religions from all over the world gather to exchange knowledge and perspectives are constantly occurring.

Today, for example, an academic planning an edited book on the status of women in world religions can enlist top scholars from all over the world in six or eight major religions to write first drafts on the status of women in their religion and then have all the authors fly to a single conference center for a few days of discussing and critiquing each other's work before each writes the final version of their chapter. I myself have participated in six or seven books based on this model, which was virtually impossible to organize before the Internet and certainly highly impractical before jet planes made it possible to attend intercontinental meetings that required only a day or two of travel.

Perhaps even more important for the improved quality of comparative religion scholarship is the fact that religious diasporas have moved scholars from all the world's religions to universities everywhere in the world. The nineteenth- and early-twentieth-century perspective of western scholars on all the religions of the world, originally based in their knowledge of Christianity and Judaism, has more recently been broadened and corrected by the inclusion in the dialogue and research of international scholars from all over the globe. For example, the faculty in my own university department includes an African religions scholar from Ghana, a Latin American religions scholar from Colombia, and an American Islamic scholar whose parents immigrated to the United States from Iran, as well as U.S. scholars of Buddhism, Hinduism, Judaism, Christianity, and Native American religions. I also research in Indonesia and teach in a graduate university religion program there, while other United States faculty in my department regularly research and teach in Japan, Israel, and India. The level of interreligious collaboration possible today due to these factors helps to correct many of the mistaken understandings that characterized earlier attempts at comparative religions.

Dealing with Bias

In late modernity when comparative religious studies began, attempts to eliminate bias aimed at objectivity and often attempted to "bracket" the categories and classifications and interpretations that we take with us into the study of anything new. They insisted they could thus clear a path for simply describing what our senses tell us, without our attempting to interpret the data. Bracketing was a well-intentioned attempt, but it quickly became clear that the human mind interprets new data based on what it has already learned.

Our minds are not really tablets that can be erased so that we can experience anything as completely new. Our minds always use prior knowledge to interpret what our bodies are seeing, hearing, smelling, tasting, and touching. Just as we use our knowledge of color learned in one part of our world to describe colors in another part of our world, our minds use prior knowledge of facial expressions and body language to understand new communities of humans. But since people and cultures can differ a great deal, sometimes using our prior knowledge causes us to misunderstand the new culture. Bracketing is not sufficient in part because we are often not even conscious of our use of earlier concepts, models, and patterns to interpret new ones.

Bias as Unavoidable

In the course of reading and discussing this text, you should be aware that as westerners, as Americans, we share a great many assumptions and convictions that are not shared with the rest of the world—and not because the rest of the world is less intelligent or less educated, as is often assumed. Every culture understands its own perspectives as self-evident. And there is a sense in which those assumptions are self-evident, in that they are responses to that culture's particular histories and events, geographies, and political structures. Understanding others' perspectives is often a matter of standing in another's shoes—if we had the same histories and experiences as people in another culture, we would probably see the world as they do. Westerners, perhaps especially Americans, are often somewhat blinder than persons in other cultures to the variety of ethical perspectives, and more likely to assume that ours is the best, or even the only truly ethical perspective. One reason for this is that we are such

a large nation that much of our social intercourse is with other Americans, who reinforce our moral attitudes and worldviews. We are also very aware that much of the world has admired the freedoms, prosperity, and power of the West and America, and we often interpret this as evidence that our way is best.

But there is another way to look at the fact of America's place in the world and its effect on our ethical perspectives. Precisely because America has been the most powerful and richest nation in the world for over a half century now, Americans have not needed to know other cultures—our very power and wealth have insulated us from dependence on other peoples, for it is the less powerful partner in any relationship that needs to understand the more powerful one. In the field of ethics, however, assuming the superiority of one's perspective is morally dangerous. In chapter 4, for example, we shall see how western assumptions about Muslim veiling can prevent understanding major shifts in social, political, and religious movements.

Postmodern approaches to avoiding bias have gone even further than attempts at objectivity. They consist of an acknowledgment that though we try our best, we will not be able to completely leave our own cultural framework behind, so that in addition to remaining aware of the need to be objective, we should disclose our own social locations to our audiences. Such disclosure, for example that I am a Christian (Catholic) white American heterosexual female university professor over fifty-five, allows my audience to approach my text with a hermeneutic of suspicion and to test my text for bias. Such disclosure opens up the conversation to those from other perspectives, which will significantly enrich the conversation.

Effects of Comparative Religious Education on Faith

Instructors in comparative religion have often insisted to the hesitant that exploring other religions does not undermine faith in one's own religion, but instead enables one to more fully appreciate its particular character and strengths. This is true for the most part. Still, instructors in comparative religion today have occasional students who belong to religions or denominations of religions that forbid the study of other religions/denominations, especially attendance at the worship services of other religions/denominations. Depending upon the characteristics of the students' specific religions, learning about other religions could raise questions about one's own, but this is most likely for students who do not know their own tradition well and/or whose tradition insists that it has a monopoly on truth. It is only honest to admit that the study of comparative religion develops students' critical facility. Religious cultures that are hostile to any questioning of the tradition or deny that any historical development has occurred in their tradition will not be comfortable with their youth learning of other religious traditions.

Yet just as studying the history of one's own religion opens up new understandings of the process of ongoing development that has characterized it, so studying another religion's ethical teaching makes us aware of the different priorities that can arise among the elements of religion in any religious tradition due to specific situations facing each religious community at any given time. As the situation facing the community changes, so does the priority that the community places on any single value or behavior.

Comparative Religion and the Media Explosion

The explosion of information media today has made the teachings and rituals of even the historically least well-known and seemingly exotic religions the stuff of countless blogs and individual postings. We cannot only find on the Web how to make a bomb, but we can also in an instant find explanations of Jewish kosher practices, Anglican exorcism rites, and "insider" accounts of the last papal conclave in the Catholic Church. While the easy availability of information on a multitude of religions has the potential for eradicating ignorance, which is one of the most common sources of religious bias, it also has other effects. The secrets and special knowledge that were once a strong support for religious officials' claims of authority are now plastered across the public's screens (not always accurately, one should note). Nor are the private personalities of religious authorities secret today. The mystery that once surrounded the Pope, the Dalai Lama, ayatollahs and imams, Hindu gurus, and other high-ranking religious leaders has been eroded by our seeing their faces on TV and Internet, in newspapers and magazines, and reading interviews with them. Most of these figures write, often with the help of ghostwriters, books that sell to millions. While for some this accessibility has facilitated learning of another approach to religious faith, for many people today, religious authorities have become all blended together in the broader class of celebrities—those who are simply celebrated for being famous rather than for any particular accomplishments. This has been one factor in the spread of agnosticism and secularism in the modern and postmodern world.

Growth of Agnosticism and Secularism

Today in most universities, in the larger American public, and even more in other developed nations, there are growing numbers of nonreligious persons. For some of these persons, the existence of divinity or afterlife is an unsettled question. Such agnostics are neither believers nor atheists. For some of them, religion is not a great interest in their lives, but for others, these unsettled questions provoke an interest in learning about or experimenting with religion as a way of finding answers. For those nonreligious who are atheists, who have decided the nonexistence of divinity and afterlife, there is no interest in learning about religion, and the place allocated to religion in modern life, especially in the public sphere, is seen as both mistaken and an unjust imposition on nonbelievers.

Even among those who count themselves religious believers, there is reluctance in many not only to accept that any one religion has a monopoly on truth, but even to accept that any one world religion is the principal source of truth. In short, there is an unwillingness to concede authority either to religious officials or to the religious traditions that these officials seek to represent.

Varieties of Disestablishment

In much of the world where democratic forms of government have sprung up, ensuring religious freedom has meant the disestablishment of any and all religions. Disestablishment, however, has taken various forms; the U.S. version, separation of church and state, is not the only one, and in many places is considered extreme. In Great Britain, for example, the queen is still the head of the Church of England, though citizens are not obliged to belong; and in Germany, citizens direct whether a share of their taxes goes to the Lutheran or the Catholic church, though it is possible to opt out. In many nations, one's religion is still listed on one's identity documents (birth certificates, passports), and not all religions may be recognized. A number of nations, for example, Israel, have different court systems for different religions, especially in matters of marriage, divorce, family law, and inheritance, though all citizens are subject to the national courts on other issues. The U.S. model of separation of church and state is seen by much of the world as the most secular, in that religion is made virtually completely private. Not only does the U.S. government not record—even in the census—the religion of citizens, but it cannot legislatively favor any religion in any way. The often-resented ban on local governments from displaying Christian nativity scenes at Christmas is but one example of the exiling of religion from public space in order not to use government power to impose any religion or its beliefs on citizens who are not members.

During most of the twentieth century, the challenge around religion in the United States was to protect non-Christians from both religious discrimination and from government-supported projections of Christian faith, for example, in the school systems, in holiday observance, and even in the prisons.[1] More recently, challenges have come from the nonreligious, who object to any public projections of religious faith, whether governmental or not. For example, some atheist groups have objected to religious programs on television stations that are privately owned but use the governmentally regulated airwaves. Their protests have been denied on the grounds that the separation of church and state does not require that religions have fewer rights than corporations or other associations of citizens; to support the atheist position in this would be to discriminate against religion, which runs opposite to the framers of the Constitution, who wrote separation of church and state into the Constitution not to limit religion, but to protect all religions from domination by one. Thus far, it has seemed impossible to find a policy that (1) equally allows all religious persons to freely express their religious beliefs, (2) without either permitting majority religions from using government power to project their practices on members of minority religions, or (3) subjecting nonreligious persons to direct or indirect proselytization efforts by religions.

Seeker Generations

It is a religiously interesting time. Influenced by all these movements, more university students than ever before are enrolling in religion courses across America, some even taking a major, a second major, or a minor in Religious Studies. Yet when asked about their religious status, most of these students reply that they are not "religious," they are "spiritual." What most of them mean is that they are interested in the questions of transcendence and theism, see themselves as serious seekers after wisdom, and find—or at least seek—riches hidden in the various religious traditions; but they no longer believe, if they ever did, that any one religion has enough of the answers to justify submitting themselves to the authority of that religion.

A UCLA-based study of American college youth surveyed over 112,000 college freshmen in 2004 at 236 public and private colleges and universities and then resurveyed 14,527 of these students (at 136 institutions) in 2007 as they were completing their junior year.[2] The study found that, not surprisingly, attendance at religious services declines steeply during college/university, while other forms of religious engagement show similar but smaller declines. Student levels of religious struggle—defined as feeling unsettled about religious matters, disagreeing with family about religious matters, feeling distant from God, questioning one's religious beliefs, or feeling disillusioned with one's religious upbringing—increase significantly during the college years.

Yet at the same time, the authors found that student spirituality increases alongside the decrease in religious practice. Measures of what they call equanimity—defined as "the extent to which the student is able to find meaning in times of hardship, feels at peace or is centered, sees each day as a gift, and feels good about the direction of her life"— show significant increases during the college years, and these increases are correlated with increases in grade point average, leadership skills, sense of psychological well-being, ability to get along with other races and cultures, and satisfaction with college.[3] An ethic of caring was also found to grow during students' college years, and it was found to be related to charitable involvement and ecumenical worldview in students.

Findings such as these will not reassure much of the religious community about the religious direction of the young, but they go a long way to defuse the very troubling assumption long made that religious commitment is the only source of moral values.

There are a number of reasons for this preference in the young for spirituality over religion. At one level it reflects a kind of postmodern skepticism about authority in general. Inevitably, knowing about many religions and cultures relativizes any one religion's claims of absolute authority or monopoly of truth, even if it often does also deepen our appreciation of specific practices and teachings in our own. There is also a great deal of individualism involved in this preference of spirituality over religion. Americans, like persons in many late-modern/postmodern societies, are relatively well educated and accustomed to making responsible decisions for themselves as individuals, as well as for others within their specialized occupations. Yet in many traditional religions, decision making is restricted to an elite few. For many today, the disparity between their decision-making responsibility in their inherited religion and that which is exercised in the rest of their lives is not comfortable. There is a yearning for greater religious autonomy. For some, nothing less than complete religious autonomy will satisfy. But for many others, the felt need is for *participation* in religio-ethical decision making, for basing religious community upon the collective processes of experiencing and worshipping Ultimate Reality and deciding how that experience and worship should direct ethical choices for individuals and communities, and not simply upon the experience of persons in the far-distant scriptural past interpreted today by small elites.

Then, of course, there are the many scandals in religions that have further undermined the claims of religious authority. Popular TV preachers jailed for fraud and tax evasion or exposed as adulterers and/or sexual abusers, religion as the rallying cry for war and terrorism, churches declaring bankruptcy from paying legal settlements to victims of child sexual abuse by priests, and internecine battles over poaching members from the fields of other sects—all of these have disillusioned many, not only the young, and have further disinclined individuals to concede authority to religious officials and institutions.

Private Religion

Religion scholars for more than a generation have deplored student individualism in religion, arguing that there is no such thing as a private religion. If one is to practice a faith, we professors have argued, one should be part of a community practicing that faith. A religion for one is like cooking for one—not worth the trouble. Is an individual really going to develop ritual for herself? How does an ethic develop within a private religion with no partners in discourse? We have argued with

Fig. Intro.1. Jim Bakker, former Assemblies of God televangelist, was convicted in 1989 of multiple counts of fraud and bribery involving his Praise the Lord club after he was removed from leadership following rape charges by an employee.

our students, often attempting to turn them back toward the institutional religions they came from, urging them to get involved and fix what was wrong, but not to kid themselves about having a private religion. To no avail. And now many of those students are parents, even grandparents, still disaffected with religious institutions, and still seekers.

It is time, I think, to realize that we cannot turn back the clock. Many traditional religions seem to be in decline, but religion around the world is fertile and fermenting, throwing up new experiments constantly. Many millions of persons are religious seekers, and hundreds of new religions are born every year. Many—perhaps most—of these new religions will not last, but some will eventually become large, venerated religious traditions. It is a time of global religious births and revivals, and university Religious Studies need to be interacting with this religious reality.

These young and no-longer-young skeptics have been crying for relevance in religion: How does this tradition speak to me in my situation? Too often, academic Religious Studies has not had an answer. This situation is changing as the dominant method in Religious Studies moves from textual, theological, and historical study of religions to social scientific study of religious belief and practice around the world. This is a shift in focus from what might be understood as "ideal" religion, studying religion in texts as handed down by the theological and liturgical experts, to studying what could be understood as "real" religion, as actually practiced by participants. This trend needs to grow, and more attention needs to be given to it. Mobility in the populations of the world, increased interest in interreligious dialogue, advances in communication technology, and the adaptations that occur with the spread of religions into new cultures—all of these have made our world a cauldron of religious change.

Is Seeker Religion "Private" Religion?

These seekers of all ages who cry for relevance between faith and everyday life and describe themselves as "spiritual"—are they all doomed to private (individual) religions? No. Some seekers are always finding new religious homes by either joining more open and experimental communities within previously existing religions, or by joining, even creating, new religious communities. Some of these associations will endure and some will not, for different reasons. One reason for dissatisfaction and shifting of religious affiliations is not only true for seekers, but for nonseekers as well: at different stages of our lives we have different ethical and spiritual needs.

Sociologists tell us that in the late teen years in most western religions the majority of young people drift away, either partially or completely, from the religious communities in which they were raised.[4] For some Christian churches, as many as two-thirds to three-quarters become "unchurched." This is a part of what the UCLA study was finding. But between their midtwenties and their thirties, well over half of these will return, at least for a time, largely because they have married and now have children. These returnees want their children to receive a spiritual and moral socialization. But most have no idea how to provide it on their own and so revert to the example of their own parents. Some of those who do not return will not affiliate anywhere; they may become seekers or atheists or simply religious agnostics.

There are, of course, dangers in this now well-recognized trend in religion. Scholars deplore the shallowness of much of the current interest in religion. Students often want to know "the basics," sometimes even only the most exotic practices, of a number of religions, instead of delving deeply into any one. There is a worry that much of the riches of individual religious traditions will be lost. In the "cafeteria" approach favored by many students of Religious Studies, one can choose to practice Buddhist meditation, Native American sweat lodge, or Jewish *mikvah*, the five daily prayers of Muslims, and Christian baptism. Critics charge that such a cafeteria approach ignores the intrinsic relationship between different aspects of a single tradition: each part is linked to the others, sharing a single worldview and metaphysics. Perhaps most important for ethics and spirituality, critics point out that at the heart of each religion is a discipline designed to connect individuals not only in mutual obligation to each other, but also to God/the Divine/Ultimacy. These disciplines are not easy paths. They involve multiple steps and much trial and error within the process of spiritual training. Critics doubt that choosing the most attractive practices from a number of religions will constitute a sufficiently coherent discipline to achieve the goals of divine communion and caring commitment to others.

Beyond Secularization Theory

Yet it does not seem as if the troops will go back to the barracks. We should be clear here. For a century, social scientists studying religion have debated the secularization theory: the idea that as the world becomes increasingly modern, with higher levels of education and persons involved in many different complex organizations, religion becomes less and less important, and the masses become increasingly secular. In the last decades, however, it has become clear that the conclusion of the secularization theory is false; religion is not disappearing. Andrew Greeley points out to the contrary that following the disintegration of the Soviet Union in 1991 religion enjoyed a strong resurgence throughout Eastern Europe and Russia.[5] In Europe as a whole over the last decades, religion has been not only both advancing and retreating, depending upon the local situation, but also changing and becoming less institutional. Religion in China has been on the rise for some decades now, and new religions are springing up all over the world. New forms of Christian Pentecostalism are enrolling many millions across Asia and are coming close to becoming the religion of the majority in some nations of Africa and Latin America.

Persons Both Secular and Religious

Yet at the same time that religion is not dying out, the role of religion in human society has definitely been changing during this end of modernity and beginning of postmodernity. Even among the religious, religion is becoming more and more voluntary—that is, chosen by the individual—instead of prescribed by one's family, even though extended families often choose to follow one of their members into a new faith. This increasing voluntariness of religious identity and membership means that religion is a serious interest for many today at the same time that religion in much of the world, certainly in the West, has been pushed out of organized public life.

Before the modern era, when a new religion arose it was taken for granted that when it enrolled the controlling powers (a monarch, the aristocracy, the military) of a nation, it would become the state religion. When one state conquered another, it almost always imposed participation in its own religion on the conquered, though often not attempting to eradicate the previous religion. Many states, for example, the Roman Empire until the fourth to sixth centuries, dealt with religious challenges to the established religious cult by simply including the new god in their pantheon. Nor is this pattern historically obsolete. Especially in Asia, where native religions have never been exclusivist as have the western Abrahamic religions (Judaism, Christianity, and Islam), we commonly see Japanese marrying in Shinto rites and dying with Buddhist funeral rituals. For religious Chinese, their practice is often a mixture of Daoist, Buddhist, and Confucian traditions. In the Hindu pantheon, there are not only a multitude of gods and goddesses that are the accumulation of different geographical areas and historical periods, but a number of deities are called by a variety of names and titles with different origins, clues as to past amalgamations of religious cults.

The western Abrahamic faiths have strongly resisted inclusion of beliefs and practices of other religions. Of course, such inclusion has taken place despite official policies to the contrary, sometimes at the initiative of religious officials, and sometimes despite their efforts. An example of the former would be the adoption of Christmas by the Christian church. Missionaries in northern Europe were faced with the difficulty of converting the local population, given that conversion would bar them from participating in the communal celebrations to the gods that marked the winter solstice. By deciding to celebrate the birth of Jesus Christ on December 25, the missionaries established an alternative reason for celebrating with Christmas trees, yule logs, mistletoe, and the foods and drink of the winter solstice celebration.

An example of the latter pattern, where adoption of practices or beliefs from other religions was opposed by religious officials yet occurred nonetheless, was the worship by ancient Jews of Yahweh alongside his consort Asherah, a Ugaritic goddess commonly worshipped in Canaan. Though biblical evidence was sparse, more recent archeological excavations, many from the eighth century BCE, have unearthed a number of artifacts that mention Yahweh and his Asherah. Most scholars now agree that monotheism developed slowly among the ancient Jews, many of whom worshipped Yahweh and Asherah—the pairing of gods being common in the Ancient Near East—until priestly monotheism, aided by the 586 BCE conquest by the Babylonians, was finally able to prevail.

Some western religions still forbid the inclusion of "foreign" practices in worship, such as the Vatican teaching that forbids Catholics from practicing Buddhist meditation. Yet the very reason for announcing such bans is that many members of the church are practicing such meditation. Buddhist meditation and yoga have become common practices among many Jews and Christians, and even among small but increasing numbers of Muslims. Today in the Unites States many people practice the purification rites of their own as well as other religions, such as Native American sweat lodge or Ramadan-type fasting, as part of seeking a higher level of religious consciousness.

At the same time, some barriers are breaking down between religious sects. In the United States for example, there was until the last forty years a fairly strong division between Catholic and Protestant Christian hymns. As the Second Vatican Council (1962–1965) reformed Catholic worship toward more congregational participation and the use of the vernacular, Catholic music directors were hard-pressed for some years to find sufficient substitutions for the Gregorian chant and Latin hymns that had prevailed before. New liturgical music was developed, but in the process people realized that except for the Catholic emphasis on Eucharist in many of the new hymns, it was difficult to tell the difference between Protestant and Catholic hymns. So old Protestant standards, such as "Amazing Grace," and even Luther's "A Mighty Fortress Is Our God," became familiar mass music for Catholics at the same time that some of the new hymns developed for Catholic worship appeared in Lutheran and Presbyterian hymnals.

Audience for This Text: Seeker-Skeptics

This book is written for the seeker-skeptical students of Religious Studies who know that there is something valuable to be found in the study of religion, however reluctant they may be to sign on to any one existing religion. We will have to wait and see how the present shake-up of religions works itself out and whether the seeker-skeptics will yet find organized religious communities that suit their needs. Meanwhile, within their search for religious meaning, they will test varied religious teachings within the structures of their everyday lives. They will attempt to see, for example, whether any of the teachings of religions on human work relate to their experience of work, how their welfare as defined by religions is connected to that of needy strangers, and whether what religions say about the roles of food and body adornment is relevant for their project of creating self-identity. This book is a resource for such analysis.

Religion, if it is alive, is a part of everyday life, not a few moments periodically outside that life. In this volume, we will examine various aspects of everyday life and the moral decisions we make concerning them—about eating, working, covering our bodies, sex, friends and family, anger and violence, and charity—looking to isolate the ethical problems felt by living persons today, the concerns that world religions have had ethical discourse about in these areas of life, and areas of overlap between the two.

The ethical systems of religions have much more in common than do their belief or ritual systems, because the members of very different religions often had very similar life experiences, and because religions did not invent basic human values, but rather built upon them. Human experience has always grounded the establishment of religions; it was through human experience that values were discovered and lifted up. The real differences that do exist within comparative religious ethics are largely the result of the different cultural, historical, geographical, and even climatological contexts in which those religions developed, as each focused on using a body of largely similar human values in resolving the particular set of problems facing it. Some values took on greater priority in specific situations.

Biblical scholars have often pointed out, for example, that because of the harshness of the semi-arid Ancient Near East, the value of hospitality became highly developed and took on an ethical priority in the religions born there (Judaism, Islam, and Christianity) that was not found in more temperate zones.[6] The very existence of trade and travel in the Ancient Near East depended upon a collective willingness to share water wells and even food with weary travelers. For this reason, many of the stories in the Christian Old Testament/Hebrew Scriptures revolve around the virtue of hospitality and meetings at wells. A number of the stories about the Jewish patriarchs in the Hebrew Scriptures, and about Jesus in the Christian New Testament, occur at wells, and a number of Muslim hadith deal with justice around owning, sharing, and using wells.

What This Text Will Not Do

It is perhaps necessary to also say what this text will not do. It will not compare meta-ethical systems of religions.[7] It will not lay out the moral worldview and basic moral principles of the world religions.[8] It is not focused on comparative religious ethics as a basis for doing interreligious dialogue.[9] It will not compare comprehensive thought systems of ethical leaders in the various religions.[10] Instead, this text will attempt to lift up values, meanings, and interpretations from religions and also from "secular" thought (most of which has been influenced by the dominant religion of the culture) that are relevant to the most basic interests and activities of contemporary human beings in North America. The text will not try to convince readers of the truth of any one religion or of the superiority of any one system of religious ethics.

Instead, the focus will be eminently practical. The text will try to demonstrate that because humans have been virtually unanimously religious from our very origins, a great deal of the treasury of human wisdom and training in virtue is to be found within the religious traditions of the world, despite the institutional problems that afflict so many of them today. A helpful glossary at the back of the book clarifies the meanings of specialized terms used in the text.

Weighing Historical Richness and Contemporary Relevance

While some scholars lament that new religions springing up do not have the depth of theology or the richness of ritual developed over millennia that are found in traditional world religions, these things, while excellent in themselves, are not sufficient if believers cannot find links to their own lives in these religions. Relevance is what many contemporary seekers are searching for.

The spiritual and ethical wisdom in the world's religions was not easily learned by the human race and was often learned at great cost. Like religions, most individual humans find that they learn their most valuable lessons from experience. We begin such learning in infancy when we learn not to touch hot things by burning our hands. With the development of multistep reasoning and analytic ability, young people and then adults are able to recognize in their own experience situations that resemble those they have heard in religious myths and codes. When we recognize an analogy between religious teachings and our life situation, impulsive responses can be checked and we are more cautious and deliberate in deciding action. The more ethical wisdom we have been exposed to, the more likely we are to have some of the necessary resources for making complicated ethical decisions today, both individually and as members of society. At the same time, as we will see in chapter 1, doing ethics will also require a great deal of social analysis of our current reality.

NOTES

1. Until the last few decades, U.S. prisons had chaplains, but only Christian and occasionally Jewish ones. More recently, in

part as the result of court decisions, both prisons and the U.S. military have enlarged their chaplaincy programs so as to be able to provide spiritual and religious care for virtually all inmates/members, though the increasing variety of religion in America makes this a daunting task. Chaplaincy in federal prisons is still Christian-oriented, however, in that a prerequisite is eighty hours of graduate education in theology, sacred texts, religious history, and ministry at a school accredited by the organization that accredits seminaries and theological schools.

2. Alexander W. Astin, Helen S. Astin, and Jennifer H. Lindholm, *Cultivating the Spirit: How Colleges Can Enhance Students' Spiritual Lives* (San Francisco: Jossey-Bass, 2010). An overview of the findings is available online at http://spirituality .ucla.edu.

3. See overview at http://spirituality.ucla.edu /findings/spiritual-measures/equanimity .php.

4. Similarly, but at much younger ages, Amish youth, usually between sixteen and eighteen, observe a period called *rumspringa*, during which they are allowed some laxity of behavior (often not nearly so radical as popularly depicted) in order that they come to a final decision about whether to accept baptism within the community, or leave it.

5. Andrew Greeley, *Religion in Europe at the End of the Second Millennium* (London: Transaction, 2004).

6. Two examples: Mario Liverani, *Myth and Politics in Ancient Near Eastern Historiography*, ed. Zainab Bahrani and Marc Van De Mieroop (London: Equinox, 2004), ch. 8, 160–92; and Andrew Arterbury, *Entertaining Angels: Early Christian Hospitality in Its Mediterranean Setting* (Sheffield, UK: Sheffield Phoenix, 2005).

7. As does Charles Mathewes's *Understanding Religious Ethics* (Malden, MA: Wiley-Blackwell, 2010).

8. Mari Rapela Heidt, *Moral Traditions: An Introduction to World Religious Ethics* (Winona, MN: Anselm Academic, 1991), took this approach.

9. See Sumner B. Twiss and Bruce Grelle, eds., *Explorations in Global Ethics: Comparative Religious Ethics and Interreligious Dialogue* (Boulder, CO: Westview, 2000).

10. For a text that does this, see Darryl J. Fasching, Dell deChant, and David M. Lantigua, *Comparative Religious Ethics: A Narrative Approach to Global Ethics* (Malden, MA: Wiley-Blackwell, 2010).

CHAPTER 1

ETHICS AND SPIRITUALITY IN RELIGION

What does it mean when students say, "I'm really not religious, but I am very spiritual"? It usually means that they do not subscribe to the rules and regulations, the organizational authority structures of religions, but that they are interested in a personal relationship with the Divine/Ultimate. It usually also means allowing such relationship with the Divine/Ultimate to instill values that will guide their decisions and actions, that will form their character and the shape of their lives. This is the core of the relationship between spirituality and ethics. True spirituality produces good ethics. Essentially, this was what both Catholics and Lutherans finally agreed following their centuries-long Reformation battles over the salvific power of faith versus works: that faith, understood as personal relationship with God, issues in good works.[1] Works without faith can be worthless, because good deeds can be performed for morally perverse and evil reasons. But faith without works is not real faith, because it is devoid of divine love, which by its very nature overflows onto others in good deeds.

The steps between experiencing a sense of divine presence within oneself or within the world and the development of ethical character and life are not simple and are certainly not automatic. As we will see, there is a discipline involved, as all religions have recognized. Each religion has held up models of persons who have mastered that discipline and thus become "holy." Edith Wyschogrod, in her book *Saints and Postmodernism*,[2] makes a convincing case that in the postmodern age, the lives of the saints are better able to inspire virtue in us than are principles and codes of ethics. Our attention is caught by stories of other humans, especially stories of drama. We are natural mimics—virtually all our early learning is based on mimicking others, much of it not even deliberate or conscious. Compared to tales of the extraordinary doings of the saints, principles and rules are dull and uninspiring; their attempts to be universal and relevant regardless of context makes them difficult to apply. But a saint's life is embedded in a particular community at a particular time; it gives example after example of how to be holy. Postmoderns want "proof" of the truth of the principles, and the life of the saint is the proof, the explanation, the living out of the principles.

Virtue Ethics

The disciplines discovered or followed by these holy people—saints, buddhas, prophets, *bodhisattvas, sannyasin*—are not for the lazy, but neither are they impenetrable. In this text we will pay attention to a number of links between ethics and spirituality. In the various ethical methods that have been proposed over the many centuries of religious thought, not all of which have been as systematic as others, one relatively recent ethical stress is referred to as virtue ethics. This form of ethics not only proposes that virtue is trained up in communities that live out certain shared values, but it also asks of any proposed action what consequences the act would have on the character of the actor (and often on others affected): Would it move the actor, and the community, in the direction of greater virtue or not?

Virtue ethics in Greek thought. Though the term *virtue ethics* is recent, this concern with personal virtue is not. As one postmodernist thinker, Michel Foucault, reminded us in *The History of Sexuality*, according to classical Greek philosophers of many schools of thought, the ultimate goal in life was to develop one's character, to develop virtues through the practices of self-control in order that one be able to carry out one's responsibilities. One first had to care for oneself by learning appropriate self-control of one's passions, appetites, and instincts in order to then be able to care for and deal justly with others and ultimately to be able to carry out one's responsibilities to the state.

Survival as overarching ethical value. The Greeks were not alone. Concern for the development of personal virtue is strong in virtually all religious ethical systems, even if it is not always the most immediate concern.

Sometimes other values take precedence. For example, when the very existence of a religious community is threatened, its survival and continuity often take priority over all other values. Until a few decades ago, Reform rabbis in the United States participated in mixed marriage rites with Christian ministers. But as the American Jewish community became aware that about half of all Jews in the United States were marrying non-Jews, and that most of the children of those marriages were not being raised as Jews, Reform, Conservative, and Orthodox rabbis formed a united front and refused to marry Jews to non-Jews unless the non-Jewish partner agreed to convert to Judaism, irrespective of the character and virtue of the couple desiring to marry. The rabbis saw no alternative to the extinction of the Jewish faith over time. Other values, such as respect for and cooperation with other religions, became subordinated to the value of the survival of the religious community.

Sometimes other values are not so much eclipsed by the need for survival as the need for survival changes how other virtues are understood. When a religious community, for example, is under mortal threat, courage often comes to be understood in terms of willingness to sacrifice or risk for the sake of doctrine, and fidelity comes to be seen in terms of loyalty to the religious institution and rejection of all outside loyalties. Martyrdom in such situations of threat can often be elevated above even the values that the martyr refused to surrender. The sacrifice in martyrdom becomes a value in itself and no longer simply a means to defend another value.

Ethicists throughout the ages have proposed a variety of ethical models. Some of these are quite distinct, while many of them include a great deal of overlap with other models due to the continuities in human experience that have persisted over the ages. Ethical models tend to be based upon reason. The assumption is that, faced with an ethical decision, humans should use reason to discern the more moral option. As we shall see, ethical models are not the only way to understand moral action.

Deontological, or Rule-Based, Ethics

A common distinction made in discussions of ethical decision making, including religious ethics, is between deontological, or rule-based, ethics, on the one hand, and teleological, or consequential, ethics on the other. Rule-based ethics is somewhat simpler to implement, provided that the rules are clear and well known and the authority of the rule's source is accepted. In that case, one simply applies the rule. Of course, rules are developed within societies to deal with known situations, and thus rule making always lags after new developments. For example, a great part of the interest in bioethics today is that so many of the questions it confronts are new, so there are no ethical rules that apply directly to many questions. St. Augustine, for example, left us no insights on the ethics of organ transplants. One who wants to know how a religion should respond to a new issue in bioethics, such as cloning or fetal stem cells, must look for general rules and principles that may be indirectly relevant.

Socialization of the young. In general, every society in the world uses rule-based ethics in the socialization of young children. Young children do not have the capacity to reason their way through situations, and so we teach them simple rules: Do not hit, Do not break, Be gentle, Be nice to your sister/brother/friend, Eat your vegetables, Clean up your messes. Parents and teachers are the ultimate authorities for young children, and children's dependence on these adults for all their basic needs provides incentive in children to comply with the rules. As children's reasoning ability matures, these simple rules of childhood later become the basis for more complex rules—such as the golden rule of only doing to others what we would have them do to us. Religions work in the same way, beginning with teaching children moral rules based on authority, and later demonstrating the religious foundations and texts underlying the rules.

Rule-based ethical systems are not always simple. Because many religious ethical systems developed over centuries, even millennia, they have become complex systems of interlocking rules that require a great deal of expertise to master. Today many both inside and outside religious communities question the relevance of certain religious ethical rules, such as the Catholic ban on artificial contraception, or Orthodox Jewish kosher laws against mixing meat and dairy products, or Buddhist bans on monks eating after noon. As living situations change in history, some ethical practices that were easily accepted in the past seem to conflict with central ethical values in the tradition.

Even when one agrees with the moral principle behind many of the rules, application is not always clear. Thus a group of people might all agree that human life begins in the womb, and that abortion is wrong, and yet be divided over whether an anencephalic fetus (one without a forebrain, including the neocortex, which controls cognition and consciousness), can be aborted as not a human person. (Anencephalics usually die before birth and cannot survive long after birth.) Those who believe that a capacity for consciousness is an essential part of being human do not recognize the anencephalic fetus as a human person, while those who believe that any human fetus is a human person will insist on its right to as much life as its biology allows.

Sometimes rules change, not only in society, but in religious law. The practice of corporal punishment in the family by husbands/fathers on wives and children, for example, was not only accepted but advocated as a part of training families in virtue in many religious texts in the past. However, in the West over the last half-century, corporal punishment of both wives and children has been increasingly questioned in one religion—and civil law system—after another as not congruent with the equality and dignity of all persons. Nevertheless, there are many persons—and whole cultures around the world—who agree with scriptural accounts of corporal punishment as a normative parenting practice, understanding corporal punishment as a necessary part of rearing children. These people see a ban on corporal punishment as throwing out the baby with the bathwater, as overreacting to cases of physical abuse of children.

Rule-based religious systems usually include a hierarchy to be invoked when the actions dictated by the rules conflict, as they sometimes will. In some cases that hierarchy is one based on the source of the rule. For example, in Islam, a rule that comes from the Qur'an outranks one that comes from *hadith* (accounts of the sayings and decisions of the Prophet Mohammed). In many religions, the hierarchy invoked in the case of conflicting rules is one of values. For example, missing a mandatory religious ritual in order to rush an accident victim to the hospital is often the religiously correct thing to do, since preservation of life takes precedence over virtually all other values across religions.

Religious Use of Rule-Based Ethics

Within many religions, the ethical system taught to the general membership is strictly rule-based; members are often encouraged to believe that the rules are absolute and exceptionless. Simplifications of ethical systems into a limited list of absolute rules made great sense in the historical past when most world religions began and developed. The masses in every society were illiterate and uneducated. More than that: the contours of their lives were very limited. Until the last century and a half, even in what we call the developed West, the vast majority of people were farmers who lived most of their lives in the same location amid a usually rather homogenous population. They inherited the very shape of their lives from their parents and grandparents, and few had any possibility of exercising much ethical responsibility. Because there were few "new" situations in the lives of generation after generation, following inherited sets of rules made sense. It did, as we would say today, "work."

More than anything else, this lack of decision-making experience in the general adult population, and their lack of the information necessary for broad social decision making in general, meant that few individuals were able to move beyond rule-based systems. In the more complex versions of religious ethics that were more or less confined to the literate, theologically educated upper clergy, a common goal in ethics was to develop personal ethical sensitivity/conscience through applying the basic rules, analyzing the consequences for all concerned, and, with other members of the religious elite, perhaps making (usually small) adjustments in the principles or rules designed to improve the consequences.

Casuistry in Rule-Based Ethics

Casuistry is a form of thought that attempts to find an answer to a new ethical problem by analyzing precedents set in different cases that have one or more similar elements to the case at hand.[3] The Jewish Talmud is an account of rabbinic discussions on, and interpretation of, Jewish law, ethics, and philosophy by the most renowned rabbis in the first centuries of the common era. It has two parts: the Mishnah, a compendium of what has been known as the Oral Law, and the Gemara, interpretive discussions of both Mishnah and Torah. Discussions, especially in the Gemara, did not always reach consensus, even when the rabbis were discussing a single principle located in sacred text. The process was often casuistic—the rabbis often drew on past cases analogous to the one they were discussing, noting the similarities and differences, and how these should affect decision making in the present case.

Casuistry as an ethical method was also prominent in Roman Catholic moral theology, though it was discredited in Protestant circles, and in the seventeenth century was attacked within Roman Catholicism, too, as lax, not sufficiently morally rigorous. Often called by different names, casuistry is relatively common within the higher reaches of religious organizations that need to give guidance to members in new situations. Casuistry calls on previous cases that have been decided, to illustrate different principles and distinctions and how they may be applied.

There is often a general fear of allowing members to utilize casuistry, in part because much of the general membership of a religion does not have the specialized knowledge of the tradition on which successful use of the

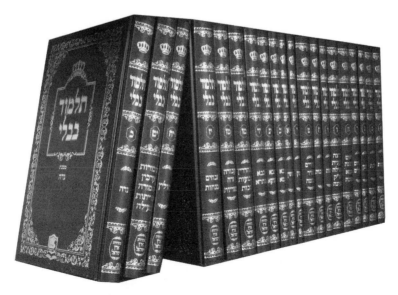

Fig. 1.1. The Jewish Talmud. Following the destruction of the Jewish Second Temple in 70 CE, rabbinic discussions of the Torah and related issues of Jewish life began to be written, and in 200 were restructured thematically to produce the Jewish Talmud as we know it.

method depends, but also out of a fear that allowing members to reach moral decisions on their own will produce chaos. In both Judaism and Roman Catholicism, rule-based ethics is generally taught to the laity, along with encouragement that ongoing questions as to how to apply existing law to new situations be referred to the rabbi in one's synagogue or to a rabbinical court of scholars in Judaism, and to one's pastor/bishop or ultimately to the Congregation for the Doctrine of the Faith at the Vatican.

This dual-level system—the masses are given rule-based ethics that may be taught as absolute, and an educated elite interprets special cases on the basis of appeal—is found in many religions. While the taught message is often that since the rules/law come directly from the divine, they are unchangeable, the interpretation of the rules/law by the elites does change with the historical experience of the community, which allows ethical teachings/practices to change, though usually very gradually.

Contemporary Approaches to Rule-Based Ethics

While there are still many defenders of rule-based approaches to ethics today, even of very absolute approaches to the rules, the contemporary situation has caused both rejections of rule-based systems by some who refuse to simply follow orders handed down from historical authority, and many attempts to reform inherited rule-based systems to make their consequences more compatible with contemporary life. The fundamental problem in such reforms, of course, is that reform can easily undermine the claims made for the authority of the rules. If some rules can be dropped or reinterpreted, why not others? For this reason, many supporters of deontological,

rule-based ethics reject reforms, insisting that at least those rules with divine origin—and sometimes their interpretations as well—are unchangeable.

Some ethical rules in religion do not rest on claims of divine origin, in the sense that various scriptures can be understood as the very words of God, but rather on claims of divine revelation as mediated through religious leaders. In Islam, for example, Shi'as and Sunnis both understand the Qur'an as the direct word of God spoken to Mohammed, and other revelation as coming through Mohammed as well, as preserved in *hadith*. But for the Sunnis, revelation ended with Mohammed, and the ethical task today is to follow the Qur'an and *hadith*, using scholarship to probe new applications of legal principles derived from these sources as needed. For the Shi'a, revelation continued through the caliphs who succeeded Mohammed and Ali, and still continues today through deputies to the hidden imams (except for the Nizari sect of the Ismaili Shi'a, whose latest imam, Aga Khan IV, is neither dead nor hidden). Among Shi'a, then, as a general rule, new ethical teachings/rules are often presented as part of revelation, and not as the result of a human process of reasoning and analysis.

Similarly, since 1870, Roman Catholicism has taught that infallible truth on matters of faith and morals continues to be revealed to the Pope and announced to Catholics. The Church of Jesus Christ of Latter-day Saints (Mormon) teaches that the president of the church is a prophet, seer, and revelator. In a less official way, the role of gurus in various forms of Hinduism can be understood either as new revelation within a long tradition of revelation or as new interpretation of past revelation. It is perhaps significant that even

Fig. 1.2. The Muslim Qur'an. Some years after the Qur'an was revealed to Muhammed, it was written down, and its surahs were organized by length, longest to shortest.

in these religions that recognize divine revelation through institutional officers of the religion, there has been decreasing use of this revelatory power in contemporary times compared to even a century ago.

Religious Reform of Rules as Problematic

Religions find it very difficult to discard teachings they have taught as divine command. But rules that have clearly been created by human beings are more easily changed. Many of these have to do with institutional rules around conduct. For example, for hundreds of years, the Catholic Church law required either fasting or abstinence from meat on many days throughout the year. But in the years following the Second Vatican Council (1962–1965), fasting was limited to Ash Wednesday and Good Friday, and abstinence from meat to those two days and all Fridays

in Lent (the period of forty days before Easter). As seen in the chart on page 22, the rules were made much less demanding.

Vatican II involved a turn toward inclusion of the laity, toward the laity accepting more responsibility within the church. Since fasting and abstinence were penitential practices done in order to atone for sin, church officials felt it now appropriate that individual laity decide how best to atone for their personal sin, rather than have rules that mandated the same practices for all. At the same time, it was felt that some residual rules around fasting and abstinence served the purpose of reminding the laity of the importance of preparing for Easter during the Lenten season, and so the rules for fasting on the first day of Lent (Ash Wednesday) and the day of Christ's crucifixion (Good Friday), and abstinence on these days and all the Fridays in Lent were retained.

Before 1965 (Pre-Vatican II)	Since Vatican II in the United States
Fasting: 1 full meal, 2 others less than half of full meal, no snacks Obliges all Catholics 21–60	**Fasting:** 1 full meal, 2 others less than half of full meal, no snacks Obliges all Catholics 18–59
Fast Days: All weekdays of Lent Ember Days Pentecost vigil Immaculate Conception vigil Christmas vigil	**Fast Days:** Ash Wednesday Good Friday
Abstinence: No meat; partial abstinence, meat only at major meal All Catholics 7 and over	**Abstinence:** No meat Obliges all Catholics over 14
Days of Full Abstinence: All Fridays Ash Wednesday Immaculate Conception vigil Christmas vigil Holy Saturday	**Abstinence Days:** Ash Wednesday Good Friday All Fridays in Lent
Days of Partial Abstinence: Ember Wednesday and Saturdays Pentecost vigil	

While the rationale for the change is clear and compelling, one common reaction to the change was suspicion: How could it have been a sin to eat meat on ordinary Fridays before the change and not a sin after the change? Because the rules had been presented as coming from God, the change made it seem as if God's rules were arbitrary. Many of the changes associated with Vatican II were received with this same suspicion, which seems to be the price of presenting all religious regulation as being of divine origin and therefore above discussion—even when,

as in this case, the rules in question were officially part of church discipline and not divine law.

Another example of changing rules to adapt to new situations is the Svetambara sect of the Jain religion of India, which, in the late twentieth century created a new order of monastics, the Samana Order. The Samanis are nuns who are exempt from the millennia-old rule that Jain monks and nuns could only travel by foot. The purposes of the new order are to minister to the religious needs of Jains who have founded global communities outside of India, and to spread Jain teaching globally, especially the ethic of nonviolence to all living beings. Samanis in this order fly from continent to continent in their ministry. Interestingly, this missionary work is not aimed at recruiting members to the religion, but at spreading its ethical message.

Problems with Reform of Religious Rules Today

Most people, and especially the young, need structure in their lives as they construct the persons they will become. They need the persons and events around them to be predictable—to follow the rules. We find ambiguity in the rules frustrating and even deceitful. Teaching the rules of religious ethics as absolute and unchangeable is sometimes part of

a deliberate attempt on the part of the leadership to create certainty and consistency in community practice. Yet we want the rules to make sense, too, and when rules are presented to us as absolute but are not clearly understandable, we question. Sometimes rules are presented as absolute that are really not, as when persons in lower leadership roles who have not yet mastered the complex ethical tradition demand unquestioning obedience as a defense against inquiries/objections they cannot answer.

Deontological (rule-based) ethics works best when the "rules" have not been imposed upon individuals as an external code, but have instead been learned within a community that teaches by example, as Wyschogrod suggested saints do. When we see over time

Fig. 1.3. These Jain Samanis teaching at Florida International University in Miami are part of a new Jain monastic order allowed to travel to minister to the Jain diaspora and to disseminate the moral teachings of Jainism.

that a rule works well, that following it has positive effects on individuals and on the life and interrelationships of our community, we are likely to incorporate that rule into our own personal code of ethics. That rule then is not external to us, but forms a part of our own ethical process.

Today many rules seem imposed. One reason that many students are disclaiming religious identities today is that the "rules" of the religion appear to them to be external impositions; they have not learned these rules through the practical experience of their communities, in part because of changes in the nature of local religious communities in the modern period. Many religious communities have become large, anonymous, and diverse. Members of the religion may not be neighbors, may not share employment or any other activity. Thus the ethos of the religious community has become more difficult to recognize and identify with.

In addition, while there have always been scandals in all human organizations, including religions, in the past many of these had been hushed in order not to threaten the faith of believers. Today every scandal is public, especially if it concerns religion. The whiff of hypocrisy makes religious scandal irresistible to the news media because it draws listeners/viewers/readers. When a religious institution has identified itself with divine authority, any moral lapse among the representatives of the institution seems to undermine the authority of the institution. Thus many ask after a religious leader is caught in some scandal: "Why should I believe anything he said?" But reflection should show us that the most basic truths will be pronounced by both geniuses and fools, saints and villains. The character of the message should not be judged by the character of the messenger.

Teleological, or Consequentialist, Ethics

Many students insist that rule-based ethics is less compatible with the postmodern period than it was with previous periods. Increasing portions of the human community are both literate and educated on the one hand and accustomed to making responsible decisions that affect the lives of many on the other. These humans want to exercise responsibility for their religious lives as they do in their work and family lives. They want to have a role in deciding what contributes to their own and their community's flourishing. These people are attracted to teleological, or consequentialist, ethics.

Teleological ethics takes it name from the Greek work *telos*, which means "end." In teleological ethics, one chooses the option that seems to produce the best end, or consequences. Rather than being based on a set of rules derived from an authority, consequentialist ethics entails choosing options with the most positive consequences. This is a very practical ethics, but it, too, is not as simple as it might seem at first. In many cases, teleological and deontological ethics end up pointing to the same option. For example, while deontologists may not speed when driving because there is a law that says one may only travel at fifty-five miles per hour on this road, a teleologist might also keep her speed to fifty-five miles per hour, not because there is a law that says so, but because she wants to travel safely and has learned that her car slips on the sharp curves if she goes over fifty-five.

When we look at the consequences of different ethical options, it is simple to say with the consequentialists that we should choose the option that promises the most positive and the fewest negative consequences. But how do we decide what are positive consequences, and what are negative? In the example above, our teleologist driver had to experiment for herself to find out at what speed danger and safety divided. We do not want to always find these things out for ourselves. Our lives are too busy to be using consequentialist method in every decision we make. As we shall see, even the most ardent consequentialists do not weigh advantages and disadvantages of every choice that is set before them every day.

Everyday consequentialism. For many moderns, thinking consequentially seems normal. We are told that if we want to have a good job that will enable us to support ourselves and our families when we grow up, we must do well in school and go to university. We have an end—to be able to support ourselves and our family—and we choose the means that will get us to that end. If we want a new set of noise-cancelling headphones or a new car, we know that we have to find ways to save money. If we want to keep a friend, we know we do not tell their secrets to others. Our actions are guided by the ends we choose to pursue. But consequentialist ethics is more than this practical thinking. It makes us look at all the consequences of our actions. For example, we want to get a university degree so that we can obtain a job that will support us and our family—and hopefully help us become the person we want to be by developing our talents. But not every job that will enable us to pay our university tuition is a good choice. Some ways of earning money are clearly both dangerous and immoral—selling drugs, prostitution, burglary. But there are others that would benefit from our weighing the advantages and disadvantages. A student in class a few years ago said that she was putting herself through school by selling

phone sex—she only had to be on call fifteen hours a week, she said, and it paid all her bills. She insisted that there was no sexual activity involved, and that she was completely anonymous to her customers, so there was no danger.

Clearly, employment as a phone sex provider fulfilled this student's primary need: it paid her bills and enabled her to earn her BS in nursing. But was paying her bills the only consequence of this employment? Instead of simply condemning the phone sex job as violating a rule that says that sexual arousal belongs in marital relationships, as rule-based ethics would have it, consequentialist ethics would ask about the variety of consequences of holding this job. For example, has she been open with parents, relatives, and friends about what she does, or is she ashamed of it? Does she become aroused in the course of her work? How will this everyday manipulation of sexual arousal in the job affect her own sexual life with a later partner? What is the effect on the customer? Does her voice on the phone encourage masturbatory habits that might be difficult for a client to break in favor of an interpersonal sexual relationship? Does this phone sex service give customers an understanding that sexual satisfaction is something that can be bought? How will extensive experience of phone sex affect the way that future sexual partners of both customer and seller are treated? Many of these questions are difficult to answer, because the experience can affect different people in different ways. But they are part of the consequences and should not be ignored.

Whose good? We also need to ask: When we are considering what consequences should count as good, from whose perspective are these consequences being regarded? An ethical egoist (one who believes that the normative position is to do what is in one's own best interest) might choose an option based on the most positive and least negative consequences for himself, without regard for the effects on others. For example, if there is a hurricane in our area and the water system is shut down, but I have the only freshwater well in my neighborhood, I could make a fortune selling freshwater to my neighbors. If I only look at the consequences for me, the decision is simple: if I sell the water for things that I don't have, I can have everything that I need and more during the emergency and will be rich afterward.

But most forms of consequentialism insist that we choose options with more positive than negative consequences overall, and do not limit our concerns to our own welfare. Some forms of consequentialism, and all religious forms, also insist that distribution of the positive and negative consequences to different persons be as equitable as possible. A judge who faces a large mob waiting to hang a man accused of child rape and murder must decide whether to convict the accused, though the evidence is completely lacking, and let him be hanged, or acquit him and risk the mob attacking the courthouse and killing the judge, sheriff, and jailers in a riot. Conservation of human life might suggest that the best consequence is to convict the man so that only one dies. This could be understood as the greatest good for the greatest number. But it is certainly not just to the accused, who may be completely innocent. And it sets up dangerous precedents for the future, in which the lives and interests of individuals, the poor and powerless, count for little against the interests of the larger community. Immediate advantages for many should not justify an unbearable burden for one or a few.

The Distribution of Goods and Evils in Consequentialism

This issue of the distribution of goods and evils in consequentialism is an important one. Some forms of ethics in religion, those associated with liberation theologies, insist that the interests of the poorest and most marginal persons must be considered first. This is called the Preferential Option for the Poor, though it does not apply only to the economically poor, but rather to all characterized by relative powerlessness. In deciding where to locate a city's newest garbage dump, for example, one often finds that because land prices are lowest in poor areas, and because the poor do not have the same access for voicing their interests to officials, the dump ends up in the backyard of the poor. This is the best consequence for all, we are told, because all taxpayers benefit by the lesser cost of locating the dump in this area. But by this same logic, all undesirable public activities will end up in the backyard of the poor, and their very presence becomes the "logical" reason for not locating the more desirable communal activities there. For if the municipal ballpark, golf course, swimming pool, or concert hall were surrounded by the dump, the halfway house for prisoners, the homeless shelter, and the noisy railroad station, who would use them? Their best location, it is inevitably argued, is in middle-class neighborhoods with none of these disincentives to attendance. By putting consideration for the poor and marginalized first, one helps their voice be heard in the discussions so that a fairer distribution of these municipal goods and not-so-goods can be achieved.

If the common criticism of rule-based ethics is that it does not involve the whole human person in the ethical process, but only entails obedience to rules requiring or forbidding certain acts, the common criticism of consequentialist ethics is just the opposite. If rule-based ethics can be too oversimplified, consequentialist ethics can be too complex. The calculation that adequate consequentialist ethics requires begins with decisions about what is good and what is bad and then involves a calculus of the impacts of all possible options on all the persons and communities involved. Such calculus is extremely demanding, and in many areas beyond the capabilities of some.

Differentiating Good from Not So Good in Complex Situations

First, let us look at deciding what is good and what is bad morally. Very few things are always bad or always good. The few things that are always bad—what we term evil—are not so difficult to discern: murder of the innocent, nuclear obliteration, torture for the sake of torture, war without just cause, deliberate extinction of species, terrorizing children, and the list could go on. Many of our decisions are not between what is always good and what is always evil, but between the good and the not so good. The same substances that in small doses are medicines to make one well can, in larger doses, be fatal to human life. Speeding may be good or not so good, depending on whether one does it in an ambulance carrying a heart-attack patient to the hospital or in a joyride with a car full of teenagers. While there are certain acts that are usually good—like telling the truth—there are some situations in which even telling the truth can be vicious and cruel, because the truth-telling was done to harm another person, or to violate a promise.

Consequentialists, then, are often dealing not with black or white, but with different shades of gray. A mother has just discovered two wadded-up, long-forgotten twenty-dollar bills in her teen son's jean jacket as she filled the washer. He wants to take his girlfriend to an upcoming concert, and in order to raise the remaining money he needs, he has arranged to spend the next day with his lonely grandfather cleaning out the attic. Does she give her son the money now, knowing he will cancel the day with his grandfather, or does she hold it twenty-four hours until he has spent the day with his grandfather? It is his money, and so holding it is a form of theft. But the grandfather is lonely and would greatly enjoy a day with the teen, who also loves his grandfather and might enjoy the day, too. Would it make a difference if the teen planned to earn the missing money by cleaning out the basement for his mother? Might it be more moral to withhold the money for twenty-four hours to benefit the grandfather than to benefit oneself? Why? We might have a variety of different responses to this situation.

For many issues today, especially the many issues involving technology, consequentialist ethics often seems beyond the capacity of most of us. In order to make a decision about in vitro fertilization, for example, a vast amount of information is required, beginning with how the ova and sperm are obtained, from whom they are acquired, and with what consequences (the consequences, or side effects, for women can be significant). Then one needs to understand how many ova are fertilized, at what stage in the development of the fertilized ova the implantation process begins, how many fertilized ova are implanted, what happens to the rest, what the range of success rates is, and who will be the legal owner(s) of any child(ren) produced and of any unused fertilized ova. Since for some of these questions there will be different answers depending on the situation, deciding about in vitro fertilization is a complicated process even before one begins to ask questions about at what stage human personhood begins, what respect is owed to human biological materials that may or may not be human persons, and whether parenthood can be shared by more than two. The "consequences" of a given act or decision can be multitudinous and easily unforeseen. Rule-based ethics can begin to look much more attractive when one is confronted by this level of complexity.

A certain level of need for consequentialist decision making is involved even for those who use rule-based ethics, for some rules can become out of date, just like foods on the grocery shelf. Perhaps the authority that issued the rule has withdrawn it or replaced it. The individual has an obligation to ensure that the rule he or she is following is still sound and authoritative. For example, if one is to be more than a robot following a command, especially in rapidly changing fields such as biotechnology, one must look at the given rule and ascertain whether the reasoning behind it took into account the present reality or reflects an earlier understanding of reality that is no longer widely accepted. Much of the ethical controversy about stem cells focused on the fact that until relatively recently *stem cells* referred to embryonic stem cells obtained from aborted fetuses. Some people continue to oppose all use of stem cells in therapy or experimentation for this reason, even though today new discoveries of manipulable adult stem cells have opened possibilities that they—instead of only embryonic stem cells—could be used for regenerating various organs and tissues. Thus even deontological/rule-based systems of ethics can be dependent upon teleological/consequentialist thinking when rules must be reformed or replaced.

Maguire's Wheel for Moral Decision Making

Daniel Maguire, a well-known Christian ethicist, has developed the wheel on page 29 to illustrate both two levels of inputs in moral decision making and the multiple sources that go into good moral decision making.[4] In the center of the diagram are the basic data of the problem, the what, who, how, where, and why of the case. The spokes of the wheel are the sources and processes that the decision maker brings to the problem. Note that questions 3 and 4 in the center ask for information that is not part of the given case details, but are the result of applying the individual's sources to the facts of the case. Rules, in the form of principles, play a role in the decision-making process, as does group experience, but the predominant method here is consequential. The wheel illustrates well the complexity of moral decision making in consequentialism.

Ethics should be practical, and ethical methods should be suited to the life situations of the persons who use them. For most of us, this means that we will both accept a number of the inherited rules, but other times pay more attention to calculating consequences in choosing moral options utilizing something like Maguire's moral wheel.

Our reasons for accepting some of the more basic rules will differ. Some will accept these rules on the basis of authority, while others will accept them only after testing them in their own experience and agreeing that they produce more good than alternatives and fewer negative consequences. Most of us accept the rule "Do not kill," but with different exceptions that might include self-defense, military service, or police work. Most of us accept the rule "Do not commit adultery," and are divided only on exceptional

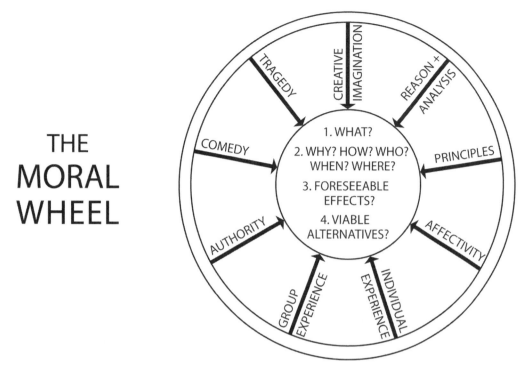

THE MORAL WHEEL

Fig. 1.4. The Wheel Model. Daniel Maguire, renowned Christian ethicist, portrays the elements of moral decision making by way of this graphical illustration.

cases, such as a spouse institutionalized long-term with Alzheimer's.

Contemporary Rethinking of Traditionally Accepted Moral Rules

Yet today there are a number of traditional moral rules that most Americans do not accept. For example, instead of making a distinction between married (moral) and unmarried (immoral) sex (traditionally called fornication) as was common in the past, the more common normative distinction that has become the centrist position in western culture today is between casual sex (of questionable morality) and committed sex (more moral), no matter whether that committed

sex is within marriage or not. This is a huge change. Many circumstances combined to influence this change, among them the availability of reliable contraception, the later age of marriage due to lengthened education, the economic necessity in most families that married women work outside the home (thus requiring education and training, and increased age at marriage), and increasing voluntarism in the selection of marital partners. Of course, there is still a significant minority of persons, mostly religious, who believe that sex outside of marriage lacks moral standing because of the absence of covenantal commitment, and another minority who see nothing immoral in casual sex.

Yet many ethics scholars point out that the new distinction (casual/committed) is prone to the same problem as the old distinction (married/unmarried): it implies that it is the external characteristics surrounding the act that make it moral or immoral, rather than the quality of the relationship in which the sex takes place. Just as a marriage ceremony does not make all sexual activity within that marriage moral, so the length and publicness of a cohabitation relationship does not mean that all activity within it is moral. Sexual abuse, for example, can occur in both marriage and committed relationships. It is not only found in casual sex.

Rethinking the Plagiarism Rule

A second example of changed attitudes is plagiarism. Increasing numbers of students reject the traditional understanding of plagiarism as cheating, or theft, when presenting the work of someone else as one's own. There are a variety of reasons given. For some students for whom education is only about jumping through the hoops in order to obtain credentials, there is no sense in wasting time to create something that someone else has already created. This attitude reflects a relatively new postmodern reality, in which the real and authentic no longer mean that which is original, of which a copy would only be a fake, a counterfeit. Instead, the real is what can be duplicated innumerable times, like a song on iTunes, or a document online. The idea that a copy is not as good as the original has little or no standing in this world. But this shift in thinking is only one part of the change in attitude toward plagiarism.

Many are no longer persuaded by understanding that education is the process of acquiring not just a license or credential, but a combination of skills and wisdom, neither of which is obtained in plagiarism. Of course, laziness also plays a part in the decision to plagiarize, as well as a willingness to deceive. Who is the loser in this shift in popular morality? Both individuals, who cheat themselves out of some valuable learning that could be useful in later life and employment, and their employers, who hired them on the basis of a school record that may have little relationship to the skills actually acquired. On the other hand, one reason that not all students see cheating as hurting themselves is that the educational process has not made an effective case for the relevance and importance—the basic purpose—of the work required. Divisions in moral thinking around plagiarism plague our educational system today, threatening basic understandings about honesty. The alarming numbers of persons claiming degrees, awards, and other achievements on their résumés that they never earned is certainly linked to this shift in public thinking on plagiarism.

Rethinking Lying and Truth-Telling

In a similar process, many people today qualify the inherited religious ethical ban on lying. There are some occupations that seem to routinely require lying. Today lying as part of a profession is not limited to secretaries ("No, he is not in today"), spies, and undercover cops. Police and medical examiners are often asked by relatives of crime or accident victims, "Did she suffer much?" The routine answer, unless there is a deal of evidence to the contrary, is "No, she died very quickly." In the same way, we tell sick and dying loved ones that yes, they look very good today, even as we cry inside for the suffering and physical deterioration that shows on their faces.

In the case of lying, we often want to know what the purpose of a given untruth is before we pronounce it a lie. While lying to deceive another in order to undermine the interests of that other is clearly wrong, lying to someone to make them feel better is not always justifiable, either. Spouses who hide from the husband or wife the seriousness of their financial troubles or their health situation by lying might say they do it to spare the spouse from worrying. But such action not only deprives the spouse of information to which he/she had a right, but also deprives them of the opportunity to affect the crisis, even if only by sharing the burden of the crisis with the partner.

Asking the Virtue Question

At the same time, as we saw above, for some the religious focus is neither rule-based nor conventionally consequential, but rather intensely personal: the best option is the one that has the effect of making the agent a better person. Even if we do not want to use virtue ethics as our exclusive moral approach, asking the question as to what effect an act will have on our own character should be part of the process in deciding upon action in a new situation.

Virtue ethics often tends to end up supporting rules. Thus even in a personal situation where a consequentialist might say that a lie—for example, a mother's denial to a child that the child's conception was accidental—could be justified because it avoided suffering in the child being lied to, virtue ethics would ask what effect this lie has on our character over time. Does it incline us to justify other untruths in other situations? What is the effect of the lie on the child if someone later tells him the truth? On the other hand, virtue ethics can sometimes support rejecting actions usually considered normative. For example, Franz Jägerstätter, an Austrian conscientious objector beheaded for refusing to

fight in Hitler's army, followed the voice of his conscience in refusing to be drafted into what he considered an unjust aggressive war on Germany's part, despite the failure of his local church community, pastor, and bishop or any other social institution to support him. He chose conscience over obedience to the state, personal virtue over moral conformity. Today the very Catholic Church that refused to support his conscientious decision has pronounced him blessed, a step in the process of canonization to sainthood.

For virtue ethics, the intention of the agent is usually of more importance than the practical consequences of the action. This makes practical sense in many situations, for we all know that the right action can be chosen for very evil ends. A mother who has gone to great lengths (change of name and location) to protect her child from the knowledge that his father was an executed murderer can be totally undermined by an enemy who maliciously tells the child "the truth" in order to cause suffering. In this case, the malicious intention makes this truth-telling action an evil one.

Buddhist ethics, in particular, stands out as virtue ethics, mostly because in the Buddhist worldview the material world is regarded as largely illusory, so that consequences within it have little importance compared to intention, which is closely related to individual progress toward the end of *nirvana*. One reason that Buddhism has kept this focus on personal virtue is that Buddhism began, and has largely remained, a religion aimed at monastics more or less withdrawn from the world. Thus worldly consequences have not carried as much weight as gains or losses in personal virtue. Buddhism has been in the past much criticized in the West for inattention to issues of justice and rights, yet praised for its corresponding emphasis on character development and self-discipline. Contemporary Buddhist ethics has, however, in Socially Engaged Buddhism, taken a strong turn toward dealing with issues of justice in the world.

Consequentialism in Social Ethics

In general, when religions turn to deal with social issues, as opposed to interpersonal relational issues, they tend to use consequentialist method, because social issues are complex, time-bound, and often dynamic. As many Catholic ethicists have noted over the last decades, Catholic moral theology (which focuses on individual moral conduct) is decidedly rule-based, while Catholic social teaching is strongly consequentialist.

Role of Social Analysis

There are seldom readymade rules in religions that directly apply to many social issues, though a number of principles are so basic that it is difficult to imagine how they could become outdated. The principle of justice, for example, that demands giving to each person what is due him or her, can be timeless, because understandings of what is due individuals changes with the times. Until the modern period, class and caste distinctions were responsible for social patterns in which some people were understood to be due much more than others because of the caste or class into which they were born. Most ethical systems today recognize different kinds of justice, based on different understandings of what is due each individual. Of course, even in late modern society, what is due each person is not the same in each situation.

Commutative justice is the justice of commerce, of exchange, in which exchanges should be of the same agreed-upon value. If you loaned me ten dollars, then I owe you ten dollars. If I buy a dozen oranges marked twelve for four dollars, then the checkout clerk should charge me four dollars and not five dollars. Commutative justice is not sufficient for human social needs, for power differentials can often unfairly influence the agreement between persons. For example, when merchants are intimidated by gangsters into agreeing to pay protection money so that their stores will not be vandalized or destroyed, that "agreement" of money in exchange for protection is not just. Commutative justice requires a level playing field for exchange, a freely chosen agreement without coercion. Social analysis is necessary to ascertain that the level playing field is present in the facts of the case, in order that commutative justice can be appropriate.

Distributive justice, on the other hand, is about the proper allocation of social goods, aimed at the welfare of the whole society. It is not necessarily egalitarian, though it sometimes is. Distributive justice can be based on meeting basic needs for those who lack them, or it can be aimed at those who are not needy, but who may invest the goods in ways that benefit the society by increasing jobs or by restoring air quality, and so on. Both progressive taxation (higher rates for higher incomes) and tax breaks for business owners can be examples of distributive justice, depending on what the overall good of the whole society requires at the moment.

While commutative justice is that which largely occurs between individuals, and distributive justice is about what societies give to individuals, social justice is about what individuals owe to society. For example, taxes are one of the things that all individuals owe to their society to underwrite the services that societies provide for all of us (roads, schools, police, fire protection, disaster relief, food inspection, etc.).

Social analysis is the tool that we use to distinguish the correct type of justice that applies in specific situations and how it can be best applied. The newer the situation, or case, the more important social analysis is in helping us understand the specific problem, the variety of options, and the consequences of those various options.

Consequentialism in Dealing with New Social Issues: The U.S. Housing Crisis and Ecology

For example, during the United States housing crisis that began in 2007, ethicists of different religions in America were repeatedly asked the question of whether it is ethical for home owners who are "underwater"—owe more on their homes than the home is now worth on the market—to walk away from the mortgage. Some argue that this is morally wrong, that these home owners made promises in the form of mortgage contracts and are obligated to fulfill these promises. Others argue that home owners should not suffer the entire burden of the financial crisis that was largely brought about by the very banks and other financial institutions that hold their mortgages. These people argue that because the drop in the value of homes was not the owners' fault, and has already victimized them (they have lost whatever equity they had built up in their homes) they should not be held hostage for decades, unable to move because they cannot sell (since the selling price would be far below the mortgage owed). In religions there are ethical values and principles relevant to financial affairs, but no

direct rules about the status of mortgage contracts. In such cases, social analysis and some form of casuistry (discussed above) must play a major role, since change in the social reality is the very reason for considering that traditional rules about keeping promises (repaying loans) might not be appropriate.

Similarly, in dealing with many issues of ecological justice, there are no rules on extinction of species or conservation of water to be found in sacred texts or moral codes. In the absence of specific rules to guide us, humans must look for general principles of justice and value in the various religious and philosophical traditions and then weigh the various options to find the ones that best approximate the justice demanded by the traditions.

Social Analysis as Defining the Moral Issues in Our Context

Some students may be surprised by the quantity of social analysis to be found in the following chapters. Social analysis frames the problematic that ethics addresses; it tells us where the ethical question is to be found. As ethicist Daniel Maguire writes:

> [T]he is is the parent of the ought. If we miss contact with what really is, our thoughts are messed up. . . . Knowing what really is, therefore, is the goal of ethical inquiry. If our judgment of the *prima facie* facts is skewed, the brilliance of subsequent discussion and analysis will be victimized by this bad start. What we say may be impressive, but we will not know what we are talking about. The first step toward prescribing what ought to be is describing what is. Description is the beginning of prescription. Description, of course, is not the end of prescription.

True ethics is creative and is as concerned with what might be as it is with what now is. . . . Many if not most ethical debates result from ignorance of what is being discussed. In fact, you could say the hotter the debate, the likelier it is that the participants to some large degree don't know what they are talking about.[5]

Certainly contemporary ethics puts a great deal more stress on understanding the circumstances of a proposed action than traditional ethics did, whether religious or secular. Much of this emphasis is due to modern realizations that the pace of change in the world has increased a great deal in the last few centuries and still continues to increase. Until the last century or two, many scholars assumed that the world was largely static, and since there was little change in humans or their societies, little attention needed to be paid to the material circumstances of proposed actions.

This emphasis on understanding the context is not limited to religious ethics but extends through many disciplines, religious and secular. Until relatively recently, most Christians read the New Testament as if Jesus had been a Christian speaking to contemporary Christians instead of a Jew speaking to first-century Jews. Situating Jesus in his own historical cultural context has made a huge difference in understanding who Jesus was, what he taught, and how he understood his mission, and therefore in how Christians understand the ethical demands of Christian faith. Similar changes have been taking place in other religions as the history and culture of foundational periods are explored contextually.

Context is important, then, at two levels. It is critical for understanding the reality in which ethical obligation exists today. But context is also important for understanding and evaluating the principles and rules that come to us in the moral traditions of religions. What was the context in which these principles and rules were revealed, and how does that context compare to ours? When we look carefully, we see that some parts of the rules in sacred texts have been set aside over the centuries as not applicable because they were rooted in a context that no longer exists. Thus the Orthodox in Israel have made no attempt to implement the punishments decreed in the Torah for moral offenses, including capital punishment for offenses such as kidnapping (Exod. 21:16), adultery (Lev. 20:10), cursing father or mother (Lev. 21:17), rape (Deut. 22:23-27), or even rebellion in a son (Deut. 21:18-21).

Though the Qur'an also lists a number of very stiff penalties for moral offenses, for example, the cutting off of right hands for convicted thieves (Qur'an 5:38), virtually no Muslim nations implement this in their penal codes, not even in those nations whose legal systems are said to fully incorporate shari'ah law. In both cases, there is increasing concern in the modern period that some punishments that may have been necessary and appropriate in more primitive living conditions are too severe in late modernity, especially given contemporary awareness of the possibility of error in judicial applications.

The issues that face us as individuals and societies today are more complex than ever before, in part because of the actions that humans have already chosen. For example, today we ask what should be done about "trash" in the space orbits around earth and who should take responsibility for it, but only a few generations ago the question would have been impossible to even conceive, since humans had not yet moved into space. Similarly, humans have over many millennia transformed much of the natural environment, so decisions in environmental ethics must take into account the environment as it exists today, not only an abstract theological understanding of nature as originally created. Whereas just a few centuries ago the overwhelming human preoccupation was simply human survival amid the intimidating power of nature, today we ask questions about how humans should preserve other species and habitats in nature. In order to answer any of these questions, we need a great deal of data about what is: what species there are, where they live, in what numbers, requiring what kind and size of habitat, how species are related (as in food chains), and what factors impact the numbers and health of species. Today social analysis is an indispensable element of religious ethics.[6]

But social analysis does not just explain the physical world to us. It also involves looking at the history of relationships, as in labor history, or the historical developments that have taken place in marriage over the centuries, or what modern medicine tells us about the maturation process in children, all of which may and should influence the decisions we make in specific situations. There are few if any types of knowledge that are not relevant to some moral situations in which humans must make crucial decisions.

Shorthand Rules in Religion

In dealing with personal quotidian behaviors, some religions have concise sets of the most basic ethical rules or practices, such as the Ten Commandments for Christians (originally of course from the Hebrew Scriptures), the Five Pillars of Islam, the Five Moral Precepts for Buddhists, or the Five Major Vows (Vratas) of Jains. These rules are a kind of shorthand. These can either be very commonsense rules

necessary if people are to live together in stable societies, or very particular rules (as in the Five Pillars) that distinguish this believer from another.

FIVE MORAL PRECEPTS (BUDDHIST)

1. I undertake the training rule to abstain from taking life.
2. I undertake the training rule to abstain from taking what is not given.
3. I undertake the training rule to abstain from sexual misconduct.
4. I undertake the training rule to abstain from false speech.
5. I undertake the training rule to abstain from fermented drink that causes heedlessness.

THE FIVE PILLARS OF ISLAM (OBLIGATORY PRACTICES)

1. *Shahada*, reciting the creed
2. *Salat*, saying five daily prayers
3. *Sawm*, dawn to sunset fasting during the holy month of Ramadan
4. *Zakat*, almsgiving to the poor
5. *Hadj*, the pilgrimage to Mecca at least once in a lifetime if possible

THE GREAT VOWS OF JAINISM (MAHAVRATA)

1. *Ahimsa*, nonviolence toward all beings
2. *Satya*, truthfulness
3. *Asteya*, nonstealing
4. *Brahmacharya*, chastity (celibacy for monks and nuns)
5. *Aparigraha*, nonpossessiveness

TEN COMMANDMENTS (CHRISTIANITY)

1. I am the LORD your God, who brought you out of the land of Egypt, out of the house of bondage. You shall have no other gods before Me.
2. You shall not make for yourself a carved image—any likeness of anything that is in heaven above, or that is in the earth beneath, or that is in the water under the earth; you shall not bow down to them nor serve them. For I, the LORD your God, am a jealous God, visiting the iniquity of the fathers on the children to the third and fourth generations of those who hate Me, but showing mercy to thousands, to those who love Me and keep My commandments.
3. You shall not take the name of the LORD your God in vain, for the LORD will not hold him guiltless who takes His name in vain.
4. Remember the Sabbath day, to keep it holy. Six days you shall labor and do all your work, but the seventh day is the Sabbath of the LORD your God. In it you shall do no work: you, nor your son, nor your daughter, nor your male servant, nor your female servant, nor your cattle, nor your stranger who is within your gates. For in six days the LORD made the heavens and the earth, the sea, and all that is in them, and rested the seventh day. Therefore the LORD blessed the Sabbath day and hallowed it.
5. Honor your father and your mother, that your days may be long upon the land which the LORD your God is giving you.
6. You shall not murder.
7. You shall not commit adultery.
8. You shall not steal.
9. You shall not bear false witness against your neighbor.
10. You shall not covet your neighbor's house; you shall not covet your neighbor's wife, nor his male servant, nor his female servant, nor his ox, nor his donkey, nor anything that is your neighbor's.

Some of these sets of rules are very similar to each other. The Buddhist and Jain precepts/vows are very similar to each other largely because Jainism so influenced both Hinduism and Buddhism in India. But some of these also match many of the Christian commandments. The Muslim list is different, in that it does not list the most basic moral rules for humans (not killing, lying, stealing, or committing sexual offenses), which are also observed by Muslims, but instead only lists the requirements that are peculiarly Muslim, those that distinguish Muslim believers from all others.

One reason why the Buddhist, Jain, and Christian rules are so similar is that they are the most basic rules for all humans, but they are not by any means the only ethical rules in these religions. They symbolize, without exhausting, the entire moral tradition of the religion. Not all religions have such concise representations of their moral system. The religions that make up what we call Hinduism, for example, have many sources/codes for guiding moral conduct. And because the Christian Ten Commandments come from the Hebrew Scriptures, in the two millennia since rabbinic Judaism was born, the

613 *mitzvot*, or Jewish laws, have become so emphasized that the symbolism of the Ten Commandments is often regarded as part of Jewish history, but not so useful as symbol today, perhaps in part due to its adoption by Christianity.

Choosing an Ethical Method

What, then, can we conclude about ethical method? What method should we choose? Perhaps the wisest because most practical path is not to restrict ourselves to one method, but to be guided by the situation. Each of these three methods of ethics—rule-based, consequential, and virtue ethics—has advantages and disadvantages. When there is general agreement between religions about a rule of conduct, and that rule does not run counter to contemporary experience, we will be inclined to accept that rule. When there are differences between religions on what one should do in a given circumstance, or when religious rules seem in conflict with contemporary communal experience, we will examine the implications of each option for both the development of virtuous character in the agent and for the flourishing of all persons affected by the decision. A certain amount of flexibility in choosing method is necessary.

This approach is pragmatic, but it is not new or original. It is what we humans do on an everyday basis. Much of ethics is about creating habits of virtue. The Christian theologian Thomas Aquinas defined a virtue as "a good habit of the mind, by which we live righteously."[7] Most of the actions/decisions we make on a daily basis are repetitive. We do not need to ask before eating breakfast each day where our breakfast food came from, who grew it, whether they received a fair price for it, or other related questions, because most

of our breakfasts follow a pattern. Once we have decided on a Fair Trade brand of coffee, eggs from a local farm, and bread from the local baker, we do not need to rethink the social ethics of our breakfast every day. In the same way, if we have made a habit of truth-telling rather than lying, we continue to follow the "Do not lie" rule without reminders. Only once in a while do we hesitate before an unusual situation, not sure that telling the truth to the distraught neighbor holding a butcher knife who wants to know his wife's location is the best option. If his wife is in the garden kissing the FedEx delivery man, the consequences of truth-telling might be very negative for all concerned.

Most of the time, we automatically either follow inculcated rules first taught us as children or follow our own ethical rules that we created by tweaking or replacing rules proposed to us in the course of our socialization. When I do not curse in front of our grandchildren, it is because I long ago accepted childhood rules against cursing. When my husband does not curse in front of our grandchildren, he is following a piece of his own ethical code that was hard-learned when we were young parents. He did not want to set the same example for his sons that his own father, a very good person but a champion curser, had set for him. But it was very difficult to retrain himself not to curse. We arrived at the same point via different methods, rule-based for me and consequentialist for him.

Conscience

As we near the end of this treatment of ethical method, some of you are probably wondering, "Where is conscience in all this?" Conscience is both freestanding and closely related to these reasoned approaches to moral decision making. Conscience is that part of humans that alerts us to a moral need to act. Conscience is not usually an answer to a consciously asked moral question; the action it demands does not often follow closely reasoned decision making. It is often impulsive, certainly compulsive, and difficult to explain or justify. "I just had to do it. I didn't have a choice," is perhaps the most common explanation following an act of conscience.

Of course, it is not really the case that acts of conscience come out of nowhere and are not connected to processes of moral reasoning, regardless of the fact that they often feel that way. In the same way that we can puzzle over where we left our cell phone, look for it for hours, and then wake up the next morning with a sudden knowledge of where it is, some acts of conscience can follow days or weeks when we genuinely do not know which way to decide on a problem. Reason has not convinced us to choose any of the available options. We are stymied until—*boom!*—we have acted. We did not see it coming, and cannot explain it. It was just the right thing to do.

Sometimes there is no question posed. A situation suddenly plays out in front of us. We respond immediately (or not) to a situation, as when a stranger sees a child in the window of a burning building and immediately runs in to rescue him. The stranger may die in the attempt or may successfully rescue the child, because the act was not a reasoned one but an impulsive one. It could go either way, but the stranger felt that she had no choice. The child's life had to be saved.

Or we do not act, do not follow the voice of conscience. We know when the moment is past, and we may feel empty, that we did wrong by not acting. We missed the opportunity. We have let down someone or some others; but even more, we have failed ourselves.

We lacked the courage to act on what we knew in our hearts was the morally correct (but difficult) course. We are ashamed; we are rudderless.

These acts of conscience that seem to come out of nowhere in fact emerge from the depths of one's personhood, from who one really is. The feeling that there is no choice concerning the act arises from an understanding that to refuse this act, to deny the voice that demands it, is to surrender all that one is. Often, the personhood at stake is one that has been carefully crafted through a series of decisions that constitutes a personal moral code. For others, the personhood at stake in heeding or not the voice of conscience is not so much one that is fully formed, but the very possibility of personhood, of character. To deny this voice feels like forfeiting all hope of becoming a person of moral character, worthy of respect.

In many cases when we fail to respond to the voice of conscience, we do so because we are seduced by what presents itself to us as the voice of reason. That voice murmurs in our ear that the consequences of doing the just or loving thing may be too grave for us to risk, that the punishments for disobeying rules can be harsh, that we should wait and see or let someone else who is better prepared do the act. But it is important to remember that reason is not the enemy of conscience or morality. Reason is a tool that can be used in both moral and immoral ways. In fact, the imperative nature of the voice of our conscience represents a moral personhood that reason has helped to craft and still supports, however quietly.

Very few of us have fully formed consciences, because these develop over time. Therefore there are many moral situations in which our conscience may be silent and we must, often painfully, discern what is the right thing to do. It is in those cases that we need to work through the moral decision-making process, choosing what seems to us to be the most moral option. The more often we work through these moral decision-making processes, the more we have formed our personal moral code, and the more frequently our conscience can speak to us.

NOTES

1. In the Reformation, Luther originally objected to indulgences—i.e., prayers and actions that could be done by a penitent to earn released time from purgatory for self or others—objecting to the concept of earning salvation. He insisted that salvation could not be earned but was the free gift of God to those of faith. The Catholic Church insisted on the power of good works as well as faith.

2. Edith Wyschogrod, *Saints and Postmodernism: Revisioning Moral Philosophy* (Chicago: University of Chicago Press, 1990).

3. For examples of casuistry in contemporary ethics, see Richard Brian Miller, *Casuistry and Modern Ethics: A Poetics of Practical Reasoning* (Chicago: University of Chicago Press, 1996).

4. Daniel C. Maguire, *Ethics: A Complete Method for Moral Choice* (Minneapolis: Fortress Press, 2010), 71.

5. Ibid., 81.

6. A handy little book explaining how to do social analysis for religious persons is *Social Analysis: Linking Faith and Justice* by Joe Holland and Peter Henriot (Maryknoll, NY: Orbis, 1983).

7. Thomas Aquinas, *Summa Theologiae* I–II, 55.4.

CHAPTER 2

RELIGIONS ON FOOD, FASTING, AND FEASTING

Food is, with water, our most basic human need. It is a need all humans share. Food not only satisfies our survival needs by filling our stomachs but also has possibilities of delighting our palate and our eyes. Because it is so necessary, food is multivalent as a symbol. Historically many different kinds of food have taken on new meanings when they were shared, given, refused, or sacrificed in a variety of religious cultures and social contexts.

Framing the Issues

Many moderns today ask what value religious teachings on food should have—after all, they were composed so long ago, in such different contexts from ours. Some people think that value should only be attached to religious teachings on food if they continue to serve a clearly useful purpose in the postmodern world. There is an assumption that many of these teachings are outdated, based on insufficient or mistaken information, and are simply superstition.

For others, religious teachings on food, like other teachings and practices in their religious tradition, are valuable in themselves both as instances of divine revelation and as connecting people alive today to ancestors and other fellow believers of the past. In this chapter we will look at some religious teachings and practices on food, the proposed purposes of such practices, and the impact of such practices today, in hopes of helping us decide on appropriate ethical approaches to food. Individual readers must, of course, decide for themselves the revelatory status of religious teachings on food.

Religions seem to have been intimately bound up with food from the beginnings of humankind. Anthropologists have found prehistoric remains of food sacrifices that appear to have been offered to the gods in hopes of their granting successful hunts. In a number of indigenous religions, including, for example, those of Northwest natives in the United States, annual offerings were, and are, made to the Master of Animals and Mistress of the Seas, both in thanksgiving for allowing humans successful hunting or fishing in the past year and in hopes of persuading these powerful deities to allow continued success in the coming year.[1] Similarly, prayers to the Rice Goddess (under many names) for good harvests are still commonplace among agricultural peoples throughout Asia.

Many religions have also included among their ceremonies feasts of food to be either consumed by the religious community as a whole or offered by individuals to the gods or to dead ancestors. Feast days of the patron saint of village churches among Latin American Catholics have been traditionally celebrated with elaborate meals for the whole village, often supplied by a local wealthy family. Anthropologists have noted that such religiously based feasts, often centered on roasting one or more large animals, predated Catholicism in Latin America. In native religions around the world, such feasts were not only a way of distributing necessary protein to poorer members of the community who might otherwise have little access to meat, but were also a way of redistributing wealth, as the sponsorship of a feast day or other celebration could deplete the wealth of even the relatively rich.[2]

In many religions across the world, from Africa to China, family members "feed" the dead of the family, sometimes by taking elaborate meals to the cemetery on special days, such as the Mexican Day of the Dead,[3] but at other times by simply pouring the first sip of a drink or the first bite of a meal into the ground to appease the spirits of the dead, so that the ancestors will lend their support to the ongoing efforts of the family to support life and prosperity.

Religious Fasting and Food Taboos

But societies and religions have not only been involved in the struggle of humans to find sufficient food for survival. They have also been concerned about what people eat, with whom they eat, and when they eat. Various societies have therefore tabooed some foods, either absolutely, as in the Muslim and Jewish ban on eating pork, or at certain times, such as the Catholic ban on eating meat during Fridays of Lent, or the food and tobacco bans that are part of the *couvade* imposed on expectant fathers in some indigenous cultures.

Many religious cultures have also demanded of their followers periods of fasting—not eating any food, and usually not any drink, as in Jewish fasting on the Day of Atonement or Muslim fasting during the lunar month of Ramadan. The purpose of such fasts is variously described as atonement for sin, self-discipline, and reconnecting with the divine.

Fig. 2.1. A graveyard decorated for the Mexican Day of the Dead celebration.

Fasting can also be a central part of voluntary rituals undertaken by individuals for purposes of purification or absolution. For example, in Javanese mysticism, individuals can decide at any time to fast for three or five or more days by not eating or drinking during daylight hours. There are further refinements in this voluntary fast. For example, a "white fast" is one in which, during the sunset to sunrise hours when one may eat, one eats only white rice and drinks only water. The purpose of such fasting is to develop the discipline and self-control that both purify one by distancing one from the material world and aid in prayer and meditation.

Caroline Walker Bynum, in her treatment of the fasting of medieval Christian women, describes how the impulse to voluntarily fast comes about, representing it as a human attempt both to link to the divine and to overcome the anxiety associated with dependence on insecure food sources by demonstrating the superiority of their wills over the interests of their bodies:

> Anthropologists and students of comparative religion who once looked for a single cause or motive for religious responses are now content to see many complex strands in fasting behavior. But it seems clear that in pre-industrial societies, where resources were limited, men and women frequently respond to the rhythm of plenty and scarcity, harvest and famine, by deciding to control it through voluntary fasting and believe that they can in this way coerce from the gods dreams and visions, health, good fortune or fertility. The earliest forms of fasting were often connected with fertility cults, with goddesses, and with women's physiological processes. Penitential or propitiatory

fasting seems to arise from this sense of nature's rhythm: if nature erratically and unpredictably humbles one through hunger, one may punish or humiliate oneself before God by similar humbling. This sense of food as a sign of vulnerability, a reminder (through flatulence and hunger pangs) of the toll the body can exact, can lead to the ascetic impulse—the desire to defy corporeal limits by denying bodily needs.[4]

Thus fasting can be analogous to other religious practices that push the body to extreme limits, aiming at inducing trance or altered consciousness that may allow communication with the divine or with spirits. Or fasting can be practiced as a way of atoning for some transgression or simply as a discipline aimed at strengthening one's control over one's body. Fasting as a voluntary ascetic practice is found in many religions, though there are great variations in the severity of fasting. Those variations may be signals of different purposes in voluntary fasting, as we will see.

Religious Treatment Concerning Food, Fasting, and Feasting

Probably the oldest understanding of divinity is as creator and renewer of nature. Fertility seems to have been central to the worship of early humans, which is understandable, as their lives depended upon the fertility of nature. An abundance of figurines of very pregnant human females with large breasts, sometimes with the heads of birds, have been found on or around altars in prehistoric sites.[5] Anthropology suggests that the earliest religious practices concerning food were prayers and offerings to the gods imploring help in obtaining food, whether by hunting or gathering, and later by harvesting crops. There are still a number of places in the world where malnutrition and even starvation, sometimes endemic and other times temporary following natural disasters or wars, make prayers and sacrifices offered to the gods in hopes of food assistance a common religious practice. Even in the agricultural areas of relatively rich nations, prayer rituals for rain for crops and for bountiful harvests are still commonplace today. In times of severe drought, even urban religious communities beg the divine for rain, lest food markets empty of food and prices skyrocket beyond individual means.

Fig. 2.2. Image of the Venus of Willendorf, an ancient fertility goddess.

Blessing the Andean Potato Crop

Some years ago near Puno, Peru, in the Andean Altiplano, I participated in a syncretic Christian/Aymaran ritual to bless the potato crop—the staple food in that area. A group of about fifteen farmers and their families who farmed small plots of land on the steep hillsides near the top of a mountain gathered together with their parish priest and me, painted their faces with colored flour paste, played a variety of native musical instruments, waved huge sunflowers like wands above their heads, and paraded, dancing, from one small potato plot to another. On the nearby mountainsides, a number of processions to other potato patches were visible.

At each plot, one potato plant would be carefully dug up to see how many potatoes and of what size were growing at its roots. It was only halfway through the growing season, but as the farmers explained, by harvesttime it was too late to implore divine help for a poor crop. Everyone exclaimed over the number of potatoes growing on each plant's roots, sometimes with glee and sometimes with dismay. Prayers asking for help with the crop, or of thanksgiving if the crop looked to be plentiful (as was generally the case this time), were addressed to Jesus Christ, to the *apus* (the spirits of the mountains), and to *Pacha Mama* (Mother Earth). Each of the uprooted plants, before being carefully replanted, received a sprinkling of wine as an offering to these deities, and then everyone in the group took a sip of wine. Immediately the group danced their way to the plot of another member of the group and began the process again.

This syncretic ritual, like many others involving prayers for bountiful crops, actually serves a number of purposes. The obvious purpose is to involve the divine in the feeding of the community: "Please give us a bountiful harvest that will last us through the winter." But another social function fulfilled in the ritual is binding members of the community together in common cause. Should some localized disaster destroy the potatoes in one family plot, other families who had shared in this ritual with the affected family would feel some need to share. (This is probably the reason why none of the plots of the ritual group were adjacent to one another, lest whatever pest affect one also affect all the others.) Those who celebrate together, who experience in the ritual a shared dependence on nature and the divine, are more likely to feel solidarity with each other: to look at the afflicted other and say, "That could be my family."

Jewish Shabbat and Seder Meals

The Jewish Shabbat meal after Friday sunset is a feast welcoming the Sabbath, the day of rest. It begins with the lighting of candles and blessings over the wine and challah (bread). Singing is traditional at Shabbat meals. The seder meal on Passover—like all Jewish holiday meals—is based on the Shabbat meal, though it is usually more elaborate, with some special features. At the seder meal ushering in the Jewish feast of Passover, which celebrates God's sending Moses to lead the Hebrews out of slavery in Egypt, the Haggadah, a special prayer book recounting the journey to freedom, is read. Among seder customs is reclining at table to symbolize the freedom achieved in the exodus, as well as drinking four cups of wine and eating matzoh, an unleavened bread representing the haste in which the Hebrews left Egypt—without the time to allow the bread to rise.

The Jewish Passover seder was the historical model for the Christian Holy Thursday

Fig. 2.3. Use of challah (bread) and wine in the Jewish Shabbat meal.

(Maundy Thursday) meal, which recalls Jesus as an observant Jew celebrating the Jewish Passover with his band of disciples in the Upper Room in Jerusalem the night before he died, at what Christians call the Last Supper. Three of the four Gospels (lives of Jesus) in the New Testament recount Jesus instituting Eucharist: he transformed the bread and wine into his body and blood, and told his disciples to follow his example.

Christian Eucharist

The Christian Eucharist holds a special place among the multitude of religious feasts, for in it many (but not all Christians)[6] understand themselves as feasting on the body and blood of Jesus himself. While non-Christians have frequently been appalled by this image of eating Jesus' body and blood, understanding this practice as a kind of mental cannibalism, for most Christians Eucharist offers the most obvious and accessible path to communion with the risen Jesus Christ. For this reason it is often called a "foretaste of heaven." The Eucharist has always been for Christians a reminder that we do not live by bread alone—that humans also have a hunger for meaning, for values, for loving and being loved in community.

During some periods of Christianity, the presence of the body and blood of Jesus in the Eucharist was interpreted to be not only superior food, but also sufficient food, as if

Fig. 2.4. The Eucharist, or Holy Communion, in the Christian tradition.

human need for material food was a moral weakness. This overemphasis on asceticism was morally dangerous, not only for human health, but also in that instead of producing material relief for those who were poor and hungry, it sometimes led to a callousness toward the material needs of the poor and even a message to the hungry to concentrate on spiritual food. At other times, devotion to the Eucharist has been very closely linked not only to individual spiritual discipline, but also to acts of charity, to concern for the bodily needs of the poor and hungry.

Cannibalistic Feasting

There is also the well-known case of the Fore tribe in Papua New Guinea, who practiced cannibalistic funerary rites for their own dead. Many women and children of the Fore died of a wasting disease called *kuru*. The practice of funerary cannibalism was finally outlawed a generation ago when science discovered that the cause of *kuru* was eating the brains of a diseased ancestor—the brain being the portion assigned to women and children.[7]

Eating the bodies of one's own dead as found among the Fore is rare among human societies, but a number of cultures have routinely eaten one or more organs of defeated enemies, usually the heart or liver. This practice was especially found among warrior cultures, in which many of the customs and practices revolve around the defeat of enemies. Though literally eating the bodies of defeated enemies suggests a gloating at their defeat, it was the organs of the most respected warriors among the enemy defeated that were usually chosen for ingestion. The organ eaten by the victorious usually represented the organ that they believed to be the seat of virtues such as courage. Some warrior societies today, for example the Mai-Mai militia in contemporary

Congo, still believe that ingesting the organs of the defeated allows one to acquire both the power and the character virtues of the defeated warriors.[8] When such beliefs become allied with magical thinking, such as the Mai-Mai belief that bullets and missiles aimed at them will become water upon approach due to the water rituals that have prepared them for battle, they can reinforce, especially in the young, a feeling of invincibility that can have tragic consequences.

Funerary feasting, Eucharist, fasting, and all religious food rituals that cause humans to recognize their dependence on the Creator and/or nature itself can encourage us to be humble, not arrogant, and to recognize our smallness in the grand scheme of things. Such humility supports a general solidarity that can produce cooperative attitudes and concern for the common good. Humility in the face of dependence also supports a kind of self-reflection (an important aspect of spirituality), a questioning of our role, our place in the world, and our behavior. Humility points us toward a reality beyond ourselves that not only depresses any arrogance on our part, but also for many people calls to us, demanding that we look inward, beyond materiality, to a realm of spirit. For many in organized religions, that spiritual realm is one of communion with a specific God; for others it is understood simply as grounding oneself in reality or connecting to another dimension in human life. There are many possibilities. Spiritual and religious cultures share an understanding that there is something ultimate beyond individual material existence, and that in order to be fully human, it is necessary to connect to that ultimacy. Various disciplines have been discovered that assist humans in this connection to ultimacy, and some of those disciplines involve food—in shared feasts, personal fasts, or food abstentions that may be individual or collective.

Fasting as Discipline, Penance, and Purification

Like feasting, fasting serves a number of different purposes. One common purpose is purification, as when persons fast in preparation for some special occasion. Until the Second Vatican Council, Catholics not only observed days of fasting and abstinence, but were obliged to fast for some hours before receiving Eucharist, lest the holy meal mingle with profane food in the recipient. Fasting for purification has had a long history among the priests and priestesses of many religious cults as a way of preparing them for close communication with the divine.

Another common religious purpose of fasting is atonement. Fasting can serve as a method of atonement when an individual or community has been judged guilty of some grievous offense against deity. A twenty-four-hour fast from both food and drink is one aspect of the Jewish Day of Atonement, Yom Kippur, on which Jews reflect on their sins of the past year and ask forgiveness.

A third purpose of fasting is discipline, to gain and demonstrate mastery over one's body. Periods of fasting have been obligatory for monastics of many religions. Still today, Buddhist monks and nuns do not eat after the noon meal, but fast until the next morning. Some groups that include fasting as part of their discipline understand it as a regime for maintaining both physical and spiritual health, crediting it with purging both physical and spiritual toxins from the self. Yet a fourth purpose of fasting can be as a form of sacrificial offering to the deity that is endured in order to persuade deity to heed our pleas for divine favor.

Sometimes these different functions of fasting are all present in the same fasting practice, as is the case in the Muslim fast during the lunar month of Ramadan. During this month, adult Muslims fast from all sustenance—all food and drink—from sunrise to sunset. Since Ramadan is based on the lunar calendar, it moves through the seasons of the year, so that in some years the fasting day may be much longer than others in areas not on the equator. Ramadan fasting can serve all these purposes—offering, sacrifice, discipline, atonement, purification—but the chief reason for the practice is that Allah commanded it.

The Ramadan fast is one of the five pillars of Islam, and Muslims take great pride in conquering this difficult discipline. Especially for Muslims who live in tropical or desert climates, twelve to fifteen hours without either food or water, day after day, is physically demanding. There is also reward, not only at the end of each day of fasting when family and friends gather to break the fast, but especially at Eid ul Fitr, when all Muslims celebrate the end of Ramadan with a major holiday filled with feasting and celebration.

Fasting for Visions

Yet another purpose of a fast could be to influence the gods to send visions, as Walker noted above. In many religious settings, including the Christian one to which Walker alludes above, fasting was understood to either induce the gods to make personal contact, or for humans to become open to such contact by taking down the everyday barriers that impede divine/human contact. Fasting became a regime for the supplicant, a regime dedicated to achieving the spiritual plane on which the divine could be experienced. Fasting has been a common practice among shamans the world over for this reason. For many mystics still today, fasting disrupts ordinary consciousness and brings about an altered consciousness in which visions and other forms of revelation can occur. Hallucinogenic substances such as peyote and

Fig. 2.5. A Turkish feast for breaking the Ramadan fast at sunset.

extreme physical exertion such as produced in the Native American Sun Dance, have been other means used to seek such religious experience through transcending ordinary reality. Fasting, then, has often been part of the discipline practiced by religious mystics and shamans who desire communion with the Divine or mediums who desire contact with spirits of the dead.

Food Fests

Religious food festivals have been routine in many cultures, particularly as thanksgiving for good harvests or hunts—the origin, of course, of the American holiday of Thanksgiving—but also for weddings and funerals. One might ask, Why feasting for funerals and not for births, which seem much more related to wedding celebrations? One important reason for lesser association between births and feasting is a historical one. Until relatively recently in human history, birth carried with it a great deal of uncertainty due to high infant (and maternal) mortality rates. A walk through any graveyard from the nineteenth century or earlier will demonstrate the multitude of infants—sometimes as high as 50 percent of live births—who died within their first year, often within days of birth. So common was this that many families did not name children until they were months or even years old. In some cultures naming a child was understood as possibly drawing the attention of demons that might attack the child, and so naming was delayed until the child was stronger and more developed.

On the other hand, death and funerals were final. Unlike those born into life who might succumb to death almost immediately, normally everyone who died stayed dead. Also, while the infant at birth had interacted with virtually none of its society other than its mother and perhaps immediately after birth its father, adult dead were more intimately connected to the life of the community, so that their passing affected a much larger group. There was also a sense that all the living had yet to pass through the veil between the living and the dead, so that it was wise to pay attention to the food needs of the dead whom one would one day join—and who in many cultures were, and are, thought able to exert considerable power over their descendants in this life as well.

Historically, festivals have been communal. Harvest festivals typically included the entire village or town. The American Thanksgiving festival, said to originally include both the entire Pilgrim community as well as the natives who had helped the Pilgrims survive the first year until harvest, is one example of harvest festival.

Jewish Sukkot. The Jewish festival of Sukkot began as a harvest festival in ancient Israel, as its biblical name "the Feast of Ingathering" denotes. It was to be celebrated "at the end of the year when you gather in your labors out of the field" (Exod. 23:16); "after you have gathered in from your threshing-floor and from your winepress" (Deut. 16:13). The Torah pronounced God's instructions for this holiday: "You shall live in booths seven days; all citizens in Israel shall live in booths, in order that future generations may know that I made the Israelite people live in booths when I brought them out of the land of Egypt" (Lev. 23:42-43). Today during Sukkot, Jewish neighborhoods in the United States often sport canvas tents (booths) in the yard, with people relaxing inside with food and drink.

Weddings across religions. Around the world, weddings have almost always been occasions for feasting, and continue to be so. There were many reasons for this. Weddings often tied together two extended families, increasing their strength and networks of support, sometimes even ending violence between them. Weddings were about the hope of fertility, new generations to further strengthen the extended families. In some cultures the feast was and is the responsibility of the bride's family, as is common in much of the United States, but in other cultures, it is the groom's family who hosts the feast; in yet others, the burden is shared between the two families.

As globalization often brings about weddings of persons from very different religious cultures, friends and families today are frequently treated to "double weddings": one wedding ceremony in each tradition, and often a wedding feast in each tradition as well. In recent years I have been to two such weddings of my students. The first was a Chinese-American student who married a Euro-American Lutheran, and the second was an Indian-American student who married a Euro-American Catholic. The bride and groom in both cases chose (with parental persuasion) to marry in two different ceremonies, with completely different clothing. Both brides wore white western wedding dresses in the Christian ceremonies, but a red cheongsam in the Chinese Buddhist ceremony and a red sari in the Hindu ceremony (in many Asian cultures, red is the symbol of fertility, of life and joy). Guests at both weddings were invited to receptions after each wedding ceremony, with lavish meals appropriate to the culture of the ceremony.

Weddings are so associated with feasting that for rich families there is sometimes no limit to the lavishness of the occasion. In India in April 2011 the food minister announced the government's intention of limiting the size and waste in weddings.[9] A rich politician had just hosted 30,000 guests at his son's wedding, complete with over five hundred food counters (each one with a different dish). The minister said that an average of 30 percent of the food prepared for weddings in India is wasted, and that such wastage is indefensible when so many millions of Indians are hungry due to rising food prices.

Funerary feasting. Funerals have always been communal. In many cultures, bells or gongs or other forms of public announcement were sounded with news of the death of each member, and all persons in the locale were invited to the funeral, which invariably involved feasting. Today, though we increasingly see notices of "private funerals," there is still some residual "feasting" at American funerals, either lunches in the church hall following funerals in the church or an invitation for all the mourners to come to the house of the deceased or that of a close relative to share a repast when the burial is complete. Today, as burials are increasingly replaced by cremations, we begin to see buffet meals for mourners at funeral homes. Frequently, especially in rural areas, friends and acquaintances of the deceased bring prepared dishes to the home of the family as a sign of support. Sometimes this food is part of the repast served to mourners, but other times it is simply a sign of sympathy intended to spare the family the work of preparing food during the first period of intense mourning.

Irish funerals historically incorporated Celtic funerary customs into Catholic practice. Nineteenth- and early-twentieth-century Irish funerals in the United States not only included food and alcoholic drink, but also dancing and card games. It was not unknown to get the corpse out of the coffin for a group picture with the mourners, or even to try to have the corpse "drink a bit."

The Celts understood funerals as celebrations of the life of the deceased, as well as a time of mourning, hence the role of food and drink.

The Garifuna (Black Carib) people of Belize practice elaborate funeral rites involving food that are outside their normal Roman Catholic faith. Within forty-eight hours of death, the body is prepared for burial and set out in the house for mourners to see. Food and rum are served to the mourners, who typically include all those in the village at the time.[10] The mourners dance to drum rhythms, which may go on all night if there is sufficient food and rum. The body is buried the next day. Beginning on the following Friday, a nine-day novena begins in which a small group of mourners meets each day at the house of the deceased for prayers said in Spanish (though the everyday language of the people is Carib). At the end of the novena, there is the ninth-day wake, in which people make final good-byes to the deceased, who is understood to have been wandering, bothering the living, since his or her spirit resurrected on the third day. At midnight of the ninth night, the crowd of mourners that has gathered outside the house while prayers were said inside is fed a feast, including rum. The eating, drinking, and dancing continue until dawn, when the novena altar is torn down and the kinswomen of the deceased wail one last time.

Sometimes the Garifuna deceased will request of the family in dreams or visions other rituals, often months or years after death, and the family is obliged to provide them. One is a requiem mass (*Helemeserun hilana*) with feasting after mass (*efeduhani laugi lemesi*), which usually takes place a few years after death. Other mourning rituals are feeding the dead (*chuga*) and feasting the dead (*dugu*), both of which are major events involving hungry multitudes and typically take place ten to fifty years after death. Garifuna mourning rituals "feed" both the dead and the living, maintaining ties between them, at the same time they separate the dead from the living, so that the living may continue on with life.

Religious Food Taboos

The most famous of all the religious taboos regarding food is the ban on eating pork that is shared by Jews, Muslims, and Seventh-day Adventists. Some Eastern Orthodox churches also discourage pork consumption, though it is not enforced. While for Jews and Adventists who follow the Mosaic law, pork is only one of the many foods that is taboo, for Muslims it is the only taboo food. There has been debate for many centuries about the reasons for this taboo. The ban appears to have been problematic in a survivalist sense, in that pigs are able to convert 35 percent of the energy in their food to meat, compared to 13 percent for sheep and only 6.5 percent for cattle. Also, while a cow needs nine months to drop a single calf, a sow can produce a litter of eight or more piglets in four months, and those piglets will gain weight twice as fast as calves. Why taboo the most efficient protein-producing animal available?

Theological conservatives have always taken the position that since the taboo on pork is the word of God, given in Torah or Qur'an, one should not question further. Nevertheless, a number of explanations have been offered, the most common by far being that of the medieval Jewish philosopher Moses Maimonides, who wrote that "[t]he principal reason why the law forbids swine-flesh is to be found in the circumstance that its habits and food are very filthy and loathsome."[11] This widespread belief that pigs are inherently dirty (generally meaning they lie in and eat feces) has been shown to be almost entirely a matter of how they are housed, a characteristic they share with a number of other species, including humans. A common modern alternative explanation is that these ancients had experience of the disease trichinosis, which is contracted from eating pork (or the meat of some wild animals) that is not sufficiently cooked, and so placed a taboo on eating pork to protect health. However, as critics point out, if that were the case, why not simply require that pork be thoroughly cooked?

Marvin Harris proposes that the reason for the historic ban on pork was rooted in the arid Middle Eastern environment shared by Jews and Muslims.[12] Pigs are animals with sparse hair and so have little protection from the sun. Also, their bodies do not shed heat well. Furthermore, they require grain, nuts, or root foods—foods also necessary for the human diet. Pigs are not ruminants like cattle, sheep, and goats, which digest cellulose (grasses) through a system of divided stomachs and cud-chewing. Pigs thrive wild in forests where they can forage for nuts, wild grains, and root foods, where there is cover from the sun and mud wallows in which they can cool themselves. When penned, they must be provided with cover from the sun, water, and a diet of grains and roots. In arid areas, pigs do not thrive and actually compete with humans for both water for wallowing and for the same food.

Thus, discouraging pigraising, Harris says, makes great sense in the Middle East. It would have been impossible for the wandering Israelites to herd pigs across the desert, and after they settled the land, pig-raising would have continued to be more costly than raising sheep, goats, or cattle because of the lack of forests. Harris supports his theory by looking at ancient cultures such as Egypt and Iraq, which shifted away from pig production as populations rose and deforestation spread. Islam, as a latter religion of the same arid area, experienced both the contextual disincentives for raising pigs and had knowledge of the Jewish religious aversion to pork. Adventists generally follow the Jewish dietary laws.

Anthropologists point out that tabooed foods are never foods that one would expect to be important food sources in the given area. One does not find taboos on fish among coastal fishers, or on pork in forested western Europe, or on buffalo among the Plains Indians. Yet food taboos are not only about telling people what is not in their survival interest to raise or grow. Food taboos can also become an important part of group identity, a sign of what group one belongs to, and a deterrent to mixing socially with other groups who might weaken or threaten one's identity within his given group.

Food Taboos and Identity

The Jewish dietary imperative to separate meat and dairy foods seems to have originally arisen from this need for distinctive identity. In Deuteronomy 14:21, and in two places in the book of Exodus in the Jewish Torah, one reads, "You should not *boil a kid in its mother's milk.*" According to many biblical scholars, this law originated in the need to distinguish (and separate) the Hebrews from the pagan Canaanites among whom they lived after the exodus from Egypt. A prominent Canaanite temple festival involved boiling a kid in its mother's milk. As Hebrew appreciation for the gift of the law increased and the need for resisting assimilation among the Canaanites continued, this prohibition on boiling a kid in its mother's milk was time and time again reinterpreted more strictly, until eventually it was understood as forbidding any mixing of meat and milk, the basis of the Jewish dietary law. Observance of the dietary law encouraged separation from other peoples, since it was impossible to share their food. Jewish dietary law also includes a number of other taboos, including those on how meat can be slaughtered: only conscious, healthy animals can be killed, and the meat must be drained of all blood.

Temporary Food Taboos

Some religions have temporary taboos on eating certain foods. For example, some indigenous religions of South America and Pacific Islands place temporary taboos on expectant fathers.[13] In a number of South American tribes, expectant fathers during the last period of pregnancy observe *couvade*, which entails taboos on certain foods and often a ban on smoking, or drinking from particular sources, and even on scratching one's body. The mother is understood to be responsible for the physical health of the child to be born, but the father's adherence to taboos is held responsible for the child's spiritual and moral health.

As we saw in chapter 1, Catholics historically observed long centuries of abstinence from meat on Fridays, though the number of these abstinence days, like the number of days of fasting, had gradually declined since medieval times and were most recently reduced following Vatican II. In general, temporary taboos on certain foods share a character with fasting and feasting, in that they serve to set apart one time from another. Dividing time into special periods is a way to break routine, to make humans conscious and reflective. Friday abstinence was understood to cause Catholics to reflect on Jesus' sacrifice on the cross for their salvation. *Couvade* was a way of attaching fathers to children by involving them in the birth process, of making fathers responsible for the welfare of children, and having them share with wives the sacrifices in reproduction.

Fasting and food taboos, like feasting, differentiate our days. Though individual humans vary a great deal in the amount of routine they can tolerate without stimulation of some kind, no humans tolerate well the boredom of unchanging sameness. Scheduling fast days, and the feast days with which they contrast, adds spice to our lives, stimulating us to think, to plan, to develop new aspects of ourselves and our relationships.

Food and Charity

All of the world religions, usually identified as Hinduism, Buddhism, Judaism, Christianity, and Islam, enjoin their members to charity, to care for the needs of others. The primary form that charity takes is the giving of food and water to those who are hungry and thirsty. The mendicant monks and nuns of Buddhism and Christianity and the *sadhus/sadhvis* of Hinduism are understood to present to laypersons opportunities for earning merit through feeding the mendicants. If fasting is an ascetic practice believed to move the practitioner closer to God, making one more open to divine communication, it also has had the advantage of presenting to laypeople in the person of the monk, nun, or *sannyasi* an immediate and recognizable religious opportunity.

When communities of monks and nuns became permanent residents in monasteries, they also practiced charity, historically offering meals to the hungry and safe overnight shelter to the traveler. Within the law of hospitality that made travel possible in the ancient and medieval world, feeding hungry people occupied a central place, which will be examined in more depth in the final chapter.

New Ethical Questions on Food, Fasting, and Feasting

Today there are some new ethical questions concerning food that have arisen in the late modern context but are rooted in the values that have been attached to food for millennia.

Vegetarianism

Food shortages for the last few years have been pressuring food prices higher all over the world. There is no doubt that a principal cause of the food shortages is good news—more and more people in places that have in the past suffered massive starvation and malnutrition, such as China and India, can now afford sufficient food. There are also other causes that are not such good news, such as large-scale use of food crops for energy (biofuels), or difficulties in global transport (e.g., lack of refrigerated transport in India). One effect of food shortages and rising prices is that many of those millions who had crept out of malnourished poverty over the last decades are being pushed back into it by rising prices, and some of those groups that remained malnourished are now facing severe malnourishment, even starvation.

There is a developing consensus between the environmental movement and those within what is called in many nations "the hunger lobby" that the appropriate ethical response to food shortages and rising food prices is a global shift away from meat-eating toward vegetarianism. The higher castes of Hinduism are traditionally vegetarian, as are many Buddhists[14] and New Agers. Some persons in all these groups have been known to suggest that meat-eating in humans is linked to higher levels of aggression (though there is not yet any scientific corroboration for this widely held view). Even among Hindus who are not vegetarian, there is a strong avoidance of beef, since the cow is a sacred symbol in Hinduism and cannot be killed or eaten.[15] Meat taboos, both the Muslim and Jewish ban on pork and those treated above, are therefore common in world religions.

Meat protein represents tremendously more energy than plant protein—for cattle, up to fifty-four times more—as well as much higher inputs of water. Meat production also produces a great deal more air pollution, most of it in the form of methane gas, which has many times the capacity of carbon dioxide to heat the atmosphere, and thus worsen global warming. In many parts of the world, forests are being cut to clear pastureland for raising meat herds—pastureland that is quickly exhausted, but very difficult to return to forest.[16]

These reasons for curtailing meat consumption do not mean that everyone is ethically obliged to immediately become vegetarian or vegan. But it does mean that we should all be decreasing our consumption of meat: shifting from steaks, chops, and chicken quarters to casseroles, soups, risottos, and pastas with, at most, small amounts of meat for flavoring, and planning meatless meals some days each week. We might still have turkey for Christmas or Thanksgiving, or a hamburger on our birthday. But per person annual meat consumption needs to drop significantly. Those in the West must take the lead in this shift, for not only are they the greatest consumers of meat, but those around the world who are becoming increasingly prosperous are imitating western styles and habits, including tremendous increases of meat in their diets. There is little chance that they will agree to go back to what was regarded as meatless poverty unless the West sets some example.

Shifting from meat to fish is not an ethical option, either. Virtually every ocean fish that humans like to eat exists in radically diminished numbers today, a few even in danger of extinction[17] (Chilean sea bass, for example). The majority of the world's fisheries have been overfished; 70 percent are now fished at capacity or exceeding capacity. Because the oceans belong to all, it is difficult to get agreement on limiting fish catches (or even catches of endangered whales) in international waters. Nations have been limited to restricting catches within their own territorial waters. The most effective way to protect the ability of the next generations to have fish in their diet is for consumers both to consume less fish and to refuse to buy seafood that is not sustainably harvested.[18]

Obesity

Another current food issue in ethical debate in much of the developed world, especially in the United States, but already seen in some developing nations, is obesity. Obesity is not just a matter of eating too much food, of course. It is also connected to what kind of food we eat and how much exercise we get. The rate of obesity in American children is alarming, and a number of partial responses are being tried, including making school lunch meals more nutritious and less caloric, and removing soda and snack machines from school property. But even in the schools there are cross-cutting trends as well, such as declines in property tax revenues prompting cuts in physical education, and cash-strapped schools accepting gifts of educational TV programming that includes advertising for high-sugar, high-salt snack foods.

Obesity in children is matched by obesity in adults. U.S. males rank third in the world in terms of percentage of the population that is obese, and U.S. females rank sixth.[19] Adult obesity is due to many of the same causes as child obesity, one of which is a shift in families from home-cooked meals "from scratch" to fast food, snacks, and high-calorie drinks. The power of advertising in the late-modern world has been one force pushing consumption of high-caloric food with low nutrition content, but it is not alone responsible. The movement of women into the workforce two generations ago in response to the decline in the buying power of men's salaries has brought about situations in which no one in many homes has the time or energy to cook meals anymore. In many families, in fact, there is no longer anyone who knows *how* to cook. The term *cook* is increasingly used for anyone who warms pre-prepared food in a microwave, and *home-cooked* is used to describe frozen meals that can be popped into the oven for ten minutes before serving. Manufacturers of prepared foods of all kinds have been competing with each other for market share by using high-salt, high-fat, and high-sugar contents to enhance taste and attract customers. Many of us have become addicted to such food. Raised in families whose mothers and grandmothers were accustomed to use food, especially rare foods such as sweets, as rewards, present generations find themselves able to procure such treats for themselves and their children throughout the day on every corner instead of only on special occasions. The result of these trends is obesity.

At the social level we do not yet have a response to this ethical problem; the lobbying power of large food corporations has thus far been successful in stalling national discourse. The only effective responses we have at the moment are individual: to read labels, reduce fat and sugar in our diets, and to eat more raw foods and fewer processed foods. And, of course, exercise. Yet it is important to push for a national discourse—even international discourse—to respond to the obesity problem.

We do not have to be intensely religious, or even overtly spiritual, to understand that life is precious, and health is one of the aspects of life that make it precious. We understand our own lives as precious, and we know that if we want others to treat our lives as precious, we must be prepared to treat their lives as precious also. We therefore have ethical obligations to see that there is sufficient food for all in our newly globalized world, and that the food that is made available to us and to others is capable of sustaining healthy life.

Organic Food

If we were to look around our world today at bans on food, perhaps the closest to historic religious bans on pork or other animals is to be found in the organic food movement. Many people in the organic movement today consider providing only organically grown food for their family's consumption as a moral duty because they see nonorganic food as poisonous.

The boundaries of the organic movement continue to expand, so that for many today "organic" food is not just produce that has been grown without pesticides, fertilizers, or genetic enhancement (GMO—genetically modified foods) as it meant in the 1960s and 1970s. Today it also includes animals, fish, and animal products (eggs) whose feed has not included animal parts, hormones, or antibiotics, and that have been raised "free-range" and not in the cages or fish farms of factory farming.

In the midst of the mad cow epidemic that killed hundreds in Britain and France beginning in the 1980s, it was discovered that mad cow, or Creutzfeldt-Jakob, disease arises from giving cows feed that includes brain tissue from diseased animals. Testing and legislation banning animal parts in animal feed have thus far prevented further outbreaks. (It seems that no one in the factory-farm movement had ever heard of the Fore experience of *kuru*!) In recent years similar concerns have been raised about the practice of feeding salmon in fish farms small ocean fish to speed up their growth (free salmon are exclusively plant-eaters).

Humanitarian concerns about the conditions under which factory farms raise pigs, turkeys, chickens, and calves have mingled with concerns about the antibiotics fed to these animals. The purpose of lacing animal feed with antibiotics is to prevent the infectious diseases that would otherwise affect herds and flocks penned in such close quarters that animals ingest feces. Since it was discovered that antibiotics fed to animals do cross into the bodies of humans who eat these animals, there is now medical concern that antibiotic resistance in humans, which has reached dangerous levels in the West, may not only be based in past indiscriminate use of antibiotics to treat colds, flus, and other minor ailments in humans, as previously thought, but may also be based in the meat we eat.[20]

Animal food on factory farms typically has included low levels of antibiotics, some of them the same antibiotics given to humans against disease. Experiments in many places, and the results of several European laws banning antibiotics in animal feed, have proven that, through use of various sterile and containment techniques, it is possible to end the use of antibiotic feed and still compete

Fig. 2.6. Production of baby chickens in a factory farm.

with factory farms that use antibiotics. Meat industries need continued pressure to abandon antibiotic animal feeds, because antibiotic resistance is a serious health threat and continues to get more serious as pharmaceutical research has not developed new families of antibiotics for human use in the last decades.[21] In April 2012 the U.S. Food and Drug Administration presented a three-year plan for eliminating the use of antibiotics in animal farming, though critics point out that it was only voluntary, not mandatory,[22] and thus unlikely to end the use of antibiotics in animals—a practice that is hugely profitable for drug companies and does not involve the initial costs to farmers that switching to new drugless production methods does.

Yet another type of "organic" food is milk from cows that have not been fed hormones to enhance milk capacity. Various studies over the last decade or so have suggested that hormones in human food, found in both meat and dairy products, may be disrupting normal sexual development in children and decreasing male sperm counts. There is also evidence that the discharge of human wastes (body waste and household waste) containing these hormones into streams is endangering wildlife species by thinning eggshells and disrupting sexual development.[23] Due to lobbying in the United States, some states now have labeling laws that mark meat that is free-range and milk from cows that have not been given hormones. In other states, however, there is not only an absence of such laws, but even strong opposition to such labeling.[24]

Regardless of how much safer the consumption of organic food seems, its higher cost has limited its appeal. Clearly the social goal should be to continue safety testing of our food and to make our national, and the world's, food supply as healthy as possible. While the shift toward a more "organic" food supply may need to be gradual lest it sharply increase the price of food and thus condemn many to an absolute lack of food, the cost of the shift is not sufficient cause to reject action toward such a shift. On the grounds of both human health and environmental integrity, we need to cease unhealthy interventions in the nourishment given plants, animals, and humans. A ban on animal feeds containing hormones, antibiotics, and parts of diseased animals could have the same purpose as the ancient ban on pig farming and consumption in the arid Middle East—maximizing the human food supply and making healthy food more available to all, at the lowest cost possible. We all need to consider how we personally can advance the movement to healthy food production both in our own consumption patterns and in our social and political interactions.

Feasting as Multipurpose

Is there anything ethical to be learned from the multitude of feasts offered up in religious traditions? Yes, for feasts are multivalent. They were designed to fill the hearts and souls as well as the bodies of those who participated, and to bind those bodies together into a community. Eating together ties persons to each other. This binding power is made up of experience that is over time woven into tradition. To be invited to sit down to a meal with others is to be trusted by them, to become an intimate. Because in virtually all communities eating together in the home is something done by close friends and relatives, an invitation to share a meal with a family gradually came to be seen as a mark of favor, an invitation to friendship. But it is not only ingrained traditions that cause us to feel bound to those with whom we share meals.

Shared pleasure of all kinds has the capacity to bind persons together. The pleasure we feel in any given moment can spill over, coloring the way we feel about those who share this pleasure with us. Eating a meal together satisfies our hunger; the special foods that make a meal a feast go beyond satisfying hunger, bringing us numerous pleasures that begin with smelling the feast-day foods, then seeing them temptingly laid out for our repast, and finally tasting them in abundance. When we share these pleasures with others, those others frequently take on some of the specialness with which we have invested the meal and the entire occasion.

Religions are practiced by communities. Feasts were one way of binding believer/practitioners of a religion together into one community. Sharing meals can produce a kind of intimacy—it reduces us all to the level of biological being that must eat to live, but it also demonstrates our aesthetic and relational capacities. Our palates crave more than simple nutrition; they crave the stimulation of different tastes and smells. We share what food we have with others because we are social and need to be in relationship.

Today this particular function of shared meals as capable of binding is critically important not only for religions, but also for our other communities, our scattered natal families, and the communities of friends that we have made. This binding function is important both for feasts and for the ordinary family table. Feasts—at Thanksgivings, Christmases, Fourth of July picnics, religious occasions (Passover, Easter, weddings, Eid ul Fitr, bat/bar mitzvahs, Divali, first communions, and funerals)—help tie us to other people about whom we care, even though our families, even our friends, may be too busy, or even too widely scattered, to gather frequently. Feasts are a reason for assembling together again to share pleasure. Humans are social beings, but we are living in increasingly impersonal, even anonymous societies, where sheer human density makes maintaining relationships difficult, as we will see in a coming chapter. Though the food at our feasts changes, and should change, over time, our need for feasting together does not.

Family Meals

In the same way, ordinary family meals bind family members together, too. They provide a relaxed time when persons who are already connected in some ways are satisfying their physical hunger, where the family members also share their lives—their activities, thoughts, and emotions. Postmodern life has put tremendous pressure on family meals because so many members of the family, even relatively young children, operate on different schedules. Unlike the situation in earlier agricultural societies when the entire household was tied to the work in the fields, today soccer games, school clubs, social or work obligations, and many other activities often pull family members in different directions at mealtimes. But families of whatever age are well advised to establish a regular time to share themselves over shared food, even if it is only once or twice a week, even if no one has the time to cook and they are all gathered around a takeout meal. In this regard, the Family Home Evening of the Church of Jesus Christ of Latter-day Saints (Mormons) is a good example of a positive practice. One night a week, usually Monday, the entire family spends the evening together, usually beginning with dinner. After dinner there is time for games, prayer, a religious lesson, or a family meeting.

While shifting our food consumption away from meat is the right ethical direction, how one decides to pursue that, and at what pace, must be an individual decision. Even if our society as a whole decides to take a policy direction that discourages meat consumption and encourages some organic route (which will not happen without a great deal of citizen pressure) there are any number of further decisions that must be made by individual households.

Every household is different. Some families may have other established meeting points rather than sit-down meals. The family of one of my siblings is centered on crew (competitive rowing). The children, from junior high through university, all row on a club team; the mom coaches and the dad drives and makes arrangements for team and boats to go to meets. They spend many hours a week together driving to and from practices because they are bound together by a shared focus (some would say obsession!). Meals are casual, often on the run for this family, but they spend a great deal of time together in a joint concern.

All families are not the same, and patterns such as this one will change as children and parents age and move on to new interests. In each new period, ways must be found for the family members to meet, and meals are one of the easiest meeting points, since everyone must eat.

Fasting: Individual Decision

Does an ethical life in the contemporary world need to include fasting? No. But that is not to say that fasting is useless. Fasting is an excellent reminder to us of the reality of those who continue to go hungry involuntarily, as well as a help to us in appreciating the food we do have available to us when we end our fast. Those of us who desire to pursue spiritual disciplines that aim at personal communion with the divine may want to consider extended but safe fasting as a cheap and easily available tool of that discipline. Fasting helps us develop control over the appetites of our bodies, which is in itself a valuable skill. Control over our bodies' demands is a form of power that can be put to good use in other areas of our lives. Being able to control our bodies' demands is a first step in feeling confident about our presence in the world and hopeful about our ability to positively impact our world.

Fasting, of course, must be an individual decision. Fasting can advance a number of goals, but these goals, such as awareness of hunger in the world, can also be achieved in other ways. If one's job is as a nurse, doctor, or social worker at a neighborhood clinic in an urban downtown, one does not need to fast to become aware of how the hungry are hurting, though fasting may be a response to that knowledge of hunger, a way of sharing the pain and contributing the money saved to the local food bank. There are also other paths to experience the divine and other ways to atone for sin—fasting is not the only way to do either. Fasting is a valuable tool—not an end in itself—but some will have other tools to reach the same ends. We also need to be careful in fasting. In this age of anorexia, if we fast for long periods, we must be careful to take in sufficient calories and nutrition to maintain our health. Religious fasting should never be a rationale for endangering our health or life.

Festivals, Crowds, and Alcohol

Feasting—large gatherings of a community to share food—is also important for our increasingly atomized lives. People who grew up in small towns, or in urban ethnic neighborhoods that put on ethnic or religious picnics or festivals, often carry wonderful memories of working together to put on the event, and feasting and dancing at the celebration itself, surrounded by hundreds of neighbors who also helped produce the celebration. Today, however, many of these festivals have gotten bigger and bigger, drawing from larger areas people who do not know each other, but who come to the event to eat, and inevitably to drink. As these festivals have gotten larger, they have become commercial, and more often than not, many involved in the work of preparing the feast are paid workers, sometimes not even from the celebrating community.

Alcohol has become a major part of American public feasts. Feasting at ball games (either tailgating parties or in the park itself), urban homecomings, Oktoberfests, and other ethnic festivals—all tend to have alcohol as a prominent feature, and inevitably, there are persons who drink to excess. Excessive use of alcohol inhibits the solidarity that should be at the heart of feasts, because it makes us less sensitive to our neighbors, more focused on ourselves and our feelings. It can lead to aggression, even violence, which in turn can divide communities and create fear and distrust.

The dangers of alcohol excess are especially heavy for the young. For many years, surveys on university students have reported that three-quarters of campus sex takes place under the influence of alcohol at parties, dances, and other celebrations, and that most campus sex could not take place without alcohol. Students are deliberately getting drunk in order to have sex that they would not choose if they were sober.[25] An alcohol fast might be a good way to learn how to feast with rationality and affectivity intact, creating connections that do not dissipate with the alcohol haze.

Politics/Law on Food

Ethical decision on each of these issues above will be personal, but each of these issues is also political, involving the whole society. Government should not design our menus for us. But it can nudge us in more ethical food directions, as it has done with the smoking issue (by raising tobacco taxes at both state and federal levels, and by banning smoking in public places). The federal government's fundamental interest in smoking was based in the need to lower the Medicare and Medicaid costs for lung cancer and emphysema. Warning labels on cigarettes, smoking bans, and high taxes on cigarettes have drastically reduced the number of smokers in North America and Europe, while still allowing smokers to decide if, when, and how to stop smoking. A shift toward vegetarianism could be promoted by similar means, since there is a collective interest in lowering human cholesterol, methane pollution, and land devoted to pasture. Governments have similar interests in decreasing obesity and the many health problems associated with how we raise food for the table.

Part of the ethical obligation of all citizens is to provide political pressure toward social goals that seem important ethically, using means that do not deprive other citizens of their right to decide for themselves. Where to draw the line between acceptable and unacceptable levels of political pressure, and exactly how free we as citizens should be to resist the direction of political/legal "nudges" will, of course, always be debated. Such debates are ethical discourse. It is through ethical discourse, based in sound social analysis, that societies eventually reach either compromise or consensus, though sometimes by way of extended stalemate.

Case Study: Food

"Dinnertime is becoming a battleground," thought Sally. "We have to resolve this issue."

Sally and Doug had three children, two older sons of eleven and nine, and a younger daughter of two. While mealtime disturbances were usually the province of the older son, Dan, who enjoyed provoking his parents to see how they would react, this time the trouble came from Pete. Following completion of a social studies unit on environmentalism at his school the previous month, Pete had informed his parents that he was a vegetarian, and refused to eat meat or fish, though he still drank milk and ate eggs. He earnestly informed his parents of all he had learned about how bad so many animal herds were for the atmosphere because of their methane production, and how much more food there would be if everyone was a vegetarian, because animals consumed more food energy than they produced in meat. He brought home maps of the major world fisheries, with levels of depletion marked. And he had some numbers about hungry people in the world, and how many children died because malnutrition and starvation weakened their bodies and made them susceptible to disease.

The first response of Pete's parents had been pride in Pete's knowledge and concern. They assured him that when he reached his majority—when he left home and prepared his own meals—he could practice vegetarianism to his heart's content. But Pete insisted that he knew his own mind now and wanted to be exempt from eating meat and fish now, in his home and when the family went out to eat. It had proved a very disruptive position. The previous week, Doug had taken the family to Dan's Little League game, and then the family and the team went to a hamburger joint. Pete did not want hamburger, chicken, or fish sandwiches. But his parents insisted that French fries were not a healthy meal for a growing boy. They ordered him a chicken sandwich—he had told them that chicken was not so environmentally damaging as beef—but he refused to eat. An hour later Doug told Sally to load the team in the van and take them home, that he would stay with Pete until he ate the sandwich. But Pete never did.

The next day was Saturday, and Doug and Sally called a family council. Sally tried to reason with Pete: "Pete, we respect your decision to be vegetarian, but you don't have the right to impose that decision on us. I have a full-time job, a house to take care of, and a two-year-old still in diapers. You cannot expect me to make two separate meals for this family every night."

Dan put in, "You've got to be nuts, Pete! No more hamburgers, hot dogs—what will you do when we go to the football games at the university, bring cheese sandwiches? And what about turkey at Thanksgiving and Christmas, or the lamb at Easter? Or jerky—you can't give up jerky!"

Doug insisted, "You are too young to be making this kind of a decision. Your body is still growing, and it needs protein. Learning to satisfy all your body needs to be healthy without meat or fish is going to take some time, Pete. Remember the fried tofu that the Rahayus brought to the potluck at church—you hated it. What if you don't like the meat substitutes that are available? You can't rush into this so fast."

But Pete stood firm. "I don't need you to make different foods for me, Mom. If you have chicken and potatoes and green beans for dinner, I can eat the potatoes and beans, and have a slice or two of cheese instead of chicken. Vegetarianism is not so hard if you still eat milk, cheese, and eggs. But I will not eat meat or fish anymore."

Below are some possible approaches to this family dilemma. What are the advantages and disadvantages of each, and why? Can you think of others that would be more adequate?

1. Doug and Sally proposed that if Pete would agree to eat some meat or fish, then the whole family would have two dinners a week without meat or fish; two nights a week the family would have meat and Pete would eat cheese, yogurt, or eggs; and three nights a week, the family, including Pete, would have casseroles, pizza, or other dishes that included meat, but in very small proportions. They said in this way, Pete was doing more good for the earth than simply not eating meat at seven dinners a week—altogether in their proposed regime there would be twelve meatless dinners in the family's week and fifteen with minimal meat.
2. Pete finally convinced his parents that his health would not suffer from the change, and that the work of his decision would not fall to Sally. It took awhile, but over the next few months the rest of the family got used to Pete eating yogurt while they ate pork chops. The most tension came to center on eating at other people's homes, like grand-parents, who were offended when Pete turned down Grandma's special pork roast, or Grandpa's grilled burgers.
3. Sally and Doug held firm on dinners. Pete was simply too young to make such a com-mitment. They conceded that if Pete wanted to pack his lunch with cheese or peanut butter and jelly, that was fine. But he ate the family dinner, or else he was grounded from all activities except school. Sally did use less beef and pork and more chicken, as well as more casseroles with less meat than in the past. But there was meat at virtually every meal. Two months later, Pete was still grounded, and the family was increasingly tense.

DISCUSSION QUESTIONS

1. Have you ever fasted? What did it feel like? Did you take anything helpful out of the experience?

2. How important are feasts in your family? Are there different kinds of feasts, and if so, what are the differences? Do you agree that feasting together binds families and communities together? Why or why not? What kinds of circumstances or conditions affect the potential for binding/bonding?

3. In your experience, what are some of the elements that make a feast most pleasurable? How important is anticipation? Describe.

4. Does it make any difference to the meaningfulness of a feast if the guests are seated or simply roaming a buffet?

5. There are many persons in our world who observe medical taboos on certain foods. Persons with heart disease are warned off red meat, cream, eggs, and fats of all kinds, diabetics off sugars and other carbohydrates, persons with gout off beans, apples, and many other foods, and increasing numbers of persons with food allergies off nuts, wheat, and other foods. How does observing such bans affect our feelings toward the banned foods? Is there more than one response that arises from observing such bans?

6. In looking at religious practices around food, it should be clear that for many religions there is a relationship between ethics, as collective discourse on right and wrong, and individual spiritual discipline. Are these two unrelated results of food practices, or are there any inherent connections between them?

7. What do you think about funeral feasting? At what kinds of funerals might feasting seem more appropriate than others? Why?

8. What level of ethical responsibility do you think individual Americans have toward (a) the hungry in other nations, (b) the practices that produce the food we eat, and (c) the unhealthiness of the American diet?

9. Discuss what you think are legitimate ways for government to encourage a shift away from meat-eating? What would be illegitimate or unwise ways? Is there a difference between illegitimate and unwise ways, and if so, what is it?

FOR FURTHER READING

Bray, Tamara. *The Archaeology and Politics of Food and Feasting in Early States and Empires.* New York: Kluwer Academic, 2003.

Bynum, Caroline Walker. *Holy Feast and Holy Fast: The Religious Significance of Food to Medieval Women.* Berkeley: University of California Press, 1987.

Counihan, Carole, and Penny Van Esterik, Eds. *Food and Culture: A Reader.* New York: Routledge, 1997.

Food and Agriculture Organization of the United Nations. *Animal Welfare and the Intensification of Animal Production.* http://www.fao.org/ethics/readings _en.htm.

Food and Agriculture Organization of the United Nations. *Ethical Issues in Food and Agriculture.*

Genetically Modified Organisms, Consumers, Food Safety and the Environment. Ethical Issues in Fisheries. All at http://www.fao .org/ethics/ser_en.htm.

Jung, Shannon L. *Food for Life: The Spirituality and Ethics of Eating.* Minneapolis: Fortress Press, 2004.

Singer, Peter, and Jim Mason. *The Ethics of What We Eat: Why Our Food Choices Matter*. Emmaus, PA: Rodale, 2006.

FILMS

Alternative Agriculture: Food for Life, 2004. Films for the Humanities and Sciences.

American Ramadan, by Naeem Randhawa, 2006. JustSayGo Films.

Da Feast! by Artemis Willis, 2009. DER Documentaries.

Fast Food Nation, by Richard Linklater, 2007. Twentieth-Century Fox Home Entertainment.

Faith, Fasting and Football, by Rashid Ghazi, 2011. North Shore Films.

The Feast Day of Tamar and Lashari, by Hugo Zemp, 1998. DER Documentaries.

The Feast in Dream Village, by Janet Hoskins and Laura Scheerer Whitney, 1988. DER Documentaries.

Food Fight: Childhood Obesity and the Food Industry, ABC, 2003. Films for the Humanities and Sciences.

The Future of Food: A Looming Crisis, BBC, 2009. Films for the Humanities and Sciences.

Slow Down and Fast. Blind Life Films at vimeo.com/3272736, 2009.

Super Size Me, by Morgan Spurlock, 2004. Hart Sharpe Video.

Tarahumara: Festival of the Easter Moon, by Charles Nauman, 1975/2005. DER Documentaries.

NOTES

1. Sam Gill, *Native American Religions* (Belmont, CA: Wadsworth, 1987), 122–30.

2. One example would be the slaughter and roasting of a black bull in the prophetic cult of the Diola prophet Alinesitoué, which served both to support community and to share protein within the community. See Robert M. Baum, "Alinesitoué: A Diola Woman Prophet in West Africa," in *Unspoken Worlds: Women's Religious Lives*, 3rd ed., ed. Nancy A. Falk and Rita M. Gross (Belmont, CA: Wadsworth, 2001), 179–95.

3. See, for example, Mary J. Andrade, *The Day of the Dead through the Eyes of the Soul* (Mexico City: La Oferta Review, 1999).

4. Caroline Walker Bynum, *Holy Feast and Holy Fast: The Religious Significance of Food to Medieval Women* (Berkeley: University of California Press, 1987), 34.

5. Some of the most interesting examples of these can be found in the published works of archeologist Marija Gimbutas, though her conclusions concerning the evidence have given rise to both strong support and strong criticism. See *The Language of the Goddess* (London: Thames & Hudson, 1989).

6. For Catholics, Anglicans, and Lutherans, the body and blood of Jesus Christ are understood to be present in Eucharist (though Catholic transubstantiation involves a total transformation of bread and wine into body and blood, and Lutheran consubstantiation understands both bread and wine and the body and blood being present, with Anglicans somewhat divided on this issue), because Jesus told his disciples that the bread and wine he gave them at the Last Supper were his own body and blood, and then told them to do what he had done. For many other Christians, Holy Communion is understood as ritual done in memory of the Last Supper when Jesus gave his

disciples his body and blood in the form of bread and wine.

7. Shirley Lindenbaum, "Understanding Kuru: The Contributions of Anthropology and Medicine," *Philosophical Transactions of the Royal Society* (Biological Sciences) 363 (2008): 3715–20.

8. "UN Team Investigates Reported Atrocities in Eastern DR Congo," AFP, January 10, 2003, http://www.preventgenocide.org/prevent/news-monitor/.

9. Andrew MacAskill and Prabhudatta Mishra, "Indian Weddings Face Menu Curbs as Minister Targets Food Waste," *Bloomberg Businessweek*, April 22, 2011.

10. Virginia Kerns, "Garifuna Women and the Work of Mourning," in Falk and Gross, Ibid., 125–33.

11. Maimonides, *A Guide for the Perplexed* 3:48.

12. Marvin Harris, "The Abominable Pig," in *Food and Culture: A Reader*, ed. Carole Counihan and Penny Van Esterik (New York and London: Routledge, 1997), 67–79.

13. Barry S. Hewlett and Shane J. Macfarlane, "Father's Roles in Hunter-Gatherer and Other Small Scale Cultures," in *The Role of the Father in Child Development* (5th ed.), ed. Michael E. Lamb (Hoboken, NJ: John Wiley & Sons, 2010), 419–20.

14. Buddhist monks and nuns are not allowed to kill or have killed for them any meat. They may only eat meat when it is what is given them by householders in their begging bowls.

15. While most Hindus do not eat beef at all, there are some groups of Hindus, including Balinese Hindus, among whom even priests eat beef. Balinese Hindus practice a very early Hinduism that does not include the use of ghee (clarified butter) for anointing sacred images or bodies for cremation.

16. T. Desjardins, F. Andreux, B. Volkoff, and C. C. Cerri, "Organic Carbon and C Contents in Soils and Soilsize-Fractions, and Their Changes Due to Deforestation and Pasture Installation in Eastern Amazonia," *Geoderma* 61, nos. 1–2 (February 1994), 103–18; Christopher Neill, Linda A. Deegan, Suzanne M. Thomas, and Carlos C. Cerri, "Deforestation for Pasture Alters Nitrogen and Phosphorus in Small Amazonian Streams," *Ecological Applications* 11:1817–28; V. Rasiah, S. K. Florentine, B. L. Williams, and M. E. Westbrooke, "The Impact of Deforestation and Pasture Abandonment on Soil Properties in the Wet Tropics of Australia," *Geoderma* 120, nos. 1–2 (May 2004): 35–45.

17. Jeremy B. C. Jackson, Michael X. Kirby, Wolfgang H. Berger, Karen A. Bjorndal, Louis W. Botsford, Bruce J. Bourque, Roger H. Bradbury, Richard Cooke, Jon Erlandson, James A. Estes, Terence P. Hughes, Susan Kidwell, Carina B. Lange, Hunter S. Lenihan, John M. Pandolfi, Charles H. Peterson, Robert S. Steneck, Mia J. Tegner, and Robert R. Warner, "Historical Overfishing and the Recent Collapse of Coastal Ecosystems," *Science* 293, no. 5530 (July 27, 2001): 629–37.

18. Monterey Bay Aquarium, *Seafood Watch*, http://www.montereybayaquarium.org/cr/cr_seafoodwatch/issues/default.aspx?c=ln.

19. *The Economist, Pocket World in Figures* (London: The Economist, 2011), 87.

20. "WHO Advises Kicking the Livestock Antibiotic Habit," *Science* 301, no. 5636 (August 22, 2003): 1027.

21. Carl Nathan, "Antibiotics at the Cross-roads: Are We Making the Right Choices to Bring New Drugs to the Marketplace?" *Nature* 431, no. 21 (October 21, 2004): 899–902.

22. Helena Bottemiller, "FDA Issues Voluntary Plan to Limit Antibiotics in Agriculture," *Food Safety News*, April 12, 2012, http://www.foodsafetynews.com/2012/04/fda-issues-voluntary-plan-to-limit-antibiotics-in-agriculture/.

23. "Hormone Disruptors: A Clue to Understanding the Environmental Causes of Disease," *Environment* 43, no. 5 (June 2001): 22.

24. "Consumers Union Applauds New Pennsylvania Milk Labeling Rules," January 20, 2008. Consumers Union Reports, http://www.consumersunion.org/pub/core_food_safety/005363.html.

25. A. Abbey, C. Saenz, M. R. Parkhill, and L. W. Hayman, "The Effects of Acute Alcohol Consumption, Cognitive Reserve, Partner Risk, and Gender on Sexual Decision-Making," *Journal of Studies on Alcohol* 67 (2006): 113–21.

CHAPTER 3

RELIGIONS ON MAKING WORK HUMAN

Some things do never change. It has always required human work to feed, clothe, and shelter human communities, and it seems that this will always be the case. We sometimes hear predictions of a human future without work, in which robots toil instead of humans. It is difficult to imagine, even if robots can be made to do most of the work that is now done by humans, that they can also be made to design themselves, or to repair themselves. But even if that were possible, the consensus of the world's religions is that it would be a bad thing for humans. For human work is *both* onerous and a necessary—and invaluable—part of the humanization process.

Framing the Issues

While it is true for humans in general that, as the book of Genesis puts it, "By the sweat of your face you shall eat bread, till you return to the ground,"[1] it is also true that since humans spend much of their waking hours in the purposeful activity we call work, much of what they learn and become occurs through work. That is, work is valuable not just because we do so much of it that it is the principal arena

in which we learn and become. It is rather because work is our principal *purposeful* activity that it is so important. Because work for humans involves goals, and steps toward those goals can be assessed and measured, it is through work, beginning with chores in our homes and schoolwork as children, that we learn who we are, our talents and capacities, our strengths and weaknesses. Further, it is through work—precisely because it requires discipline and persistence—that most of us develop our talents and learn to deal with or overcome our deficiencies, as well as learn cooperation with others. It is chiefly through our work that we participate in and contribute to our communities. And while it is still the case that through work many humans have their chief interaction with the nonhuman natural world, it is increasingly the case for humans that we no longer recognize nature in most of the materials with which we work, not even in the food we eat. Unlike virtually all children in past centuries, schoolchildren in much of the developed world today have to be taught that the Little Red Hen they read stories about is the same as the fried chicken they eat, that the cute pink pigs in cartoons are the source of ham, bacon, and pork chops. Unlike humans in past ages, we take for granted the natural sources of the materials we fabricate—the water, the wood, the oil, even the animals.

Social Analysis of Contemporary Work

But before we move on to see what religious wisdom of the past concerning work can contribute to our current situations and understandings, we need to do some analysis of human work today. Because there have been so many radical changes in the nature of human work in only the last two centuries, the social analysis here is more complex than in many other issues.

The first thing to note about human work today is its diversity. This diversity is partly the result of the fact that parts of our globe are still largely preindustrial, while others are industrial, and yet others are postindustrial.

Work in preindustrial and industrial areas. In preindustrial areas, work for most of the population is still largely agricultural. In some parts of our world, the most common pattern of agriculture is even subsistence agriculture, with plots too small for mechanization to be feasible. In these areas, the population often exceeds the ability of the land to support it, and the result over time has often been environmental degradation. Farmers have attempted to cultivate marginal land on hillsides, causing erosion that loses topsoil and clogs streams. Land has been deforested both commercially and for fuel, causing further erosion by wind and water, and sometimes even modifying climate patterns and causing or aggravating droughts. Where there has not been enough industrial work to engage the excess population from agricultural areas, unemployment and poverty also result.

Other areas, often within the same nations as preindustrial areas, are industrial, with some of the same labor abuses and negative health and environmental effects as were seen in the developed nations 60 to 150 years ago. Industrial areas have much greater labor specialization than preindustrial areas. In industrial areas there are many different kinds of industrial laborers, from engineers and machinists at the more skilled end, to unskilled manual laborers who load trucks and boxcars with the manufactured goods at the lower end of the skill (and pay) scale. In general, as agriculture became more productive, workers were freed to work in factories, and as factories became more productive, more human resources could be put into research to create even more new products and more efficient processes. With each step in this process, human labor adapted to new kinds of work. Today there are new skills used in manufacturing (e.g., miniaturization and robotization), even in the manufacture of traditional industrial products such as steel, cars, rubber tires, shoes, and textiles.

Work in postindustrial areas. Yet it is in postindustrial areas of the world that labor has been the most transformed. The majority of work in postindustrial areas is relatively high-tech service work. Many more jobs in postmodernity today are in the service areas of banking, finance, and healthcare, as well as in research jobs in agriculture, medicine/healthcare, and engineering/design. These jobs either didn't exist at all in the past (e.g., biotech research), or employed only a few workers compared to today (e.g., banking and finance). In postindustrial areas, labor specialization has become so intense that often workers within the same industry have no understanding of the training, skills, and contribution of fellow workers.

Problems Arising from Specialization

Labor specialization. For many skilled workers today, especially those considered professionals, their closest colleagues are often not those in the same company or workplace, but those of similar training who perform similar jobs in other institutions, often far distant. Physicians who work for insurance companies, or hospitals, or the navy, or even in private practice, for example, often associate more with physicians in other institutions than with nonphysicians in their own institution or office, and belong to local medical associations or even the AMA (American Medical Association) as well. Another example: I am a religious ethicist in a state university religious studies department that has thirteen full-time faculty, five half-time faculty, and a slew of adjuncts, but my closest colleagues are not the faculty members in my department, all of whom specialize in other religions, methods, and/or time periods and regions than mine. My closest colleagues are other religious ethicists, professors scattered in dozens of universities across the United States and the world, either members of the Society for Christian Ethics, the Ethics Section of the American Academy of Religion, or persons I have served with on the editorial boards of ethics journals or in the writing of ethics anthologies.

Across the world of work this pattern grows: workers identify with and associate with the members of their ever-more specialized subfields. Knowledge of our world and of processes for manipulating it have become so specialized that there appears little room—and virtually no respect—for generalists.[2] There are clearly some benefits from this specialized organization of work. But there are also some disadvantages.

Increasingly, we do not know how to talk to one another across the differences in training and work. We are isolated in our specializations. Specialization is not completely new. Even fifty years ago in universities it was not an easy thing to get professors in English and Social Work to hold serious conversations, or engineers and marketers in industrial corporations to feel collegial. But today the barriers are up between ever-increasing subfields.

The complexity involved in this process of further and further specialization results in a situation in which fewer persons have the ability to comprehend, much less manage, large corporations, institutions, much less large governments or economies. For example, following the housing crisis that began in 2008 from the sale of toxic mortgage-backed securities, there was a consensus that neither the firms selling the securities, the banks buying them, nor the rating agencies giving them AAA ratings had any idea what level of risk was involved in these securities. Each group down the line assumed that the firms who put them together understood them and vouched for their safety. None of the groups processing the sales thought it important to understand how the securities worked, precisely because they were so accustomed to complex specializations being impenetrable to others. To this day, it has been impossible to know the value of any particular group of these securities, even after initial defaults affecting them.

Specialization in media. Of course, work is not the only area where this problematic level of specialization occurs. Many social commentators have remarked that the explosion in media, especially the explosion in news media, over the last two decades has created a situation in which people in general, of both the political left and the political right, the old and the young, those who like reality TV and those who don't—all tune in to only the radio, TV, and Internet news and programming aimed at their particular segment of the population. Consequently, we—and the workers in particular stations and networks—see our world from only one perspective; our worldview and ethical stances are never challenged by contrary evidence or opinions. Libertarians only tune in to those channels and programs that are suspicious of government policies and look for plans to violate freedom, and those who believe that government regulation is in the common good tune in to liberal channels that do not cover complaints with or problems in government regulation. These trends in work and in media are related and have a tremendous impact on the character of individuals and society.

Attempts to overcome effects of specialization. There are, of course, many attempts to overcome the divisions caused by specialization. At the most superficial level, many companies and institutions have company picnics for all the families of their employees, for example. But when we look at the groupings at those picnics, we see that they tend to be employees who share similar training and jobs. After initial greetings, the secretaries and their families are in one corner, the human resources people in another, the attorneys in another, the engineers in another. Everyone is polite, and if there are games all groups compete together, but there is little or no opportunity either for discussing the organization of work or for developing personal interactions in which workers hear life stances or stories that are not congruent with their own. When we live completely within our specializations of work and worldview—our comfort zone—we are neither exercising critical analysis nor learning tolerance. Instead of enlarging our

range of experience by sharing our differences, our closest associates tend to reinforce the narrowness of our experience, thus confirming us in our original stances. The most we can hope for in the way of challenging diversity is that some of our colleagues within our subspecialty come from backgrounds dissimilar to ours and still carry some of that different "flavor" with them.

Specialization requires education. Many of the new jobs in postindustrial society involve communications and information technology, scientific research, or other technical expertise, and thus workers require significant training. While many nations and communities recognize the need for more and more education within their populations, the progress is uneven, even in rich nations. In the United States in June 2011, 72 percent of the high school class that had begun tenth grade in 2008 graduated from high school.[3] This was the highest graduation rate since the 1980s, but it still meant that 28 percent of students who began tenth grade failed to complete high school. More than a quarter of young adults do not have a high school diploma in an age when employment at more than the minimum wage increasingly demands education *beyond* high school.

Moreover, the high school graduation rate for males is considerably lower than for females (68 to 75 percent), and for black and Hispanic males is only slightly above half (58 percent). This difference persists in higher education: by age twenty-four, 27.6 percent of women and 18.7 percent of men have been awarded bachelor's degrees, while only 11.1 percent of all non-Hispanic blacks and 10.1 percent of Hispanics and Latinos have earned a bachelor's degree.[4] Lower rates for blacks and Hispanics with bachelor degrees are related to lower rates of high school graduation, which are, in turn, related to incarceration rates.

In graduate education in the United States, women have earned more master's degrees than men since 1986, and since 2009 women have been awarded more doctoral degrees than men.[5] The U.S. Census statistics for 2008 and 2009, the last years available at this writing, show that American women make only 77.5 percent of the wages of American men when both work full-time.[6] So the gender group that is most educated and therefore most employable is also the group that is lower paid. This is bad news for children and families in general.

Excluded from work. But high school dropouts are not the only persons unprepared for work in the contemporary workplace. There are a variety of persons, including persons mentally or emotionally disabled, those who are chronically ill, and some severely physically disabled persons, who are not employable in the ordinary workplace. It is not the case, as we shall see, that there have always been large groups of disabled persons excluded from work. For much of the past, most of the disabled were not excluded from work, because they did not survive to an age where work was even a possibility. In many very poor populations even today, persons considered permanently unable to contribute to family and community resources are not considered to have the same rights to draw upon limited resources of food and medicine. Thus in some poverty-stricken regions the incidence of the disabled who grow to adulthood, compared to those who are not disabled, is much smaller than in wealthier communities. Overall, many of the chronically ill and physically disabled are only alive into adulthood due to improvements in modern medicine, and many physically disabled

persons are accessing work and more ordinary lifestyles due to recent improvements in technology and social planning (wheelchairs, Braille readers, and handicapped-accessible buildings, for example).

Obviously, some persons who are chronically ill, profoundly mentally disabled, or emotionally disabled to the point that they might endanger themselves or others cannot be expected to work. But many of those persons who are mentally and emotionally disabled have only been excluded from work by the changes in the nature of work in late modernity/postmodernity.

Other exclusionary changes in modern work. As we will see in chapter 7, one of the changes in modern work was the shift of most production during the nineteenth century from the home to the factory. When production took place largely in the home, family members with mild forms of disabilities could often take part in production. They had family supervision, and parts of the production process could be adapted to their special needs. They could take part in the work of the home according to their abilities, just as children did. When production moved to factories, there was excess labor for the jobs available, and factories were not willing to hire the disabled. There was usually a set wage, and from the owner's perspective, it made no sense to pay a disabled person the same wage as a nondisabled person when they could not produce for as long or as fast, or needed supervision to stay on task.

The nature of the disability most likely to exclude persons from work has also changed over the modern period. When 90 percent of the human population was engaged in agriculture, which was the general situation in virtually all societies in the world until about 1900, it was the physically disabled, not the mentally disabled, who were most excluded from work. Most agricultural work required physical strength and mobility. While overseers or landowners needed to keep records, plan seed orders, keep to calendars, and negotiate with middlemen, the bulk of their laborers needed only to follow simple directions as to physical labor. In these circumstances, most of today's mentally disabled persons (those with mild or moderate mental or emotional disability) were employable, and often able to marry and raise families. There was a place for the "simple-minded" in many farming communities, especially on farms owned by other members of the same family.

Today, however, there are few jobs that do not require literacy—not only the ability to read, but even the ability to use computers at some minimal level, if only to use ATMs to get one's pay that has been directly deposited to one's bank account. Repetitive assembly work, which many of the mentally disabled were very competent to perform, is increasingly relegated to machines, and where it has not yet been, the pace and accuracy required in assembly has increased to the point that even many nondisabled workers cannot keep up. In the United States, where public transportation systems are almost nonexistent and driver's licenses require not only passing written tests but relatively quick reflexes for the driving tests, the mentally disabled cannot even qualify for pizza delivery jobs.

As the requirements for employment rise, more and more of our population is deemed economically superfluous—not only the chronically ill, the mentally and emotionally handicapped, and some physically handicapped, but also large parts of the uneducated and unskilled population.

Illegal work. Another issue within social analysis of contemporary work is illegal and coerced work, of which trafficked labor is a major part.

Trafficked labor includes many different levels of coercion of workers, as well as kinds of work (only a small part of trafficked labor involves sex workers, though that is the media focus). Some workers seek out traffickers, hopeful of higher wages in developed parts of the world that they can send back to families or take home to start a business. Some young workers are entrusted to traffickers by parents, who believe the stories of high wages, good working conditions, and large remittance checks. And some workers are simply kidnapped. But most end up working long hours in prisonlike conditions. There is general awareness that labor trafficking is a growing problem around the globe. Sometimes trafficking simply involves illegal transport of undocumented workers—men, women, and children—into a different country, but often it involves *de facto* slavery in inhumane working and living conditions. Attention to trafficking is only a few decades old. Nations devote a great deal of police and security forces to trafficking across borders, and there is growing concern around the world about the abuses of human rights and the flouting of law involved in labor trafficking. The more desperate the living conditions for the poor in the nation of origin, the more risks people are willing to take to escape.

Child labor is another special issue within a social analysis of contemporary work, but we will postpone treatment of it until we deal with religious traditions on work. Child labor is difficult to deal with, especially in regions where the transition from family agriculture to industry is still taking place. Many families understand that when they were farmers, their children worked in the fields alongside their parents, contributing to support of the family. Parents often do not see the difference between children of ten or twelve working on the farm and working in a factory, especially in situations where their earnings can make the difference between the family surviving or not. Many nations are struggling between ignoring child labor laws and leaving it to families to protect their children, and enforcing bans on child labor that seem to handicap families while attempting to protect, perhaps overprotect, children from exploitation.

Religious Treatment Concerning Work

One role of religion in human history has been both to legitimate (or condemn) existing social practices and proposals, and sometimes to help refashion existing social practices from its own perspectives or in its own interests. Thus in the texts of many religions, we find allusions to, even descriptions of, longstanding social practices around work that are approved, condemned, or advocated by religious authorities.

Hinduism on Work: The Asramas

In Hinduism, the *asramas* are the four stages of human life; each is characterized by the work—the purposeful activity—that predominates within that stage. Though the *asramas* were historically only applied to males, with females considered neither appropriate recipients of education nor bearers of fiscal responsibility, this has changed in the modern world, in which Hindu women are increasingly well educated and found in professional employment. Neither were women in the

Fig. 3.1. Young boy grinding sugar cane in Liberia.

tradition considered capable of autonomous pursuit of *moksha* (salvation through achieving no-self), but today we find in Hinduism female *sannyasin/sadhvis* pursuing *moksha*, and even female gurus with numerous male and female followers.

The first stage of the *asramas* is that of the *Brahmachari* (student), which begins about age twelve and lasts until the midtwenties. *Brahmachari* are not married, are traditionally assigned to a guru who supervises their studies, and are initiated into this stage through a ceremonial ritual that admits them to the status of twice-born, able to wear the sacred thread. Traditionally this initiation and the *asramas* themselves were closed not only to women, but also to members of the *shudra* or peasant caste, though now these exclusions have been largely lifted.

From the midtwenties to about age fifty a Hindu is expected to be a *Grihasta* (a householder), which entails marrying, raising a family, and, especially but not only for males, earning a living that will support his extended family. This is the stage in which the individual's activity fits what moderns understand by "work." Work is earning a living that will support not only one's immediate family, but all kith and kin who require support. This stage is, more than any other stage, understood as one of self-sacrifice. The *Grihasta* works for the benefit of others to whom and for whom he is responsible. The more onerous this work is, the more honor and merit accrue to the *Grihasta*. It is accepted that for many, if not most, *Grihasta*, work in the world is burdensome, certainly draining, and sometimes even dangerous and/or demeaning.

The third stage, which begins about age fifty and may end around age seventy, is that of *Vanaprasta* (forest dweller or hermit in semiretirement from the world). Normally by this time in a man's life, if he is still living, his children have married, and his son(s) has/have become *Grihasta* and had children, in effect taking over the father's *Grihasta* responsibilities. This frees the father to withdraw from the world and engage in a level of contemplation not compatible with the responsibilities of a *Grihasta*. The fifty- to sixty-year-old withdraws to the forest or other hermitage, sometimes with a spouse. Ideally, the meditation and spiritual discipline learned in this stage lead persons to move on to the final stage of *Sannyasi* (the renounced one in full retirement), which usually begins around age seventy, and involves living a life dedicated to prayer and meditation, with no care for whether one lives or dies, subsisting as a wandering beggar, with no care for status or recognition.

Buddhist Treatment of Work

This Hindu organization of working life in the *asramas* contrasts with Buddhist organizations of work. In Buddhism believers are divided between householders (laity) and *bhikkhus/bhikkhunis* (monks and nuns). A simple explanation of the difference is that householders marry, raise families, and work to support both their families and the *bhikkhus/bhikkhunis*, who devote themselves to meditation and learning. Such an explanation is not only simple—in some ways it is simplistic. For *bhikkhus* and *bhikkhunis* also work, and some significant part of their work is often even manual labor.

As Thomas Borchert points out,[7] monastic communities are communities that must be maintained, often with property that must be maintained. While in some places monks in major temples employ others to perform some of the menial labor necessary to maintain monks and property, especially in East Asian nations (China, Japan, Vietnam), monks work in some way to support the monastic community. Monks farm, cook, clean, launder, repair, and perform many other mundane forms of work in addition to learning/teaching and meditating. These work activities are not merely time-outs from their principal work of meditation. They are, in fact, part of the discipline, just as begging their food has been a part of the discipline. Especially for young monastics who are not yet capable of long periods of fruitful meditation, periods of purposeful physical activity can relieve restlessness and restore the ability to concentrate. Furthermore, taking care of the daily needs of the monastery makes the monks more aware and appreciative of the labor that others expend for them.

Begging as work. Buddha ordered that his monks (both men and women) beg for their sustenance. This reliance on the work of begging served a number of purposes: it reinforced the nonattachment to the material world that was at the center of his teaching. Their dependence was a constant reminder to the monks not to be arrogant with the laity; it freed monks to have more time for meditation; and it served the laity by allowing them to earn merit by supporting the monks. The karma earned in feeding monks becomes a kind of seed that grows, affecting who laypersons become through reincarnation.

Even from the beginning of the monastic orders, though, food was not the only need of the monks. The retreats where the nomadic early monks were to spend the rainy season had to be built and maintained. Later, when lay generosity had provided permanent monasteries, a variety of kinds of work developed in each monastery, sometimes including growing crops, taking care of domestic animals, and domestic labor, in addition to work

more commonly associated with monastic life, such as study of texts, copying texts, teaching, and meditating, both singly and communally. In majority Buddhist nations such as Thailand, monks and monasteries do receive some government support. In many south Asian nations, monastic dependence on lay generosity often does not require door-to-door begging by monks. Instead, every morning householders can be seen walking to the temples with gifts of large tureens of food to feed the monks.

Mindfulness in work. Despite the Buddhist teaching that the material world was to be understood as illusion, monks were expected to apply themselves to physical work with the same mindfulness that Buddhists are to bestow on all their activities, no matter how repetitive and boring. Mindfulness is the seventh of eight elements in the Eightfold Path, and one of the most basic of Buddhist practices, to be utilized in all activities. Westerners sometimes interpret Buddhist emphasis on mindfulness in terms of western appreciation of efficiency, and there is no question but that mindfulness in many forms of work does increase efficiency. But that is not its principal value within Buddhism. Mindfulness is rather a mental discipline, a way of learning the ability to concentrate, to channel one's thoughts, and to ignore distractions of all kinds that could keep the practitioner from going astray from the path that Buddha laid out.[8] This mental and spiritual discipline obviously can have nonspiritual, nonsalvific benefits in other areas of life, such as labor efficiency. But mindfulness can also lessen efficiency in some situations. Mindfulness calls us to pay the proper attention to those persons with whom we interact, rather than treating others as anonymous, faceless machines, and this takes time. Humanizing our interactions through mindfulness can slow down our output. But mindfulness can also help us avoid letting fears, dislikes, boredom, or other feelings distract us from what we should be doing.

Right livelihood. Perhaps the most pointed of all Buddhist teachings regarding work is the precept from the Eightfold Path that enjoins Buddhists to right livelihood, which is interpreted to mean that one's work should not involve dishonesty or suffering to other living beings. Work that entails suffering to other living beings has traditionally included trade in weapons, as well as raising animals for slaughter, or being a slaughterer or butcher or hunter. Today, as Peter Harvey suggests in his *Introduction to Buddhist Ethics*,

> [w]hile the early texts give only a short list of types of "wrong livelihood," in the modern context, a Buddhist might add others to the list. For example: doing experiments on animals; developing pesticides, working in the arms industry, and perhaps even working in advertising, to the extent that this is seen as encouraging greed, hatred and delusion, or perverting the truth.[9]

Interestingly enough, in the Buddhist lists of duties of husbands and wives, the housework duty of wives is directly mentioned and is listed first in the list of their duties, while the work of husbands is only assumed but never mentioned. Of course, without remunerated work, a husband would not be able to afford the clothes and ornaments that he is supposed to provide the wife according to his station:

> In five ways should a wife as western quarter be ministered to by her husband: by respect, by courtesy, by faithfulness,

by handing over authority to her [in the home], by providing her with adornment. In these five ways does the wife, thus ministered by her husband as the western quarter, act in sympathy with him: her duties [in the home] are well performed, she shows hospitality to kin of both, is faithful, watches over the goods he brings, and shows skill and artistry in discharging all her business.[10]

Thus Buddhism teaches that some forms of work are not licit, that work is part of the task of humans, monastics and laity alike, and that it should be done with full concentration (mindfulness).

Islam on Work

Islam assumes that all will work and that work is good and necessary for humans. Muslim teaching and law have also made clear that some kinds of work are *haraam*— to be avoided, forbidden, evil.[11] Muslims are not allowed to grow grapes for wine or produce crops for any other form of alcohol, to make or sell alcohol, to engage in or profit from prostitution, to extract interest, gamble, hoard food to raise prices, or institute wars. All of these activities are considered *haraam* because of the harm they pose to the Muslim community, the *umma*. For Americans, one of the more surprising activities understood as *haraam* might be running lotteries. The historic wisdom here is that people should not be encouraged to pursue wealth without work, because it undermines a work ethic and encourages laziness and daydreaming.

The Muslim ban on interest. The ban on extracting interest (*riba*) on loans has in Islam, unlike Christianity, extended into the contemporary period. As in the ban on lotteries, the Islamic idea is that wealth should come from work, not simply from having money that can be lent to make more money. It is considered wrong for a person or banking institution to loan money to a person or business to expand the business and expect both the loan and interest to be paid back regardless of whether the business prospers or fails. In Islamic thought, if the lender expects to obtain a portion of profits made, she should also accept a portion of the risk because the risk is the work that earns the interest. Therefore, Muslim banking involves investing in businesses as partners.[12] A mortgage with a Muslim bank begins with the bank buying a lease on the house for a certain number of years, based on the actual neighborhood rental value. The house is registered in the name of the new home owner. The owner then pays monthly rent to the bank, until the end of the lease, when the property both in name and in use becomes that of the home owner.

If the home owner defaults on the rent, the bank and the home owner can either agree to rent the house to someone else who will over time pay off the bank's interest in the use of the home, or the house can be put up for sale, with the home owner and the bank splitting the proceeds, depending on what proportion of the lease the home owner has fulfilled.

Islamic no-*riba* banking has been spreading rapidly around the world. A number of no-*riba* banks now operate in the United States, and some major U.S. banks are now offering no-*riba* divisions in order to attract Muslim customers both in the United States and many other parts of the world. Malaysia has the most developed system of no-*riba* banking, and finds that about one quarter of customers are not Muslims, but persons attracted by the principle of no interest.

Other *haraam* work. For some Muslims, singing, dancing, music, and photography are also *haraam* occupations, but there is some ambivalence in the tradition on singing, music, and dancing. There are no Qur'anic verses forbidding these, but there are some *hadith* that are honored in some communities and not others. It is not difficult to imagine the reasons for such a teaching—professional entertainers in many religions and cultures have been considered as lacking in morality, because often they are involved in licentious behavior (commercial sex, gambling, alcohol).

Photography has been listed among banned occupations for Muslims, because when photography entails depictions of living beings, it violates the Muslim tradition on *aniconism*, the proscription against creating images of sentient living beings. The original ban stemmed from the prohibition on idolatry. The most absolute ban covers images of God, then of Mohammed, and then Muslim prophets and the relatives of the Prophet. All depictions of humans and animals are discouraged in some *hadith*[13] and by a long tradition of Sunni Islamic authorities, though Shi'as and Sufis have generally been less inclined to interpret all figurative depiction as idolatry. Thus in Islam, especially in the Sunni tradition, there has been little place for sculptors and not much for painters; painters are limited to still lifes and landscapes without humans or animals. One of the most noted modern implementations of this ban on figurative depiction was the 2001 destruction of massive (165-foot) statues of Buddha dating from the second century CE in Afghanistan, which occurred under orders of the Taliban, a conservative Sunni organization then ruling Afghanistan.[14]

Christianity on Work

In early Christianity, any occupation that might involve shedding human blood was banned; Christians were not allowed to serve in the army or as guards or executioners. Those who had shed blood could not be buried in Christian burials. Once Christianity turned away from its pacifist first centuries, there were few forbidden occupations, though a great deal of concern about executioners, sometimes deploring execution as an occupation for Christians, and at other times demanding hooding for executioners to protect their identity from discrimination and revenge.

Priests and religious were fairly consistently forbidden to shed blood and thus banned from participation in war. Despite this ban, over the centuries various clergy, even bishops, sometimes went to war, especially in the Crusades. Most carried the mace (a stick connected by chain to a metal studded ball) instead of a sword in deference to the ban on shedding blood; killing with a mace was usually less bloody than with a sword.

Beginning in the sixteenth century, pacifist Christian churches that developed out of the Reformation (e.g., Brethren, Amish, Quakers, and Mennonites) reverted to the much earlier Christian pacifism and continually resisted calls for military service, often at great cost, as well as avoided police-type work. In the past, however, Christian nonviolence (unlike that of Buddhists, Jains, and Hindus) did not require nonviolence to nonhuman beings, though this issue is now being raised in many different denominations due to growth in concern for both animal rights and ecology.

Condemnation of usury. The practice of usury was one of the few regularly condemned occupations for Christians from the fourth century to the early modern era. As in Islam, the Catholic Church regarded any charging of interest as taking advantage of the poor or unfortunate and so forbade the practice first to clergy in 325 CE, and then to the laity a century later.[15] The ban was only lifted in the early modern period when it became clear that most lending at interest facilitated commercial expansion, not aid to individuals or families in distress. Christianity has not shared Islam's concern that those who lend money at interest should share in the risks as well as the profits, and so removed the ban on usury. Yet today in Christianity, and in many religions that allow usury, there is strong condemnation of excessive rates of interest charged to the needy, rates that entail enriching the lender through the suffering of the poor.

Monastic work. Christian monasticism displays much of the same lived pattern of manual work combined with meditation that we saw in Buddhism. Beginning with the Rule of St. Benedict in the early sixth century, manual labor was clearly a planned part of the monastic discipline and not merely a necessity for the survival of the monks.[16] For example, chapter 48 of the Rule of St. Benedict stresses the importance of daily manual labor, never less than five hours a day. Ways were sought to integrate prayer and work. Monks working in the fields (far from the chapel) were not excused from daily prayers, but were directed to find ways to participate in collective prayer even from a distance. Chapter 35 stipulates that all monks take turns at working in the kitchen preparing and serving meals. As in Buddhism, Christian monastic rules (Benedictine as well as later Franciscan, Dominican, and others) set aside a number of times during each day and night for (prayer and) meditation. The work of monks in both traditions involved spiritual

Fig. 3.2. Christian Orthodox monks planting potatoes at Gethsemane Hermitage on Lake Seliger, Russia, 1910.

disciplines that governed both labor (manual, intellectual, or begging) and spiritual/intellectual labor.

Ritual breaks from work. Also like Buddhism, work in Christianity tended to be taken for granted as the principal activity of laity, with women working within domestic space and men working both around and outside domestic space. For Christian laity, however, work-time was frequently interrupted or otherwise affected for religious reasons, including the prohibition of work on all Sundays. For much of Christian history, work was also interrupted or postponed due to processions and fasting on the four annual Rogation days,[17] as well as by obligatory mass attendance on all holy days of obligation.[18] In traditional Catholic nations, holy days were like Sundays, generally work holidays, until secular democracy became the norm, at which time churches gradually adapted to people having to work on holy days, and so scheduled evening and sometimes very early morning masses to allow members to fulfill their mass obligations without endangering their jobs.

The prohibition of Sunday work for Christians is now hardly observed in the West; it has lost out to consumerism and the call for entertainment. Throughout North America and much of Europe and Latin America, stores and restaurants, nightclubs, movies, and other places of entertainment find Sunday one of their busiest days, entailing Sunday work for millions.

Work in Judaism

Shabbat rest. In Judaism, work as central human activity is taken for granted and is assumed to be draining. The center of Jewish ritual and prayer is Shabbat (from sunset Friday until sunset Saturday), which is primarily a day of rest during which all work ceases. Among Orthodox Jews, who observe as much of traditional Jewish law as possible, the prohibition on Shabbat work includes operating all machines, including stoves, cars, and elevators. Orthodox Jews must live within walking distance of their synagogue. The Shabbat meal is typically celebrated Friday night; this allows the work of preparing the meal to be done before Shabbat begins, as it cannot be prepared after sunset without violating the ban on work. The only exceptions to the ban on work on Shabbat are actions aimed at saving lives, such as rushing a heart-attack patient to a hospital by ambulance. Conservative and Reform Jews are somewhat more relaxed in their views of what constitutes work on Shabbat but still attempt to maintain it as a day of rest.

Although Shabbat is also a day of special prayers and of feasting compared to ordinary weekday meals, the focus is on rest and replenishment of one's body and spirit from the preceding days of labor. Work is also prohibited on Jewish holidays.[19] However, holidays are not typically so restful for women as Shabbat, for while most Shabbat work bans are also in place for holidays, kitchen activities—including cooking, baking, and carrying water—are not banned on holidays.

In Jewish communities around the world, Shabbat and Jewish holidays are relaxed times for feasting, recreation, and spending time with family and friends as well as for prayer. In contemporary communities some of the emphasis has shifted with changes in work in the postmodern world. Where Shabbat once primarily represented rest for the body from debilitating physical labor in various forms of manual labor, today Sabbath rest is understood to be as much, if not more, rest for the human spirit, which is battered in our quick-paced, heavily networked, competitive, and fast-changing workplaces in which workers of all kinds carry heavy responsibility for the welfare of others. The Genesis creation story, claimed as the basis for Shabbat rest in both Judaism and Christianity, reminds us that we, like God, need rest from even the work of creation, no matter how satisfying that creation is to us.

Usury in Judaism. Concerning bans on moneylending at interest, Judaism is governed by two verses from the book of Deuteronomy that prohibit taking interest from fellow Jews, but allow Jews to charge non-Jews interest:

> Thou shalt not lend upon interest to thy brother: interest of money, interest of victuals, interest of any thing that is lent upon interest. Unto a foreigner thou mayest lend upon interest; but unto thy brother thou shalt not lend upon interest; that the LORD thy God may bless thee in all that thou settest thine hand to, in the land whither thou goest to possess it.[20]

This law covered not just lending money at interest, but also lending things such as

Fig. 3.3. A family enjoying a day of rest.

goats or sheep, that procreate and increase over time. In the agricultural economy in which Deuteronomy was written, even most money loans were for purposes of investing in things like seed or animals, which increased. The interest was understood as a part of the increase. Lending by Jews to non-Jews was especially likely to be commercial—intended to grow a farm or business—and therefore interest seemed more appropriate. Within one's own community, where loans would more likely be to cover need, profit in lending (interest) was forbidden. At the same time, this distinction was a dangerous one, in that it was always open to being interpreted such that justice was only owed within one's own group.

In this quick overview of selected religions on human work, we see some convergences. There is a recognition in all these religions that work is necessary, that it is draining, and that therefore respite from work is necessary.

Buddhism, Jainism, Hinduism, and Islam in particular remind us that some types of work are not justifiable, that they do damage to the community of living beings, both human and nonhuman.

Work and Justice in Religions

Justice has long been a concern of religions, especially in the West, where justice was a prominent theme in the prophetic traditions of Judaism, Christianity, and Islam.

Work and justice in Judaism. The Jewish prophets railed against those who denied workers a fair wage, or who took advantage of their desperation in bad times by lending at high interests. The prophet Amos reported:

Thus says the Lord: I will not revoke the punishment of Israel for three sins or even four, because they sell the righteous for silver and the needy for a pair of sandals— those who trample the head of the poor into the dust of the earth and turn aside the way of the afflicted. (Amos 2:6-7)

The dispersion of Jews throughout Europe following the destruction of the Second Temple in 70 CE and the hostility of Christians throughout Europe that produced constant discrimination and periodic violence against Jews, made the justice themes of the Jewish prophets continually relevant to quotidian Jewish life in Europe. An early-modern Jewish Zionist immigrant to Palestine from Russia in 1904, Aaron David Gordon, was influential in creating a Zionist synthesis of religion, labor, and nature that can still be located within contemporary Israel. Gordon taught that because European Jews had been largely excluded from agriculture and had been herded into urban ghettos, they had lost touch with nature. Exiled from both homeland and nature, Jews, he thought, needed to find a new spirituality to revitalize life. In his essay "Human-Nation," Gordon wrote:

Man [sic] in his own narrow confines of life is like the worm burrowing within a bitter herb, ignorant of a better and greater world beyond his little restricted domain. A human being must broaden his horizons to include the larger life, the infinite world around him, the world with which he must maintain relations.[21]

For Gordon, and for the many Jewish settlers in Palestine who admired and followed him, a true Jewish spirituality involved immersion in nature and reconnection to the oneness of the cosmos. Gordon taught that this spirituality would emerge from manual labor on the Land of Israel. Gordon wrote that "the Jewish people has been completely cut off from nature and imprisoned within city walls these two thousand years. . . . We lack the habit of labor—not labor performed out of external compulsion, but labor to which one is attached in a natural and organic way. This kind of labor binds a people to its soil and to its national culture."[22] Gordon himself became a kind of prophet for the new immigrants to collective farms in Israel. The theme of justice in his religion of labor also led him to the practice of vegetarianism, on which he left some writings that sound eerily contemporary.[23]

Work and justice in Christianity. Jesus in the New Testament, perhaps most pointedly in the Beatitudes (Matt. 5:3-12), blessed peacemakers, various groups of the poor and weak, those who "hunger and thirst for justice" and those who are "persecuted for righteousness' sake." Many of the parables that he used to describe the coming of the kingdom of God were about human work, especially about farming. There is the parable about the sower and the seed that fell on different kinds of ground (Matt. 13:3-23; Mark 4:1-20; Luke 8:4-15), the parable of the weeds sown alongside the seed (Matt. 13:24-30), the parable about the mustard seed (Matt. 13:31-33; Mark 4:30-32), and the parable of the shepherd and the lost sheep (Matt. 18:10-14; Luke 15:3-7). There are also others about fishing (Matt. 13:47-50), housework (Luke 15:8-10), workers in the vineyard (Matt. 20:1-16; 21:28-33 and 33-41; Mark 12:1-11), the dishonest steward (Luke 16:1-13), and the servants entrusted with various sums of money while their master traveled (Matt. 25:14-30; Luke 19:12-27). These parables have various themes; some commend loyalty and honesty toward one's employer that will be rewarded just as God rewards the faithful, but others also urge the exercise of shrewdness in achieving salvation.

Perhaps the most pertinent parable of Jesus for the theme of justice and workers is the parable of the workers in the vineyard (Matt. 20:1-16), who were each given a full day's wages, though some had worked a full day and some only a few hours. A full day's wages for day laborers was barely enough in first-century Galilee to feed one's family the next day; if a day laborer was only paid a fraction of the day's wage, his family went hungry. The parable taught that God, like this vineyard owner, is both just and generous, giving to each what is needed and not merely what is earned.

As a Jew, Jesus respected the Shabbat, though he was clear that "Shabbat was made for man and not man for Shabbat" (Mark 2:27). Yet as a Jew he also understood that rest for the body was not the only Shabbat rest that humans need:

> "Come to me, all who are weary and carry heavy burdens, and I will give you rest. Take my yoke upon you, and learn from me, for I am gentle and lowly in heart, and you will find rest for your souls. For my yoke is easy, and my burden is light." (Matt. 11:28)

Human souls need rest also, especially in the late-modern world of population density, constant communication, and high-stress employment.

Religions and worker justice in the late-modern United States. In Christianity, the theme of justice for workers has been constant, but it was especially prominent in the late nineteenth and early twentieth centuries in both Europe and the United States.

Catholics and worker justice. In the United States, both before and after the papal encyclical *Rerum novarum* on the rights of labor in 1891, the Catholic bishops were very involved in supporting Catholics in the union movement, primarily through the Association of Catholic Trade Unionists. As later immigrants to the United States, Catholics were poorer than other Christian groups, and were concentrated in cities and in industrial factory work, with much less presence in either agriculture or small towns. Nineteenth- and early-twentieth-century Catholic pastors and bishops were much less likely than Protestant ministers to have in their congregations factory owners or managers, and therefore were less conflicted about supporting industrial laborers and their organizations. Following the second papal encyclical on the rights of labor, *Quadragesimo anno*, in 1931, Catholic labor schools were set up by the U.S. Catholic bishops (150 of these schools existed in the United States at their high point) to train union rank-and-file leaders in the labor teachings of the Church and provide practical skills for building and maintaining effective unions, as well as to train priests in the social teachings of the church. These schools lasted until the mid-1950s, though the one in Boston is still active. Also in the 1930s, the Catholic Worker Movement began with the creation of *The Catholic Worker* newspaper and movement by Dorothy Day and Peter Maurin. During the 1936–1937 New York Maritime Strike, the Catholic Worker Movement set up headquarters on the docks to provide striking workers food and shelter.

Protestant Christian labor justice. Protestant labor justice programs began in 1920 with farmworkers on the East Coast, where the Council of Women for Home Missions sponsored daycare centers for young children of laborers. In 1926, the newly created National Migrant Ministry, part of the National Council of Churches, began providing health, vocational training, and religious services at migrant labor camps. By 1939, there were Migrant Ministry programs in fifteen states. The California Migrant Ministry program, which by the 1960s included both Protestant and Catholic clergy and laity, worked with Caesar Chavez for years attempting to get his National Farm Worker Association recognized as a union to negotiate for migrant workers' rights. Their ministerial presence made known to growers and politicians the churches' support for the movement and helped Chavez maintain the peaceful nature of the strikes and protests that preceded recognition and regulation, despite the violence and humiliation the migrant workers regularly experienced.[24]

It is often forgotten that when Martin Luther King was assassinated in 1968, it was not in a campaign against segregation, but in a campaign for recognition of the union formed by the sanitation workers of Memphis to work for just compensation and safer working conditions. The sanitation workers of Memphis, Tennessee, who were predominately but not completely African American, had asked for his help in forcing the city to change its refusal to recognize the union and negotiate. Eight days after the murder of King, the city recognized the union and signed a union contract.[25]

Jews and U.S. labor justice. Christianity was not the only religion active in supporting the union movement in the United States. During the heavy waves of European immigration to the United States in the second half of the nineteenth century and the first

Fig. 3.4. Tomb of Martin Luther King Jr. in Atlanta.

decades of the twentieth century, Jews from Europe helped fill the ghettos and factories of the Eastern Seaboard cities of the United States Jews were the single most prominent group in organizing the labor movement in the United States, and disproportionately prominent in the resulting leadership of many unions. In the 1930s the Jewish Labor Committee was formed by Jews active in a number of American unions to challenge the rise of Nazism in Europe, but in the 1950s, after the Second World War and the defeat of Nazism, it shifted its focus to combatting prejudice and discrimination of all kinds among American and Canadian workers.

Today the successor of many earlier labor justice movements within Catholic, Protestant, and Jewish communities is the Interfaith Worker Justice program, begun in 1991 in Chicago. In addition to reporting to government and raising court challenges to the illegal activities of some large corporations (e.g., Walmart forcing employees to work time off the clock) and industries (migrant workers denied overtime pay), the IWJ sponsors a "Seminary Summer," an annual program that places student ministers, priests, rabbis, and imams with union affiliates so that emerging religious leaders can participate in worker justice campaigns and learn about labor issues.

Religions and child labor. Today a variety of religious and secular organizations as well as governments are involved in attempts to protect children from inappropriate and dangerous labor—which persists, usually in poor areas of the world. One important governmental tool in discouraging child labor has been import bans on categories of items from

Fig. 3.5. Child labor is relied upon in many parts of the world, as shown here in Morona Santiago, Ecuador.

individual countries where child labor laws are routinely ignored in the production of those items.

Most religions explicitly condemn exploitation of children. Christians often quote Jesus from the Gospel of Matthew about children:

> "Truly I tell you, unless you change and become like children, you will never enter the kingdom of heaven. Whoever becomes humble like this child is the greatest in the kingdom of heaven. Whoever welcomes one such child in my name welcomes me. If any of you put a stumbling block before any of these little ones who believe in me, it would be better for you if a great millstone were fastened around your neck and you were drowned in the depth of the sea."[26]

In Jesus' time, children were accorded little importance in themselves. Then, and for many hundreds of years after, including some places still today, children have so little worth that they are assigned the most onerous and dangerous work. The above message about children was not the more modern message that children are innocent and their innocence should be protected. Rather, in Jesus' day children were not innocent or protected, but exploited because not considered important. Jesus recognized that it was the weakness and dependence of children, like that of the poor, the sick, and women whom he also championed, that made them open to the love message of Jesus and his discipleship of equals in which all persons were valuable. Inclusion is considerably more attractive to the marginalized than it is to the elites who are already at the center of the community.

A special case: Islam on child labor. Islam, in contrast to most other religions, has a long and well-developed body of legal thought on the issue of child labor,[27] which seems to be linked to the development of its treatment of orphans and their property. The care of orphans was an important concern of Mohammed, as he was orphaned very young. While Islam understands work as the human vocation (Qur'an 9:105—"work, soon will Allah observe your work, and his Apostle and the believers"—is often quoted in this regard), it understands children under seven as lacking the capacity to distinguish good or bad, and therefore decrees that children under seven should not be allowed to buy, sell, employ, or be employed by anyone, even with the agreement of parents. They are allowed to perform tasks in the family business only, supervised by family, for training purposes only, not for purposes of increasing profit, and there must be no harm or potential harm to the child.

From ages seven to fifteen (eighteen for the Hanifi legal school and some in the Maliki school of thought, both Sunni) a child is thought to be able to distinguish legal and illegal, good and bad. But the child is still considered vulnerable, and so should not work outside the family business. Yet Muslim religious authorities realized that families frequently found it necessary for older children to earn salaries to support the family, and so directed that if it were necessary for children in this second stage of development to work, the contract and work requirements must be approved by the parents, not only by the child, and the work contract must be geared to the interest of the child. It must provide the child with safety, integrity, education in a useful trade, and fair wages.

At fifteen (or eighteen for Hanifi and Maliki Sunni schools), the child is considered to pass into adulthood. If the parents examine

Fig. 3.6. Children mining casserite and wolframite with their fathers in an artisan mine in Congo.

the child's maturity and find it appropriate to the child's age, then the child is to receive any due inheritance and be able to enter into work agreements independently. Of course, as is often the case, religious legislation is easily overlooked both in situations of extreme poverty and in the presence of systems of exploitation of the powerless, so that unsupervised and exploitative child labor is today found in some poor Muslim nations.

Though established many hundreds of years ago, the outlines of this (Sunni) Muslim child labor policy seem particularly modern, especially with the Hanifi/Maliki use of eighteen rather than fifteen signaling entrance into adulthood, since in late modernity extended education has effectively postponed the beginning of adulthood.

New Ethical Questions on Human Work

Following this very brief survey of some of the highlights of religious treatment of human labor, we need to turn to current questions. What wisdom can these religious teachings and activities point us to as we try to make sense of our work and the circumstances in which we work today?

Probably the most important thing that religions tell us is that while work can be exhausting, boring, and deadening, it is also necessary for us as humans, that it plays a role in constituting our very selves. It is not only necessary because most of us cannot feed ourselves and our loved ones without work. Even those who are comfortably off, even the rich, need to work. Their work can be volunteer work, or it can be paid. It can be full- or part-time. It can be growing a garden, weaving, writing, service on the neighborhood watch, or delivering hot meals to the seniors in their neighborhood. Everyone needs work of some kind in order to be connected to our community, to develop their talents, and to learn discipline.

Finding Appropriate Work

So we all need some organization in our lives, and work is the usual way we organize our lives. But work also allows us to contribute to our society. Whether as a bank teller, a factory worker, a cashier at Walmart, a nurse, a police officer, a teacher, or a clerk at a rental car agency, our jobs serve the needs of others. Religions warn us to stay away from jobs that do not serve others in some capacity, especially those jobs that clearly harm others. Each of us must decide for ourselves what that category of jobs that harm human society includes. Some will decide that working in a slaughterhouse is not a right livelihood, but that photography is fine; others will decide that making or selling alcohol is wrong, but joining the police force is not. Yet others will decide that working with pesticides is wrong, but selling lottery tickets is fine. Our decisions should involve good social analysis so that we understand the consequences involved in each of our options, as well as our personal principles, talents, and preferences.

Some of us will need jobs that give rein to some streak of creativity in us; others will be fine with limiting their creativity to hobbies, so long as they can feel efficient on the job. Some of us will be employers, or management, or human resource officers, and will need to ask if the policies we enforce are fair to the workers involved. If they are not, and efforts to change them are unsuccessful, our need to feel truly useful in our work may push us to other employment.

Some of us will take on work that involves physical risk. Some work will include both physical and spiritual risk, as when police or other agents work undercover for long periods, and acting their role well involves serious and repeated temptations that threaten a personal ethical code. Note than none of the religions insist that members abjure work because it entails physical or spiritual risk. All societies need people who will take on some necessarily dangerous work. Today we are very aware of the risks to military and first responders in disasters, but they are only one part of socially necessary but dangerous work.

Part of choosing work—or leaving behind some kinds of work—should involve knowing oneself. Some few people are able, for example, to work for decade after decade with dying children, relapsing alcoholics and drug addicts, psychopaths, and despairing, dying families in refugee camps without losing either their capacity for compassion or their zest for life and love, because they are able to recognize ways in which the needy for whom they work also feed them. Others are not so strong and need work that involves more obvious replenishment of their spiritual wells and less drain on the spirit. Yet others need work that more or less constantly feeds their spirit. We must all experiment to learn our own needs in work, as well as, of course, our talents. We should all recognize as well that these needs change over time. If we are caring for a dying relative at home, we might want to ask to switch from hospital ICU nursing to outpatient clinic for a time. On the other hand, those newly married, or new parents, might feel energized by their domestic status to take on spiritually challenging jobs.

Supporting Those Who Cannot Work

Religions remind us that our work as "householder workers" should also support both the needy in general and those religious (monastics) who depend upon our generosity in order to make their own social contributions, whether as teachers or examples of progress on spiritual paths. How generous are we in support of those who cannot work or whose work does not sufficiently support them?

We as individuals, and our society as a whole, need to come to grips with the fact that our society cannot afford having a smaller and smaller share of workers supporting—or refusing to support—not only growing numbers of the retired who have put in their years of salaried work, but also those unprepared to take on any but the most unskilled work which is fast disappearing, as well as all those who are today considered disabled in the face of ever-more demanding contemporary labor.

There is little excuse for the United States to have a high school dropout rate of 28 percent, which then serves as the primary basis of unemployment. We need a reorganization of our work system, beginning with education, training, and retraining programs for the undereducated, underemployed, and unemployed, but also one in which some of the different groups today labeled disabled can play as much role as possible.

Religions, work, and disabled persons. Concerning the disabled, religions certainly do not have a sterling record. Only in the last few years have American religions begun to recognize that their churches, temples, mosques, and synagogues did not include the varied groups of disabled persons who belonged to the families of their members. Most religions had neither accessible worship spaces nor any outreach to those they physically excluded. Programs in religious education for the mentally disabled that would

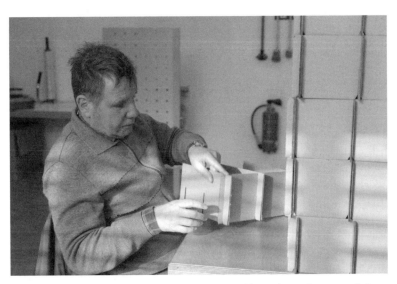

Fig. 3.7. Mentally handicapped man doing assembly work at a factory workshop for the disabled.

prepare them for ritual participation are still rare. Recognition of the need of physically or mentally disabled persons to work has been even farther from the minds of religious leaders than issues of access and outreach. Only in the last few years has there been any theological treatment of disability,[28] and ethics lags behind theology in this regard.

American and Christian thinking on disability has suffered from the same dualism that has hampered much of traditional thinking: that people are either normal or abnormal, healthy or sick, intelligent or not, educated or not, even educable or not. But the fact is that in each of these areas there is a wide range of capacity. Many physically disabled persons today are able to perform at or above the levels of those not physically disabled because so much of modern work does not involve physical strength or mobility/agility. But those who are mentally or emotionally disabled need not be excluded from all work, either. Much of our difficulty as a society in placing these people in work that would be fulfilling for them as well as allowing them to participate in and contribute to society lies in the fact that there is no flexibility in our laws or work policies. A person must either qualify for disability or be able to compete in the market with all other persons for employment. A more rational plan would be to structure some work that can be done in ways that currently high-functioning but formally disabled persons can perform, and compensate that work at levels appropriate to their productivity, so that high-functioning disabled persons would have some salaried work but also be able to draw at reduced rates on disability payments. The simplicity of either/or systems in the field of labor (either disabled or employable, either paid at minimum wage or above or not working at all) is simple but not efficient either for our economy or for the welfare of our disabled population.

Currently there are workshops for the disabled, supported by government funds and run by nonprofit community organizations, that attempt such a mix, but they generally have dramatically insufficient levels of work. Especially since the economic crash of 2008, the able-bodied unemployed compete with the disabled workshops for piecework contracts. Workshops for the disabled are also not organized for efficient work because too many are forced to provide both daycare for the severely disabled and paid work for those disabled who are capable of it. This is a field that needs the attention not only of the disabled and their families, but of religious communities and all their members, as well as corporations, social organizations, and government.

Work and retirement. One of my colleagues recently confided that she wants to retire, but her retired partner has already become the domestic in the house, doing the shopping, cooking, cleaning, and gardening in addition to her own hobbies. That leaves my friend, who has no hobbies at all, feeling that until she discovers some other "frame" for her life as a retired person, she needs to keep working, even though she has no financial need. There is a long anecdotal tradition in the United States of retired men dying quickly for lack of such a frame for their lives. Women have usually seemed to adjust to retirement better—at least they have lived longer after retirement—because after retirement from paid employment they still had the continuity of domestic work. What had been a "double burden" while they were working often became a helpful "frame" for their lives after retirement. Today domestic situations are changing and giving men more options for sharing domestic life-frames after retirement. My father, a retired physician, had never washed a dish or turned on a vacuum before retirement; but as my mother, a retired teacher, had increased difficulty with arthritis, he gradually took over laundry, cleaning, and even some cooking. After retirement, the ratio of work to rest, relaxation, and recreation changes, but some work is still necessary, even if it is primarily the work of sustaining self.

Persons looking toward retirement need to be able to anticipate greatly expanding what are now current hobbies, whether that be care of grandchildren, gardening, reading, needlework, or woodworking, volunteering at a local school or food bank, or visiting family and friends. These are not work in the sense of drudgery, but activities that will organize one's day, allow one to interact with others, and involve planning and goals for the future. These activities can allow one to be creative and useful. The absence of such activity—of any reason to wake up in the morning, or anything to look forward to—is part of the terror that nursing homes often represent to the elderly, who want to be active and useful. They want to be able to work in some capacity, to have some control over their lives, some purposeful interaction with others, and some organization of their day other than simply the institutional hours of rising, eating, and going to bed.

Work and rest. Because work can drain our spirits, the reminder from religions of the importance of rest should be taken seriously. It is not only repetitive drudge work that can be draining. Sometimes creative work can be the most draining of all because of the responsibility that so many creative workers have for the groups in which or for which they work. Think of neurosurgeons or drug researchers or inventors of new computer technologies, not to mention military officers in war or directors of biotech laboratories: the life or death of individuals, companies, or whole communities falls on their shoulders.

We all need rest, and rest is not merely time off. We need to replenish bodies and spirits. Some people will replenish bodies with exercise, a spa, and/or healthy food, and spirits with friends, music, a good book, or a tailgate party and football game. We all need to find our own way. We need to learn to recognize what our bodies and our spirits really need, and to help the people we love learn to recognize and achieve what their bodies and spirits need in the way of work and rest.

Work specialization and religious communities. What can religion tell us that can be of help in dealing with the isolation that work specialization imposes on our society? Perhaps this is one of the most important functions of religion today, one that is not always realized: forming communities. Many religious communities are successful in creating community out of persons of the same racial, ethnic, and class background, regardless of differing occupations, though usually less successful at attracting and integrating different racial or ethnic groups, especially when these differences coincide with differences between middle-class professionals and members of the working class. Creating communities out of members of religious congregations is ever-more difficult in increasingly diverse and secular America, but religions have been more successful at it than other organizations.

Religious communities that are most active in addressing local community needs are likely to be the most successful in bringing together persons of different occupations, classes, educational levels, races, and ethnicities. Shared concern for justice, for the ethical health and welfare of the larger community, and for the spiritual and physical needs of human persons are attractive to many persons in all groups. Many have found a new community home when a local church, temple, or synagogue organized help details following local tornadoes or floods, or memorials for children killed in school shootings. But churches are not the only means of creating community. There are many organizations that both serve the needs of society and provide members with social circles. Veterans' groups (American Legion, VFW, and others), Rotary, Elks, Lions, Eagles clubs, Masonic groups, and other organizations based in either nationality or ethnicity, have outreach projects that serve various social needs and initiate events that bring together families of members for social recreation. We are more than our work specializations and do not have to be limited to these groupings.

It has been noted that young people today are not joiners of such groups. Perhaps the organizations of their parents or grandparents are not for them and they will found their own social groups. But there is room for concern that more and more youth distance themselves from both churches and established social clubs, and as yet we see few replacement organizations. Social organizations are valuable in that they schedule events that interrupt work, bring people together for relaxation and recreation, and also gather persons into projects that meet important community needs that would otherwise go unmet. When we belong to such groups, some of the burden of planning for recreation and relaxation is taken from us.

Humans need work both to sustain ourselves and to support our growth as persons, but religions remind us that work is not our only need. Our bodies and spirits also need rest and community with others.

Case Study: Work

"How did the interview go? Did you get it? What is the job?" demanded Bryan of his girlfriend, Zoe, who had just come from her first job interview after three weeks of intensively filling out applications.

"I don't know what to think about it," Zoe said. "They offered me the job. The salary is okay, $40,500 to start, with evaluations and raises every half year for the first three years. It includes a week of paid vacation, a 5 percent pension that vests after eighteen months, and health insurance that I didn't understand but sounds all right. There would be two weeks of paid orientation, shadowing people doing the work now."

"That's fantastic," Bryan shouted, "we both have jobs now!"

Zoe raised her hand in a "Stop" gesture. "I haven't taken the job yet," she said.

"Why not?" Bryan asked. "What's wrong?"

Zoe had gotten an interview with a new bank that had moved into the area. Following the housing crash and recession that began in 2008, the banking scene had changed a lot. Old banks were bought by bigger banks, foreign banks had entered the scene, and new local and regional banks had formed. She had been surprised by the job ad. It had demanded a university degree, but not a business degree or a major in economics. Instead, it had said that psych majors were preferred, especially those with experience in working with the public. Zoe had a brand-new degree in psych but little interest in becoming a clinical psychologist. At the same time, she had no idea how her psych studies could be useful in banking until she went to the interview, which was arranged a few days after her application had arrived at the bank.

"If I understand the job correctly," Zoe explained, "it has two parts. One is simply handling paperwork having to do with foreclosures. There is an eighteen-month backlog in those, and after the foreclosure mess is over, I would be moved into the community investment department. The foreclosure paperwork sounds boring, but I expected boring. I don't know what I'd be doing in community investment.

"I had to take a typing test and a basic stats test—but the standards were not terribly high. The other part of the job has to do with handling the people who contact the bank about foreclosures on their homes and small businesses. That is where they want me to use my psych training. I am supposed to be as helpful as possible to these people in explaining the foreclosure process, referring them to agencies that provide counseling, shelter, etcetera, for the victims of foreclosure (though the bank does not like to use the word 'victims'), and screen out any that I think might become violent or even suicidal and report those upstairs. I didn't get a clear picture of what they do with these referrals, but I gather something is done, because there have been a few incidents with disgruntled clients that scared the execs upstairs. I guess suicides over foreclosures are bad publicity, and banks don't need any more of that."

"You don't sound too enthused about it. I had thought that any job that paid 40K would have you floating on air," noted Bryan.

"I thought so, too," said Zoe, "and I'm surprised. All the way home I was asking myself what do I want in a job? What can I reasonably expect to find in a job? And I guess that if I'm honest, I feel let down by this prospect—which is right now my only prospect! I had thought to have a job where I made some social contribution, work I could be proud of. But this job makes me feel like I would be part machine and part bodyguard. Neither one is comfortable."

"But Zoe, we both knew that whatever job we got would be entry level, and that there would be parts of it that would make us machines or servants bringing coffee and lunch. I can't even imagine what some of our friends who graduated six months or a year ago and still don't have a job offer would say about your reservations!" protested Bryan.

"I know I'm being unrealistic," responded Zoe. "That's what makes me so down. Now I realize that I secretly hoped for a job that would be fulfilling. Is that too much to ask?"

This case could be dissected and resolved in a number of ways. With which of the following do you identify, if any? Why or why not?

1. It is not too difficult to imagine what Zoe's parents would say to her if they heard this conversation. Almost all parents, even before economic depression and recession, would advise adult children to "take the job and keep it until you find a better one." They might be willing to discuss Zoe's questions about what would be fulfilling work or work

that contributed to society, but they would want that conversation to take place with an employed adult child—in order that the parents not be forced to take on support of the adult child at the expense of their own retirement.

2. In the years following the 2008 recession, banks got a lot of bad publicity for their poor or nonexistent screening of loan applicants and the terms offered to those applicants, not to mention their investment in risky securitized loan packages. But those families who lost homes and businesses in this debacle do need help, violence needs to be averted, and banking functions need to be restored because they are fundamental to a healthy national economy. It is not clear what Zoe's reservations are based on. Banking is not glamorous at the moment, but because banking serves an essential social function, its reputation will rise.

3. Zoe is right to feel ambivalent about this job offer. In working with the bank clients undergoing foreclosure, she is sure to have divided loyalties. If she is to be effective in meeting the needs of these clients, her concern must be for them. But she is paid by the bank and required to report those she suspects might be violent or self-destructive to the bank officers. What if she should find—in a circumstance widely reported to occur—that a family in the midst of foreclosure due to job loss now has new permanent work and cannot only continue mortgage payments but make up missed ones, if only the penalties and fines are removed? The bank's interests would be much better served by the family making the originally agreed mortgage payments than by selling the house at auction in a market with drastically reduced home values. Does she have the authority to halt a foreclosure? It does not sound like it.

DISCUSSION QUESTIONS

1. Do you agree with religions that there are some jobs that should not be done? How would you describe jobs that should not be done—what is wrong with these jobs?

2. What kind of job do you want when you complete your education? What parts of the job are must-haves, and which are nice-to-haves?

3. When you think of the work of your parents, relatives, and friends, do you see any that would for you be deleterious to your growth as a just and compassionate person? A happy person?

4. Do you think that disabled persons would enjoy more social status if they were thought of as workers, or not? What would be the possible advantages and disadvantages of seeing more disabled persons as workers?

FOR FURTHER READING

Albrecht, Gloria H. *Hitting Home: Feminist Ethics, Women's Work, and the Betrayal of Family Values.* New York: Continuum, 2002.

Chusmir, Leonard H., and Christine S. Koberg. "Religion and Attitudes toward Work: A New Look at an Old Question." *Journal of Organizational Behavior* 9, no. 3 (July 1988): 251–62.

Creamer, Deborah Beth. *Disability and Christian Theology: Embodied Limits* and Constructive Possibilities. New York: Oxford University Press, 2009.

Ferriss, Susan, and Ricardo Sandoval. The Fight in the Fields: Caesar Chavez and the Farmworkers' Union. Ed. Diana Hembree. Orlando: Paradigm/Harcourt Brace, 1997.

Haggis, Jane. "Ironies of Emancipation: Changing Configurations of 'Women's Work' in the 'Mission of Sisterhood' to Indian Women." Feminist Review 65 (Summer 2000): 108–26.

Honey, Michael K. Going Down Jericho Road: The Memphis Strike, Martin Luther King's Last Campaign. New York: W. W. Norton, 2007.

Interfaith Worker Justice. A Worker Justice Reader: Essential Writings on Religion and Labor. Maryknoll, NY: Orbis, 2010.

Lazerov, Tama. "Religion and Labor Reform in Antebellum America: The World of William Field Young." American Quarterly 38, no. 2 (Summer 1886): 265–86.

O'Brien, John J. George G. Higgins and the Quest for Worker Justice: The Evolution of Catholic Social Thought in America. Lanham, MD: Rowman & Littlefield, 2004.

Smith, Ted, David A. Sonnenfeld, and David Naquib Pellow, eds. Challenging the Chip: Labor Rights and Environmental Justice in the Global Electronics Industry. Philadelphia: Temple University Press, 2006.

Trimiew, Darryl M. God Bless the Child That's Got His Own: The Economic Rights Debate. Atlanta: Scholars, 1997.

FILMS

The Dark Side of Chocolate: Child Trafficking and Illegal Child Labor in the Cocoa Industry. Films for the Humanities, 2010.

Disabilities in the Workplace: Working Out. Films for the Humanities, 1993.

Finance, Trade and Islamic Regulation in Asia. Films for the Humanities, 2010.

Prophetic Witness. National Interfaith Committee for Worker Justice, 2001.

NOTES

1. Genesis 3:19, The Holy Bible, English Standard Version (Wheaton, IL: Crossway, 2001).

2. Michel de Certeau, The Practice of Everyday Life (Berkeley/Los Angeles: University of California Press, 1984), 7–8.

3. Jason Koebler, "High School Notes: U.S. High School Graduation Rates Improve," U.S. News and World Report, June 13, 2011.

4. Bureau of Labor Statistics, "America's Young Adults at 24: School Enrollment, Training, and Employment Transitions Between Ages 23 and 24 Summary," http://www.bls.gov/news.release/nlsyth.t01.htm.

5. Claudio Sanchez, "Women Outnumber Men Earning Doctoral Degrees," National Public Radio, September 15, 2010, http://www.npr.org/templates/story/story.php?storyId=129874290.

6. U.S. Census Bureau, Current Population Survey 2009, http://www.census.gov/cps/.

7. Thomas Borchert, "Monastic Labor: Thinking about the Work of Monks in Contemporary Theravada Communities," Journal of the American Academy of Religion 79, no. 1 (March 2011): 162–92.

8. Thich Nhat Hanh, The Miracle of Mindfulness (New York: Random House, 2008).

9. Peter Harvey, An Introduction to Buddhist Ethics (Cambridge/New York: Cambridge University Press, 2000), 188.

10. Buddha, *Sigalovada sutta*, D 3.189. See Harvey, *Introduction*, 100, for the larger selection from which this one is taken.

11. For one Muslim example, see "The Importance of Suitable Occupations," http://www.taajushshariah.com/Articles%5Csuitable_occupation.htm.

12. Mohsin S. Khan, "Islamic Interest-Free Banking: A Theoretical Analysis," *Staff Papers: International Monetary Fund* 33, no. 1 (March 1986): 1–27.

13. *Sahih al-Bukhari*, 3:34:318; 7:62:110; 41:4914, *Sunnan Abu Dawud*, 41:4913, *Sahih al-Bukhari* 7:73:133; *Sahih al-Bukhari*, 7:72:838.

14. W. L. Rathje, "Why the Taliban Are Destroying Buddhas," *USA Today*, March 22, 2001, http://www.usatoday.com/news/science/archaeology/2001-03-22-afghan-buddhas.htm.

15. John Noonan, "Authority, Usury and Contraception," *Cross Currents* (Winter 1966): 56–63.

16. Charles Herbermann, ed., "Rule of St. Benedict," *Catholic Encyclopedia* (New York: Robert Appleton Co., 1913), http://www.newadvent.org/cathen/02436a.htm.

17. Rogation days and Ember days are no longer binding on all Catholics.

18. Today in North America those holy days of obligation number six, including Christmas Day; January 1, feast of Mary, Mother of God; November 1, All Saints Day; the Ascension of Jesus (forty days after Easter); August 15, the Assumption of Mary; and December 8, the Immaculate Conception of Mary.

19. These holy days include Rosh Hashanah, Yom Kippur, the first and second days of Sukkot, Shemini Atzeret, Simchat Torah,

20. shavu'ot, and the first, second, seventh, and eighth days of Passover.

20. Deuteronomy 23:19-20.

21. Matt Plen, "A. D. Gordon: The Religion of Labor," http://www.myjewishlearning.com/israel/Jewish_Thought/Modern/Secular_Zionism/AD_Gordon.shtml.

22. A. D. Gordon, "People and Labor," quoted in Plen.

23. In 1921, the year before he died, Gordon wrote letters to Nathan Bistritzky, who had asked him to contribute to an anthology on vegetarianism. Selections can be found in "A. D. Gordon Writes about Vegetarianism," http://anonymous.org.il/artegordon.html.

24. Susan Ferriss and Ricardo Sandoval, *The Fight in the Fields: Caesar Chavez and the Farmworkers' Union*, ed. Diana Hembree (Orlando, FL: Paradigm/Harcourt Brace, 1997).

25. Michael K. Honey, *Going Down Jericho Road: The Memphis Strike, Martin Luther King's Last Campaign* (New York: W. W. Norton, 2007).

26. Matthew 18:3-6, New Revised Standard Version.

27. Mohammed Adam El-Sheikh, "For the Good of the Children: An Islamic Response," in *Ethics and World Religions: Cross-Cultural Case Studies*, ed. Regina Wenzel Wolfe and Christine E. Gudorf (Maryknoll, NY: Orbis, 1999), 310–18.

28. Nancy Eiesland, *The Disabled God: Toward a Liberatory Theology of Disability* (Nashville: Abingdon, 1994); Deborah Beth Creamer, *Disability and Christian Theology: Embodied Limits and Constructive Possibilities* (New York: Oxford, 2009).

CHAPTER 4

RELIGIONS ON BODY COVERING, APPEARANCE, AND IDENTITY

Recently I returned yet again to work and visit friends in Indonesia, and the first thing I noticed at the Jakarta airport when I arrived was the crowds of young Muslim women. They were, as always in past visits, wearing *jilbabs* (headscarves) that cover their hair and wrap around their necks. Most but not all Muslim women in Indonesia wear *jilbabs*. But the sight was startling, because the same young women were also wearing skinny jeans or tights and long-sleeved cotton sweaters that clung to every curve. I remarked on this to my Muslim hosts at the university, that the skin-tight jeans and tights seemed to defeat the purpose of the headscarves, which have often been justified as a mark of modesty lest the bodies of women incite lust in men.

Their response was illuminating: that the contemporary purpose of the headscarf in Indonesia is about identity and not primarily about modesty. I knew that in various Muslim nations where head coverings for women were not traditional, especially in parts of Africa and Asia, contemporary Muslim women have donned the headscarf not worn by their mothers as part of the global Muslim revival.

They wear the headscarf as a sign that they, too, are full Muslims. Within this revival in various countries women are also reclaiming their right to attend mosques and to receive formal religious education,[1] contrary to some national traditions that excluded women from both, understanding them as extensions of their husbands and fathers, who were responsible for women's religious behavior and knowledge. The headscarf on the heads of university-trained doctors, engineers, bankers, and other female professionals today signals not only a willingness, or even demand, to

Fig. 4.1. Display of headscarves in a Kuala Lumpur store.

exercise responsibility in the modern world, but also a desire to exercise responsibility in the *umma*, the Muslim community.

I had not known that the headscarf as symbol of Muslim identity in Indonesia had so completely displaced the headscarf as symbol of female modesty that there would be no outcry from Muslims at such a combination of clothing. Such a thing would have been unthinkable fifteen years ago—and probably still is in some parts of Indonesia less cosmopolitan than Jakarta. Interestingly, the contemporary revival of the headscarf among Indonesian Muslim women has led to its becoming subject to fashion. New stores featuring a myriad of styles and colors of headscarves, from simple white cotton to chartreuse silk with designs in gleaming gems, as well as jeweled and enameled pins with

which to secure the headscarf on the shoulder, have not only arisen but have thrived and expanded quickly. These are among the most crowded stores in major cities.

Framing the Issues

As I thought about my friends' response, I was reminded that body covering as a sign of identity is actually a common religious practice, and not at all a phenomenon limited to Islam. Throughout the ages, religious societies have marked the bodies of their members in various ways, including but not only through regulations concerning dress. These regulations have served a number of different purposes and meanings. One purpose has been to identify religious leaders and distinguish them from ordinary members. Think of the

Fig. 4.2. Buddhist monks in saffron robes collecting alms, Laos.

Fig. 4.3. Newly married Asian couple.

saffron robes of Buddhist monks and nuns, or in Catholicism, the brown robes of Franciscan monks, the red robes of cardinals, or the black suits and round white collars of secular priests.

But religious leaders have not been the only members of religions to wear distinctive dress. Sometimes ordinary members wear distinctive clothing for special occasions, such as the wearing of white by participants in Umbanda rituals or Catholic First Communions, or even the wearing of white wedding gowns in Christianity or red dresses in Asian weddings. Among Christians, there have been special gowns for christening babies, as well as robes for immersing adults in baptism.

In some religious communities that set themselves apart from the wider society, different dress for all members is a prominent way of marking their separation. Think of the black suits, tassels hanging from the waists, and side-curls of Hasidic Jewish men,[2] or the full-coverage dresses and small bonnets of Amish women and the wide-brimmed hats and suspenders of Amish men.[3] It is in this

Fig. 4.4. A woman wearing a burka enters a merchant's shop in Afghanistan.

category that the Muslim headscarf falls, as well as the more enveloping and obscuring *burka* found in some very conservative Muslim communities.

Color Symbolism

In the West, white clothing has generally denoted purity, innocence, and, in relation to weddings, virginity, while black garments have signified death and have been customary garb for funerals. In other parts of the world, for example in Islam, white has designated death and so is used in funeral coverings for the dead body. In China and much of Asia, brides dressed in red symbolize both joy and fertility. In many other parts of the world, red, and even more often purple, have been clothing colors that have been at times restricted to the highest classes of society, frequently to royalty. The dyes for these colors were rare and expensive, which in itself restricted their use to the rich. But in societies where individual members of the lower classes were amassing wealth that would allow them to purchase expensive items previously available only to royalty, there were sometimes sumptuary laws passed, often in the name of preventing ostentation and waste, that limited the colors and fabrics of dress, or the types of carriage, or the frontage of houses, differently for different classes.[4] While sumptuary laws were most often civil laws and not religious laws, they were most often justified in religious and moral terms. Like the differences within religions between the clothing of leaders and that of members, such sumptuary laws served to set up boundaries between economic classes of people, not only to make clear which group was due the greater respect, but perhaps more centrally to inhibit movement between the classes. These laws were understood as one facet of maintaining stability in society, a task to which religions were dedicated: maintaining the social structures dictated by the gods.

Modern Clothes Make Modern Minds?

So intimately have we humans understood the link between body covering/appearance and personal identity that the Russian czar Peter the Great, who demanded that his nation abandon its feudal past and join European modernity, in 1701 issued the following astounding decree:

> All residents of the city of Moscow including those serfs who come to the city to trade, but excluding the clergy and agricultural laborers, must wear German dress. Outerwear must consist of French or Saxon coats, and underneath men must wear camisoles (sleeved vests), breeches, boots, shoes and German hats. And they must ride in German saddles. Women of all ranks—women of the clergy, wives of officers, musketeers, and soldiers—and their children must wear German dress, hats, skirts and shoes. From this day forward, no one will be allowed to wear Russian dress, Caucasian caftans, sheepskin coats, pants or boots, nor will anyone be permitted to ride in Russian saddles. Finally, artisans will not be allowed to make or trade [in these goods].[5]

Peter thought that wearing "modern" clothes would incline people to think of themselves as moderns and to have modern ideas. Certainly the efforts required to outfit the entire city of Moscow in German clothes and saddles would involve a great deal of commerce with Western Europe. Was it so extreme to assume that with modern clothing, and the travel and commerce necessary to secure it,

Fig. 4.5. Illustration of Peter the Great, seventeenth-century czar of Russia.

became another support for the revolutionary dream of civil equality. In short, the link between body covering and identity works both ways: body covering can express an identity that has been inherited or imposed, but a decision to change body covering can be a claim of control over oneself, a step in constructing a new identity for oneself or one's group.

Youthful Experiments with Identity

Modernity has seen the triumph of egalitarianism in many aspects of life, and this trend has tended to undermine the legitimacy of using clothing to distinguish class, caste, or other social groupings. In late modernity—postmodernity—there has been a strong movement among the young globally to experiment with religious clothing, as well as with religious rituals and behavior, from different groups. This experimentation is sometimes limited to donning, for example, a monk's robe for a Halloween party (which would have been sacrilege in an earlier time), but can also include the widespread wearing of rosaries or cross earrings as jewelry, the wearing of Rastafarian dreadlocks, of tams or brims, or even the widespread use of mandarin-collared jackets, which were originally derived from the official wear of Chinese Confucian mandarins (bureaucrats), all by persons with no connection to these religious societies. This experimentation is part of the contemporary process of constructing a personal identity, an individual "look" or *persona*.

This construction of one's personal—and public—identity is understood as a crucial task in postmodernity, and often involves, at the level of body covering, not only clothing but also hairstyles, tattoos, and even cosmetic surgery. Identity construction is a much more complex and demanding process than

modern ideas would also penetrate the Russian capital?

In reality, Peter's idea was radical in ways that he could not have foreseen. His decree actually began part of the process that led to the eventual Russian Revolution. For what was "German" clothes in Peter's time eventually, due to his decree, became "city clothes" in Russia. After the emancipation of serfs in 1861, the peasantry, especially those who relocated in the cities, began adopting these "city clothes."[6] City-dwelling factory workers who had recently been serfs realized that the more they looked like other city dwellers by adopting Western dress, the better they were treated. This experience of dressing "up" ever before in history. For in postmodernity, mobility and population density have made all of us more anonymous. We must make more of an effort to become individuated selves, for birth brings with it fewer and fewer permanent personal characteristics, and we have fewer persons around us with longstanding intimate knowledge of us that they can reflect back to us.

In this same postmodernity, we are surrounded by many more decisions and choices that must be made within this construction of self than ever faced our ancestors. In contemporary advertising alone there are many more pressures pushing us toward one choice or another, with ads and celebrities insisting on the importance of each choice of shoe or jeans for what these say about the person we are or are becoming.

Religious Treatment Concerning Body Covering, Appearance, and Identity

Modesty has historically been another purpose of dress regulation, especially in the Abrahamic religions—Judaism, Christianity, and Islam. But dress regulations for purposes of protecting modesty have generally either been applied only to women, or much more extensively to women than to men. Within the heterosexist patriarchy that has characterized most of human history up to the present, human society has been regulated from a male perspective that took for granted that sexual attraction and desire were always heterosexual. Because power was in the hands of men, society, faced with the need to keep sexual order, found it easier and more convenient to restrict the behavior of women than to restrict the behavior of men. Many men have understood male sexual desire as

uncontrollable, and thus thought it better to prevent its being aroused except in the very limited space of the marital bed. To prevent male desire from leading to rape, adultery, fornication, and out-of-wedlock children, women were made to cover their bodies and restrict their movements to those areas deemed safe from male lust; such areas were often limited to the home, and even to parts of the home in some societies.[7]

Class played a role here, of course. Not all women could be restricted to their homes, for some women in every society have always been used as cooks, maids, governesses, nannies, barmaids, and laundresses, as well as prostitutes serving the larger society. Thus the degree of restriction placed on women became an important indicator of class; the most restricted women belonged to the richest, most respected households, and the least restricted women—who were often assumed to be sexually promiscuous because unrestricted in their movements—were parts of lower-class households. These divisions were usually understood as both class and religious divisions: the more restricted women were seen as more respectable, more moral, and more pious than those who must work in the world.

In Europe, only with the rise of the middle class in the early modern period did this association of social class and moral virtue (especially of women) change; the upper classes became understood as increasingly degenerate at the same time that women's court fashions revealed more and more bosom and ankle. The hardworking—and rising—middle classes, whether Calvinist, Quaker, or emancipated Jew, came to be seen as more pious, more moral, and their women certainly more modest than the aristocracy whom they were displacing.

Over the last two centuries in the West, restrictions on covering women's bodies began to erode, but slowly. Years ago when my family moved to a new town in Indiana and attended the local un-air-conditioned Catholic church, my young sisters and I were denied communion one August Sunday because our dresses were sleeveless, though otherwise completely covered us from neck to below the knees. In this church, modesty decreed that women were to cover their arms at least to the elbow, regardless of the temperature. Today in much of the United States, even clothing worn to Sunday services has become very casual, and often includes bare shoulders and arms, and even shorts for men and women. Part of this shift to a wider range of dress styles, and more openness to greater female undress over the last few decades, has been the result of greater social emphasis on comfort and casual wear even at work, away from the earlier formality of three-piece suits for men and skirts, hose, and hats for women. But a second cause for the growing casualness and undress is that the women's movement has brought about a widespread rejection of the assumption that women's dress and behavior should be limited in order to control male lust and aggression. The women's movement has instead insisted that men be held responsible for controlling their own sexual arousal. And so the corsets and girdles of the nineteenth- and twentieth-century West, designed to suppress any vestige of female softness and curves, disappeared; skirts shortened, and pants gradually began to replace skirts as appropriate attire, even for church.

Moreover, as feminism promoted better understandings of women as both desiring agents and objects of male desire, the one-sidedness of earlier dress restrictions came under fire.[8] Some women asked: Perhaps there should be some emphasis on modesty in men also? In this area, too, there is a movement toward equality, though it is still popularly debated whether sexual desire in women is analogous to sexual desire in men.

Clothes? And What Kinds?

Among Jains, there are two major sects, and a major cause of the division is the dispute over how monks should be dressed. Digambara monks are naked ("sky-clad"); for them, non-possession is taken to the extreme of never wearing clothes or shoes. Digambara monks do not even own a begging bowl, so that they must accept food in their hands. Digambara female monastics are clothed, in part because the Digambara believe that women must first be reborn as men before they can achieve liberation—thus female monastics are never in the highest stages toward liberation. Svetambara male and female monks, however, are clad. They wear white robes and teach sexual equality.

Fashions change in all societies, and religious understandings of modesty often change with them. Many Christian churches in the past required that women wear skirts, and not pants, which were considered to display too much of the female figure. In some parts of the world this tradition endures still today. Yet in other parts of the world (e.g., China) skirted robes were historically the normal garb for both sexes among the elites.

Christianity on head coverings for women. Until the 1960s in most Christian churches, women wore head coverings based on a biblical passage from St. Paul that distinguished the relation of men to God from the relation of women to God:

But I want you to understand that Christ is the head of every man, and the husband is the head of his wife, and God is the head of Christ. Any man who prays or prophesies with something on his head disgraces his head, but any woman who prays or prophesies with her head unveiled disgraces her head—it is one and the same thing as having her head shaved. For if a woman will not veil herself, then she should cut off her hair; but if it is disgraceful for a woman to have her hair cut off or to be shaved, she should wear a veil. For a man ought not to have his head veiled, since he is the image and reflection of God; but woman is the reflection of man. Indeed, man was not made from woman, but woman from man. Neither was man created for the sake of woman, but woman for the sake of man. For this reason a woman ought to have a symbol of authority on her head, because of the angels. Nevertheless, in the Lord woman is not independent of man or man independent of woman. For just as woman came from man, so man comes through woman; but all things come from God. Judge for yourselves: is it proper for a woman to pray to God with her head unveiled? Does not nature itself teach you that if a man wears long hair, it is degrading to him, but if a woman has long hair, it is her glory? For her hair is given to her for a covering. But if anyone is disposed to be contentious—we have no such custom, nor do the churches of God. (1 Cor. 11:3-16 NRSV)

In the 1960s in Christianity, women's collective rejection of the expectation that they cover their heads in church signaled the beginnings of a movement of women claiming full and equal membership in the churches. Head coverings had been customary for women, but there was no legislation on head covering in most Christian churches. In Islam over the last three decades, many scholars point to the voluntary donning of head covering as signaling a similar movement among women.[9] Many in the West have misunderstood the Muslim women's movement because head covering was only viewed with a western lens.

Sacred thread in Hinduism and Buddhism. Body coverings can represent different kinds of identity in different periods of history. The sacred thread in Hinduism, called by a variety of names, originally could only be worn by men of the three upper castes, and excluded the fourth caste, the Shudra (originally peasants) as well as the class of Dalits, untouchables. But today in Hinduism, the sacred thread serves as a coming-of-age symbol distinguishing all male children from adults, regardless of caste. It is most often assumed in rituals for adolescents, though in some places the thread is not bestowed until just before marriage (rites of passage into adulthood have been linked to marriage in a number of cultures in the past). Among Buddhists, who also wear the sacred thread, the ceremony administering the sacred thread can be done at all ages and to both genders. The most common sacred thread contains three strands, which serve to remind men (and in Buddhism, women) of three debts they owe: to their teachers, to their parents/ancestors, and to the sages and scholars who discovered the knowledge that has been passed to the wearer.

Changes in the Hindu *bindi*. While the *bindi* (or *tilaka*, most often a bright red dot), worn on the forehead of Hindus, used to be common to both men and women, today Hindu men are much less likely to wear them. In most of India, a *bindi* on the forehead of a woman signifies that she is married, though in southern India unmarried girls now wear them as well. The original purpose of the *bindi* was to signify the presence of the third eye, the mind's eye, which denotes an association with the gods, meditation, and spiritual devotion. The most distinctive *bindis* are those worn by followers of Vishnu and his avatar, Krishna, which cover a large part of the forehead and may extend down to the tip of the nose. But followers of Shiva and the goddess Shakti also wear distinctive *bindis*, consisting of three horizontal stripes on the forehead with a vertical band or circle in the center. Thus what was originally a symbol worn by gods, priests, ascetics, and the most devout worshippers became widely adopted by the Hindu masses, and now is principally seen on Hindu women.

Fig. 4.6. Indian woman with the most common form of *bindi*.

The *bindi* illustrates that body covering can serve to symbolize a number of different kinds of identity at the same time: a general identification of the wearer with spirituality and wisdom, an identification with a particular religion or sect of a religion, and identification of one's marital status. Just as Muslim headscarves in Indonesia have become fashion items in themselves, the *bindi* is also subject to the impact of fashion: today many Hindu women are eschewing the traditional vermillion color of the *bindi* and choosing colors that match their dress.

Dress as Individualizing; Dress as Conformity

We should not be surprised or upset that religious symbols such as the *bindi* or the headscarf become fashion items. Fashion is yet another way of expressing one's identity. All over the world, more forcefully in some cultures than others, adolescents intent on separating themselves from their parents in order to become independent persons use body covering as a primary signal to themselves and to others of their individuality. The jeans, tie-dyed shirts, beards, and long hair on both males and females that symbolized young radicals in the U.S. antiwar movement in the 1960s and 1970s were picked up by other parts of the population until they largely failed to function as symbols of anything. Leather clothing signaled rebellion during those years but today is often found on criminal biker gangs, aging stockbrokers, and teen Goths.

Today in the United States, pants with crotches hanging at the knees and displaying a variety of boxer designs on the butt are seen everywhere in urban areas, mostly but not exclusively on African American males. To the dismay of parental generations and the ridicule of others, this style has spread to some younger groups among the middle class, both African American and white. Faced with this and any other widely adopted fashion, we must ask how some body decoration, be it clothes, jewelry, tattoos, or shoes, can individualize us, express our own personal identity, at the same time that it is the fashion statement seen on every corner. The answer is that as human beings, especially in our youth, we are always trying to disassociate ourselves from some people (usually parents or other source of restriction) and to associate ourselves with others, usually the youth group to which we aspire. We want to be a part of a community—we just want to choose that community. And dressing like the community we want to be a part of is an important part of both our assuming the desired identity and being accepted by the desired community. We need to be careful about what groups we want to affiliate to.

Until the second half of the twentieth century in the United States, pierced ears marked a female as foreign-born or born to recent immigrants. Southern and Eastern European immigrants whose females had had pierced ears for generations stopped the practice in order to blend into America. Today I still have my great-grandmother's gold earrings, because as the oldest of my grandmother's female grandchildren, I was the first woman in three generations to have pierced ears. Today pierced ears do not signify foreignness, or even femaleness, since so many men now wear earrings. Fashions, even prominent fashion symbols of identity, can change quickly.

Sometimes clothing color can signify membership in a particular group, such as urban gangs, or the Buddhist *sangha*. In the past, gold or silver crosses around the neck used to mark one as a Christian; if the cross was a crucifix (with the image of Jesus hung on the cross), one was assumed to be Catholic. Today, however, the cross, and to a lesser extent the crucifix, too, has been adopted by groups professing many other or no religious beliefs.

Women's dress as bearing tradition. Changes in dress fashions do not always affect social groups in the same way. It is interesting that in the more than three hundred years of the modern period, it has usually been women who have been expected to retain the traditional dress that proclaimed group identity. Christine Ruane explains of the period following Peter the Great's edict during which women were required to retain items of traditional dress: "It was women's bodies which were intended to represent national identity and thereby heal the social and cultural breech created by Peter the Great."[10] Often in the Andes over the last few decades I have seen a farm family on the way to market, the man dressed in ordinary western clothes with shoes, sometimes seated on a mule or horse loaded with bags of produce, the woman walking in bright, full-skirted traditional dress and hat, barefoot, often carrying a huge load of vegetables in a sack on her back. Today a similar pattern is seen in parts of the Arab world, and in much of Africa as well: men in western dress, women in traditional garb. If in many religions men are the keepers of the religious history, doctrine, and ritual, the lived culture and values are usually understood to reside with the women.

There is a great deal of speculation about why this gendered pattern of adaptation to modernity should be so common. Many understand it as the result of mothers being the principal socializers of the young; if the tradition is to be passed on to the young, those who care for them must both teach and represent it. Others point to the fact that under colonial and neocolonial regimes, households had to earn currency to pay taxes, which usually entailed men working in the colonial economy, learning something of the colonial language and mores. They were consequently much more exposed to modernity than women. There are probably many local variations on these causes.

Minorities have often used clothing to aid in identifying members of the same group. Until very recently homosexuals in various communities throughout the world developed a variety of covert ways of signaling each other as homosexual in order to avoid more open inquiries, which could be dangerous; many of those covert ways involved body covering. Such little things as where one carried one's keys, or handkerchief, or whether one wore an earring, or where one wore that earring, could identify one as gay. Even when the body covering is adopted for more theological or cultural reasons, it often endures because it is useful in identifying members of the group. Amish recognize other Amish, Sikhs other Sikhs, and Hasidic Jews other Hasids by their clothing and hairstyles, which set them apart from others and help prevent assimilation into the larger society.

Many people deny that there are any moral values in body covering. How can it be wrong to express one's identity? Modesty is often dismissed as a value, precisely because it means such different things in different societies. Let us explore what an ethics of body covering might include.

Identities Are Chosen

Perhaps what distinguishes today from past ages is precisely that we are increasingly conscious that we choose who we will be much more than did persons in the past. This change

is most radical in the developed nations of the West; in some parts of the world there has been much less change. But overall, until the coming of modernity with the eighteenth century, the vast majority of the people of the earth inherited most of their identity. Most would live their entire lives in the same society, often the same village in which they were born, surrounded by extended family and lifelong neighbors. They inherited their ethnicity, their language, their religion, their culture, and usually their occupation and economic status from their parents, with virtually no opportunities to change any of these. Many of these people had little if any choice in their marriage partners. The majority were illiterate and had comparatively little ability to control the size of their families or their health.

Voluntary Society: Voluntary Religion

By comparison, at least in much of the world today, our societies could be characterized as voluntary. Today it is not odd to hear high school students ask each other, "Where do you want to live when you grow up?" and for them to respond not with the name of some street or neighborhood, which is what this question would have elicited in the past, but with the name of another city, or even country.

Religion is one of the options; we can choose to belong or not to belong to a religion; we can choose which religion if any we want to belong to; and increasingly we can decide to what extent we want to comply with the norms of a religion we do decide to join. Westerners take for granted that they will choose their area of training and profession, that they will choose their marriage partner, and that they are free to choose a new religion or none if they become dissatisfied with the one they were born into. Perhaps the strongest mark of the voluntary society is that persons choose to socialize primarily with friends they have personally chosen as intimates, rather than with extended family and neighbors, who may now be far distant (as chapter 7 will elaborate).

Among so much individual choice, it is difficult to avoid understanding our very selves as chosen by us. Yet we do not choose all aspects of our lives, to be sure. We cannot control whether we are born to Sudanese subsistence farmers who have never seen a road, or New York bankers, whether we are born into a dangerous war-torn nation or a peaceful, prosperous one. We do not control what genes we inherit, how healthy or sick they may make us, or how many resources are available to us as we are growing up. Perhaps the best way to understand how our self is constructed is that the circumstances of our birth and youth present us with some choices—some of us many more than others—and the choices we make in those circumstances determine to a great extent the self we will become. We are both free and constrained.

We are responsible for those parts of our identity that we choose, and so, too, we must be responsible for those same parts when we signify them with body covering. One who chose to wear the swastika armband of the Nazis when not all were obliged to wear them must be responsible for the message that the swastika conveyed, and still conveys today. Today there are youth who take up the swastika out of angry rebellion—sometimes not fully realizing that it symbolizes, perhaps even more now than during the Nazi reign,[11] a racial narcissism, a blatant disregard for human life, for law, and for the promises

of treaties, as well as a capacity for efficient and impersonal violence. A symbol that may have been donned in a moment of anger carries a message not only to others, but also to the self who donned it. The symbol can exert its own "push" on the wearer, both through self-reflection and by observing how others respond to one's wearing it. One adolescent who puts on a swastika may be drawn into a group that more fully lives out its dangerous meanings, while another may remove it out of shame upon seeing that others respond to it with revulsion. To the first youth, the swastika may become associated with feelings of power and the end of social isolation, and to the second, it may appear as that which isolates him from others and marks him for shunning. In short, the way we choose to dress, how we identify ourselves to others, puts us on a certain life path. That path can be changed, but the longer we follow any one path, the more difficult changing it will be. We need to be careful about choosing that path, that identity.

This does not mean that we should avoid experimentation. We all must engage in a certain degree of experimentation in body covering in order to discover what kind fits us most comfortably, what professes to others the person we want them to see. Most of the choices before us in body covering are harmless; the worst that can be said of most is that they seem to conservative observers to be gaudy, boring, tasteless, ugly, or pointless. But beauty is truly in the eye of the beholder, as is ugliness. One of my nieces wears six or seven earrings in each ear and is the envy of younger nieces, regardless of the many warnings by her elders about how soon she will come to regret having so many holes in her body.

Sometimes our clothing announces what are at the moment important parts of our identity. At a recent NCAA Women's Basketball Tournament, I saw a number of University of Louisville fans dressed in red-and-black striped knee socks, black shorts, red shirts, and wholly shaved heads entirely covered in red and black paint. These students, both male and female, left no doubt where their loyalties lie. Sports teams of all kinds evoke great passion, but universities' teams are objects of near reverence, a reverence displayed in body covering. Around my home I see University of Kentucky bumper stickers, T-shirts, and jackets on everyone. Businesses close when UK plays in the NCAA tournament, though very few of their owners have ever been to UK. Other people wear their American patriotism on their bodies, in the form of flag lapel pins or flag ties or shirts, while yet others proudly wear the T-shirt proclaiming their city, their church, or their club. In some ways, we are what we wear.

New Ethical Questions on Body Covering, Appearance, and Identity

Some decisions about body covering do have moral import, however. Some choices we make can start us on a path of insensitivity to the interests of others, an insensitivity that can lead to greater offenses in the future. For some people today, there can be no moral excuse for wearing animal fur. For them, wearing animal fur symbolizes an understanding of these animals' lives as completely without value, as things to be used at will by humans even when there are alternatives that serve us just as well. Wearing particular animal furs (lynx, leopard, ocelot, etc.) is seen as even more reprehensible, as it represents illegal hunting of endangered species and risks the extinction of that species. Other people

will condemn not only the hunting and use of the fur of endangered species, but also the ghastly conditions under which animals are raised on most "fur farms," and yet insist that fur-bearing species that are abundant in the wild, even regarded as vermin (such as rabbits in much of Australia), should be exempt from a clothing ban.

Whether one decides to simply avoid wearing all fur, or decides to be discriminating about what type of fur one wears and how it is produced, it should be clear that we are responsible for the effects of our clothing choices. If we know that the fashionable sneakers we have been saving for are produced by children working twelve-hour shifts in some sweatshop in Africa, then we need to think about choosing different sneakers.

The response of most of us to such a statement is that life is too short, too busy, to constantly be researching who makes which product where, with what kind of working conditions. In fact, most of us choose to be ignorant about exactly these facts, as if chosen ignorance excuses our bad choices in the same way that invincible ignorance excuses. (Ignorance is invincible when there is nothing we could do to penetrate the ignorance.) But when ignorance is chosen, it is not invincible; we are responsible. There is not much moral difference between seeing the newspaper headline about the cashmere coat we are saving for being produced by poorly paid trafficked workers and deciding not to read the article, and hearing a sustained series of slaps, thumps, and childish screams next door and closing the window. When ignorance is chosen, it is culpable. This does not mean that we must, or even can, know everything about all the items we wear. But we need to make some efforts to buy responsibly.

Bodies, Youth, and Beauty

Once upon a time in the United States, the most common gift for high school graduation was pen and pencil sets, or among the wealthy college-bound, perhaps a manual typewriter. Today a common high school graduation gift, at least among females, is a nose job by a plastic surgeon.[12] Plastic surgery has become ubiquitous. Nose jobs, breast augmentation, neck lifts, lid lifts, facelifts, liposuction, tummy tucks, butt lifts—the generic terms for plastic surgery options are heard everywhere around us. All are part of a cultural fixation on youth and beauty. Advertising exists to make us self-conscious about how we look every minute of every day, to make us compare ourselves to the young and beautiful who populate advertising. While women are the primary targets, in the last decade an increasing amount of cosmetics, colognes, and designer clothes have been aimed at men, using similar advertising tactics.

Usually when some action or practice is considered morally wrong, it is because it is harmful to someone else or their interests. As we have said above, clothing and body decoration are one of the ways that we try out, and finally announce, our own identity. When we buy into the cultural fixation on youth and beauty, the damage done is mostly to ourselves, though it does also affect others. Instead of accepting our bodies as they are, or as we can make them through exercise and care, we pursue what for virtually all is the impossible task of competing with the media images we are shown. Though we know at a conscious intellectual level that the images are not real, that they are edited and retouched at numerous levels, we nevertheless react to their constant repetition by granting them normative status. The shift to TV broadcasting in HD beginning in 1998 was a shock to many viewers, who discovered for the first time the facial blemishes, bumps, large pores, and pasty makeup on the faces and bodies of the stars they had long admired and envied. Many stars, given the new clarity, demanded that cameras eschew close-ups, and others

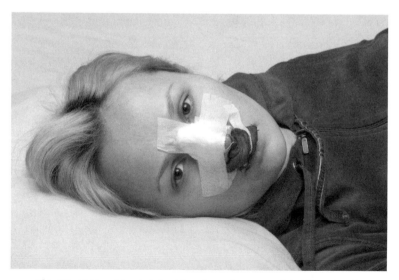

Fig. 4.7. Girl in a blood-stained bandage after a nose job (rhinoplasty).

demanded more makeup. Interestingly, many viewers were not so much disillusioned about the images of beauty in which they had been led to believe as they were disturbed at being forced to admit that their idols were not necessarily perfect in appearance.

Of course, the waste involved in attempts to improve on natural beauty is another issue for ethics. When there are hungry people, people without basic medical care, not only in our world, but in our county, how do we justify thousands spent on a cosmetic surgery that, for example, will simply delay some part of aging for five to eight years? As in every other area of our lives, we are responsible for how we use the resources of our society and our earth.

This is not to say that plastic surgery is always wrong. For many, especially those born with birth defects, injured in accidents, or scarred by surgery (e.g., mastectomy), plastic surgery can help restore social life and confidence. But as either pursuit of perfection in appearance or a denial of aging, repeated plastic surgery can signal, or even induce, serious character problems. Almost none of us is completely beautiful. No one can escape the inevitability of aging and death forever. How much better to spend one's time in maturity exercising and keeping one's body and mind as healthy and flexible as possible, than to spend it pursuing one more expensive wrinkle cream or surgery!

Part of wanting to look our best is wanting others to like us. When we want others to want to be with us, to anticipate our company and prefer it to that of others, we try to look our best. We dress up, wash our faces and hair, and use various deodorants, colognes, and perfumes; some females put on makeup and impossibly high heels. It is natural to want to look our best for those we love and for special occasions. But today technology has so expanded the options for "looking our best" as to make us question how these many possible "improvements" to our bodies impact ourselves.

Hundreds of years ago in the West, cosmetics were understood as artifices that only actors and actresses used. Like acting itself, cosmetics were regarded as morally problematic, if not outright sinful, because they were deceits. In acting, one pretended to be someone whom one really wasn't, and using cosmetics allowed one to also present a false self to the world. Wigs, kohl, and rouge were the principal types of cosmetic artifice condemned in the seventeenth, eighteenth, and early nineteenth centuries in the West. How could one trust a person who could and did appear as someone else in addition to their "real" self? The very fact that actors and actresses used these artifices made them scandalous for many others, until and unless such artifices caught the fancy of royal courts, at which time they no longer represented immoral artifice but fashionable luxury to be imitated by all.

Other types of body-altering equipment, such as peg legs or hooks as replacement hands were not regarded as deceitful, at one level because they could not even try to pass themselves off as natural, and more centrally because they partially restored natural functions of the body. Today we make this same distinction, exempting some additions to the body from moral censure (blood, artificial skin, bone marrow, dental implants/crowns and bridges, replacement organs and joints, rods and screws to strengthen bones, etc.), instead treating them as health measures under "medical care." This is also true of eyeglasses, contact lenses, hearing aids, cochlear implants, pacemakers, and other mechanical devices attached to the body that are understood to support life or central body functions such as hearing or sight.

Notice that many of the above devices are associated with the elderly, understood as necessary to replace aging biological equipment: eyeglasses, hearing aids, pacemakers, replacement joints, dental implants/bridges, and metal rods and screws. Yet with the elderly, too, we make a distinction between surgery meant to correct an aging heart valve and surgery to restore a receding hairline, between removal of cataracts and an eyelid lift.

Normal vs. Enhanced

When we speak of the possibility of genetic modifications to the body, we try to make this same distinction between restoring a person to what is the "normal" human condition and attempting to "enhance" an individual's condition beyond normal. Thus many of us approve the use of growth hormones to help children who otherwise would not grow to average adult size, but not to create basketball stars or movie idols. Many would similarly approve genetic intervention to prevent mental retardation but not to create geniuses.

Most of us approve these applications of traditional thinking about artifice in and on the human body, not because we have given great thought to it, but because we, like peoples of the past, have a need to both respect and know ourselves, and to be respected and known by others. We sense that too much artifice in the way we present ourselves to the world interferes not only with our ability to know and respect ourselves, but also with our ability to trust in the respect shown by others to us—is it real or only based on the artifice that we have used in presenting ourselves to others? Our body and its coverings and decorations are symbols of our identity. When we cover or replace our own body parts that symbolize us in some ways (such as the prominent nose we got from our grandfather) with anonymous parts, those parts of our body cease to represent us in some way. Not having our nose represent us may seem like a good thing if we always hated it and disliked our grandfather, and it may be no great problem in the larger scheme of things. But how many parts of myself can I replace without coming to feel that my body is anonymous, that it is no longer me, and that respect or love expressed to that body by others is not really addressed to me? This is to say that the moral danger may come not from a nose job, a boob job, a chin lift, or hair replacement surgery, but from our acceptance of the idea that our body is not us, that individual parts of it are not worthy of respect, and that changes to our body can make us more worthwhile.

The dangers of such thinking for humans become quickly apparent. If changes to our bodies can make us worthier, then failure to make those changes can make us less worthy, too—less worthy of respect, less worthy of care, less worthy of rights. If we can think ourselves less worthy for not making possible "improvements," how much easier would it be to think of others who have not "enhanced" themselves as unworthy?

Media—including magazines, ads, television, movies, and music videos—present images of perfect bodies, perfect features, perfect skin. The images there do not merely conform to preexisting notions of perfection but actually define for us perfect bodies, features, skin, teeth, hair, and so on. The feelings of inadequacy they spawn in us are deliberately created to persuade us to buy the enhancements offered. We know that the images are not real, and we recognize the commercial motivation that underlies them, but knowing this does not make us immune.

Dissatisfaction with our bodies can become a foundation for dissatisfaction with ourselves, which in turn can cause us to doubt the professions of love of those around us, and consequently not to return their love. Not only can we waste lots of resources chasing what is an elusive and often impossible dream, but we put off pursuit of more valuable goals and experiences in the meantime.

What about Modesty?

Is modesty outmoded? This is a tough one. Young women have grounds for resentment when they are told that if they don't cover themselves up, then they are responsible for any lewd approaches, even sexual assaults, that may befall them. They rightly point out that they can be the victim of lewd approaches or sexual assault regardless of what they wear, and that men should be able to control their arousal. Many reject the idea that male arousal is uncontrollable: "Of course they can control it, but so long as they can convince us that arousal is uncontrollable, they can do what they like, without ever learning self-control," remarked one of my students last year.[13]

On the other hand, clothing should be appropriate to the event and the group. While one can never please everyone with the way one dresses, we should try not to seriously offend others. In Muslim Indonesia, even at hotel swimming pools or the beach, one does not wear (except perhaps in Hindu Bali) a bikini unless one wants to be seen as thumbing one's nose at local belief and culture. One does not wear shoes of any kind into a mosque or Japanese home or temple. One respects the local people by following their customs unless there is some moral problem with the local custom (like bribing officials).[14]

Even when we are not in another culture, we need to anticipate the reception that particular body covering or decoration choices would evoke, and choose only the clothing that evokes the responses we desire. There is often a fine line to be walked between being honest in our clothing about who we are and being respectful of others whom we do not want to offend. Some years ago we were preparing to take our sons to my grandfather's funeral, and a heated discussion with my oldest son ensued. His father and brothers were in dark suits, but he came to the car dressed in jeans, jean jacket, and cowboy boots. When we objected and told him to put on a suit, he responded that he was not a suit wearer, and he would not "fake the relatives out" by wearing one. He considered this his "best" set of clothes; he insisted he had put on his newest jeans, his new boots, and a clean shave for Grandpa, and that he knew that "Grandpa would like it." I had my doubts that my grandfather, a retired banker, whom I had never seen without a suit and tie until he was bedridden, would "like" this outfit. But my son did make me think. If my grandfather had been there, he would have laughed and said it was not worth arguing over, to let the boy wear what he wanted. And it occurred to me that this was not just rebellion—if he had wanted, my son could have refused to shave, put on old clothes, or simply disappeared when it was time to go. Instead, he had dressed in what he, at least for the moment, considered his best. He was trying to find the line between respect for others and being his own person. As it would happen, when we got to the funeral, he felt right at home. Half of his many cousins were angry at being forced into suits, and the other half had angry parents embarrassed at the unkempt appearance of their children.

Case Study: Body Coverings and Decoration

"Oh, Jessica, how could you?" exclaimed her mother, Barbara, upon seeing her daughter walk in the back door with a startling blue, green, and red snake tattooed up her right arm and onto her shoulder blade.

"Mom, I have wanted one of these since I was thirteen, and you and Dad always said that when I turned eighteen I could decide for myself. Well, last week, as you know, I was eighteen, and now it is finished. I've been saving for it for six months," gushed Jessica with satisfaction, stroking the colorful snake.

That night as they prepared for bed, Barbara and her husband, Jessica's stepdad, Hugh, discussed the tattoo. Hugh admitted that while he wasn't fond of tattoos, this one was very striking and somewhat attractive. To which Barbara responded, "I only hope the place she got it is sanitary and the needles were clean. But Hugh, I am almost sure she will come to regret it. Some of my friends have spent small fortunes paying to erase tattoos off their daughters when they got a little older. This one is so large!"

"Maybe she won't want to erase it, Barb. After all, millions of kids have them today. It's not like she will be the only middle-aged woman with a tattoo later on. It is just an aesthetic concern, isn't it—that she look nice and not be limited by having to either cover it up or showcase it?"

"No, I have an initial health concern—HIV/AIDS can be spread through these needles—but she agreed to be tested in the next six months. She's not being stupid about that. And I do have the aesthetic concern—she is an attractive young woman, and this tattoo seems to me like voluntarily paying to have acne for the rest of your life. But it is more than that. This is clearly an identity issue for her, and that is what scares me the most. With whom is she identifying? I look around at the people I see with tattoos, especially the big ones like hers, and it scares me. They are the bodybuilders, bikers, druggies—I don't see doctors and nurses, lawyers and dentists, architects and engineers with these things crawling down their arms and legs or covering their backs. Is this her announcement of the direction she wants to take in her life? That's what scares me!" said Barbara with a sob.

"Sweetheart, I think you are overreacting. Remember when we were at dinner at Gert and Bill's (Hugh's boss in his engineering firm) a few months ago? Bill was telling us about his adventures at Columbia in the late '60s. He was part of the occupation of the president's office at Columbia! He was arrested twice in antiwar protests, wore his hair to his waist, and used both LSD and pot. But it was a phase. You heard him. By the time he finished school, the U.S. was pulling out of Vietnam, he had to cut his hair to get a job, LSD became illegal, and he decided he didn't need pot enough to risk another arrest and loss of job. He still tends to be antiwar, and active in a bunch of social justice projects—but he bathes regularly and has a respectable job and good income. Most of his friends from university are similarly conventional today. Kids go through identity phases; they try things out. Let's just hope that if and when Jess figures out she doesn't want this serpent, she has the funds to pay for removal herself!" said Hugh with a chuckle.

The next weekend, Jess and Barbara were both in the laundry room, Barb pressing Hugh's shirts and Jessica doing her wash. Barbara asked her daughter, "Jess, can you tell me what it is that attracts you to this tattoo? What do you mean it to say about you to others? I'm sure you have some idea of the message it sends, at least to other young people around you."

Barb's questions could be answered in a variety of ways. Below are a few. Which of these do you think are most commonly given? How complete are they? Why? Can you think of others that would resonate in popular culture today?

1. Mom, I don't care what other people think. I got this tattoo for me, because I like it. It doesn't have a message. Just like I painted my bedroom purple and black. Even though you hate it, it's just what I like.
2. It's how I want to see myself, Mom—as vivid, not fading into the wallpaper—and powerful. I have always felt weak, partly because I am so small. A butterfly could be vivid but is easily crushed. I think seeing this on my skin reminds me of the kind of person I want to be.
3. I am so tired of people telling me what to do and who to be—you and Hugh, Dad and his new wife, my teachers, Rev. Parker. Part of the message here is "Leave me alone! Let me decide who I want to be." I have to choose my own friends, my own life. And by the way, now that I am eighteen, I have decided not to enroll for spring semester. Randy and Celia and I are going to take a motorcycle trip across the country. It will be educational, too."

DISCUSSION QUESTIONS

1. Should people judge others on the basis of their body covering? Is it possible not to? Why?
2. What messages do you try to broadcast by your choice of body covering? Are these messages ever misunderstood? If so, why?
3. Can you name some examples of clothing that would be unethical because of how they were made?
4. What does modesty mean to you? What, if any, would be an example of body covering that would be objectionable on the grounds of immodesty? Is modesty relative to particular occasions, or is modest clothing the same in all situations? Why or why not?
5. What does modesty mean, if anything, for males?
6. Anna does a major makeover of her wardrobe, accessories, and hair color/style every year or so, and has for over fifteen years. Last year she was Goth; this year she looks like a field of bright tulips. She says it keeps her on her toes, keeps life from being boring, and makes her more interesting. Her friend Kristen thinks that in so doing Anna is trying out personalities and character but never sticks to one. Do you see anything problematic in this practice? Why or why not?

7. Do you think that sumptuary laws could be effective today in preventing people from spending to excess on decoration for body (or home)? Would such laws contribute to supporting people in becoming more ethical or undermine that process? Why?

8. What kinds of concerns should set (voluntary) limits on the amount of resources we expend on decoration? (Resources here involve not only money, but also time and effort.)

9. How and to what extent should environmental responsibility put limits on how we decorate our body and its surroundings?

FOR FURTHER READING

Arnold, Rebecca. *Fashion, Desire and Anxiety*. London: I. B. Taurus, 2001.

Carrel, Barbara Goldman. "Shattered Vessels That Contain Divine Sparks: Unveiling Hasidic Women's Dress Code." In Jennifer Heath, ed., *The Veil: Women Writers on Its History, Lore, and Politics*. Berkeley: University of California Press, 2008.

Geoffroy-Schneiter, Bérénice. *Vanishing Beauty: Indigenous Body Art and Decoration*. With Photographers Bertie Winkel and Dos Winkel. London: Prestel, 2006.

Hunt, Alan. *Governance of the Consuming Passions: A History of Sumptuary Laws*. London: Macmillan, 1996.

Killerby, Catherine Kovesi. *Sumptuary Law in Italy 1200–1500* (Oxford Historical Monographs). Oxford: Oxford University Press, 2002.

Kopp, Hollie. "Dress and Diversity: Muslim Women and Islamic Dress in an Immigrant/Minority Context." *The Muslim World* 92, nos. 1–2 (March 2002): 59–78.

Lacroix, Paul. *Manners, Custom and Dress During the Middle Ages*. Oxford: Benediction Press, 2008.

Mirza, Zaynab. *The Mehndi Kit: Learn the Traditional Art of Henna Body Decoration*. New York: McGraw-Hill, 1998.

Mutahhari, Murtaza. *The Islamic Modest Dress*. Qum, Iran: Dar us Seqafe, n.d.

Ribeiro, Aileen. *Dress and Morality*. New York: Palgrave Macmillan, 2011.

Roach-Higgins, Mary Ellen, and Joanne B. Eicher. "Dress and Identity." *Clothing and Textiles Research Journal* 10, no. 4 (June 1992): 1–8.

WEBSITES ON ETHICAL BUYING

http://worldofgood.ebay.com/Eco-Organic-Clothes-Shoes-Men-Women-Children/43/list?clk_rvr_id=334061110641&keyword=fair+trade+clothing&geo_id=641

http://www.greenpages.org/

http://www.greenamerica.org/livinggreen/nosweatshops.cfm

http://www.handmadeexpressions.net/pages/fair-trade-fashion

http://www.nytimes.com/2006/09/25/technology/25ecom.html?pagewanted=all

http://shopwithmeaning.org/fair-trade-clothes-and-clothing-companies/

NOTES

1. Saba Mahmood, *The Politics of Piety: The Islamic Revival and the Feminist Subject* (Princeton: Princeton University Press, 2004).

2. Lis Harris, *Holy Days: The World of a Hasidic Family* (New York: Simon & Schuster, 1985), 9–30.

3. Bill Coleman, *The Gift to Be Simple: Life in the Amish Country* (San Francisco: Chronicle Co., 2001).

4. Alan Hunt, *Governance of the Consuming Passions: A History of Sumptuary Laws* (London: Macmillan, 1996); Frances Elizabeth Baldwin, "Sumptuary Legislation and Personal Governance in England," Johns Hopkins University dissertation, 1923, available at http://www.archive.org/stream/sumptuarylegisla00bald#page/n7/mode/2up.

5. Christine Ruane, *The Empire's New Clothes: A History of the Russian Fashion Industry, 1700–1917* (New Haven: Yale University Press, 2009), 49.

6. Ibid., 50–53.

7. Susan Wadley, "Hindu Women's Family and Household Rites in a North Indian Village," in *Unspoken Worlds: Women's Religious Lives* (3rd ed.), ed. Nancy A. Falk and Rita M. Gross (Belmont, CA: Wadsworth, 2001), 104.

8. There is a large body of evidence that testosterone in both males and females supports libido and sex drive; persons with lower than normal levels of testosterone for their sex suffer from low sex drive and inhibited sexual arousal, and increasing testosterone levels in these men and women increases sex drive and sexual arousal. See, for example, S. Davis et al., "Testosterone for Low Libido in Postmenopausal Women Not Taking Estrogen," *New England Journal of Medicine* 359 (2008): 2005–17; J. Frank, P. Mistretta, and J. Will, "Diagnosis and Treatment of Female Sexual Dysfunction," *American Family Physician* 77 (2008): 635–50; M. Nusbaum, P. Lenahan, and R. Sadowsky, "Sexual Health in Aging Men and Women: Addressing the Physiologic and Psychological Sexual Changes That Occur with Age," *Geriatrics* 60 (2005): 18–28.

9. Here I must stress the importance of the word *voluntary*, which here refers to individual women choosing to adopt the headscarf in areas where the headscarf has not been mandatory. Though this has been a widespread phenomenon, it would be a mistake to conclude that all women who wear the headscarf have donned it voluntarily. Generally, where adoption of the headscarf is more common among educated middle-class women than among poor women, the likelihood of voluntary adoption is higher.

10. Ruane, Ibid., 52.

11. Because so many Germans—and certainly the rest of the world—did not fully know or understand all the policies that the swastika symbol represented until after the war, people today may have a fuller understanding than people of the 1930s and early 1940s.

12. Victoria Clayton, "Way to Go, Grad! Here's a Check For a New Nose! Is Cosmetic Surgery an Appropriate Commencement Gift for Teens?" MSNBC May 5, 2011. http://www.msnbc.msn.com/id/17932515/ns/health-kids_and_parenting/.

13. On this topic see young writer Wendy Shalit's controversial book, *A Return to Modesty: Discovering the Lost Virtue* (New York: Free, 1999).

14. See, on this point of appropriate behavior, Bernard T. Adenay, *Strange Virtues: Ethics in a Multicultural World* (Downers Grove, IL: InterVarsity, 1996).

CHAPTER 5

RELIGIONS ON SEXUALITY AND MARRIAGE

In the West, for perhaps the first time in many centuries, the traditional association of morality and ethics with religion has been broken for large parts of society, many of whom associate religion with moralism and hypocrisy instead. This is especially true around issues of sexuality, where scandals have ripped apart Catholic and Protestant churches, as well as various eastern New Age religions and Orthodox Jewish neighborhoods. It is likely that there were proportionally as many sexual offenses committed by religious leaders in the past, but their existence was more often silent and unacknowledged. A major part of many of the contemporary scandals involving religion involves revelations of past silence and suppression, both within religions and by secular officials who did not enforce civil law within religious communities.

At the same time, within postmodern thought many of the standards traditionally used to assess sexual morality—and much of the language of sexual ethics—has come under question and been found wanting, especially among the young. Because both the context in which sexual activity takes place

and the concepts used to express it have gone through so many comprehensive changes in the last few centuries, there is a tall task for social analysis in understanding sexuality in our present context.

Framing the Issues

When most people in North America think of sex and religion together, they think of Christian prohibitions around sexual activity: no fornication, adultery, sodomy, bestiality, incest, or masturbation. In fact, virtually all of these prohibitions can be found in the history of most religions, given that until very recently human societies and their religions understood reproduction to be the primary purpose of sex, and stable marriages to be the structures within which those reproduced should be reared. This pronatalism, or priority for reproduction, was necessary in all societies until modernity, due to the huge tolls that infant, child, and maternal mortality, disease, wars, famines, and other natural disasters could take on populations. Survival was a struggle, and constant replenishment of the community was essential. Sexual acts not open to reproduction (masturbation, homosexuality, oral/anal sex, and bestiality) and acts understood to undermine familial structures (incest, adultery) were therefore prohibited. Fornication was banned not only because it produced offspring outside a family structure, but also because it violated the patriarchal right of fathers to choose the fathers of their daughters' children.

Challenges to this procreative understanding of sex took two major historical forms. One was the early-modern methods of disease control (not so much medicine as sanitation and sterilization), which sharply decreased death rates from epidemics. Infant, child, and maternal mortality rates plummeted, raising population growth rates to levels that neither families nor polities could effectively deal with. This demographic challenge (called the *demographic transition*)[1] set the stage for the second challenge: the late-modern invention of effective contraception methods

that allowed the separation of sexual activity and reproduction. Combined, these two began a general rethinking of sexuality, its purpose and meaning, apart from reproduction. This rethinking, especially pronounced in the West, also gradually led to, first, the decriminalization of homosexuality, and more recently, to a still-growing acceptance of the movement of gays, lesbians, bisexuals, transsexuals, and queers (GLBTQ) for equal rights in society. However, this movement is still hotly contested even where GLBTQ movements have secured many of the same rights as heterosexuals.

The Modern Contraceptive Movement

Some methods of contraception had been known since ancient times, but these had nowhere near the effectiveness of the methods that would appear in late modernity. The contraceptive movement in the West began

Fig. 5.1. Gay pride parades now take place around the world, such as this parade in Milan in 2008.

in France in the eighteenth century among aristocrats concerned that decreases in infant and child mortality created problems for passing on the family inheritance: there were now too many surviving children to be provided for. Contraception spread from the aristocracy to the French middle class, and from there to the middle and upper classes in Britain and the rest of Europe. It was not until the twentieth century that knowledge of contraceptive methods was extended from the European working classes to the American working class. The most common methods until the 1960s were *coitus interruptus* (withdrawal), and barrier methods: condoms made of animal gut or (later) rubber, and vaginal sponges made of various materials. While not totally effective, faithful use of these methods could usually cut by half or more the number of children a family might otherwise have. But the oral contraceptive, new barrier methods, injectables, and implantables have transformed contraception with effectiveness rates that are as high as 95 to 99 percent.

The Legacy of Slavery

There was yet another part of the history of Christianity on sex—and of most other religions as well—that became a very negative legacy. Though Christianity arose out of Judaism, it grew and developed within the Roman Empire and its culture. In Roman culture, free male citizens—heads of households—ruled over wives, children, slaves, and servants, and their authority included sexual use/disposition of those under them. Sexual use of slaves, both male and female, included not only the master's personal use, but the gift or loan of the slave to another for sexual use. Sexual use of other males by free males was accepted so long as the free male was the active penetrator. In the prevailing

understandings of the erotic in the Roman Empire—aspects of which still linger in our culture—the passive role in sex, whether for female or male, was stigmatized, but not the active role of penetrator. As William Stacey Johnson writes:

> The upshot was the creation in Rome of a glaring double standard among men: for a freeborn Roman male to allow himself to be sexually penetrated by another male was considered shameful, even criminal; however, for him to gratify his own sexual urges with a male slave or other social inferior was considered appropriate. Indeed, it was even expected as part of the definition of Roman manhood. . . . Hence, it was not unusual for a Roman soldier to demonstrate his dominance by sexually humiliating a defeated enemy. Similarly, for a Roman citizen to pleasure himself sexually by using a noncitizen slave was considered to be normal and acceptable.[2]

This understanding influenced not only later negative attitudes toward women and gay men in the West, but it also impacted views on the nature of sexuality itself, suggesting that sex was not sex without penetration, and that sex was something dominants did to inferiors that demeaned them, that the pleasure in sex is based in the experience of domination.

American slavery. The Romans were not, of course, the only people who used slaves as sex toys or sex as a weapon symbolizing defeat of enemies. The history of African slavery in the Americas not only greatly contributed to our current understandings of sex as domination, but also inscribed in our cultural memory racist images of African women as seductive and promiscuous. Such images originated to obscure the responsibility of white slavemasters for coercive relationships with their female slaves. The image of African males as highly sexed and dangerous animals reflected masters' fear of repressed anger and revenge in male slaves.

Such understandings of sexual activity and pleasure, totally devoid of mutuality and relationality but instead based in domination, became over time culturally linked to Christian attitudes valuing sexuality for its procreative potential despite its potential for dangerous sexual pleasure. Together these attitudes produced a number of easily recognized views: that sex involves domination by one and submission from the other; that lesbians do not have sex because there is no penetration; that people of African descent are more sexual than others; that missionary-position sex (woman under) is the optimal position; and that males who rape other men are not homosexuals (only their victims are). Contemporary society is still wrestling with the remnants of both procreationism and the eroticization of coercion and violence.

Development and Effects of Patriarchy

Before turning to what useful insights religions might offer into contemporary sexuality and marriage, it is necessary to discuss some effects that patriarchy has had upon religion. In many indigenous nature religions where the fertility of nature is often venerated as female, the union of male and female in sex was often used as a symbol of creation, power, complementarity, cooperation, and balance. But frequently, beginning with the agricultural revolution of 8000 BCE and continuing today, the ancient and continuing human drive to control survival by controlling the powers of nature (planting seeds; domesticating pigs and cattle; building dams

to prevent floods, irrigation systems to avoid droughts, grain storage to avoid famines, and cities for protection against weather and human attacks)—these ever-growing methods of controlling the raw forces of nature were accompanied by attempts to control the reproductive power of women by subordinating them to men. The likeness that men saw between women and nature—reproduction—led to associating growing control over nature's power with justification for also controlling women's fertility. Women became understood as things, resources, like animal and plant fertility, to be manipulated. Many of the sacred texts of the world religions—all of which date back a millennium or more—in places compare women to fields to be plowed by men, or root stock to which men graft their own offspring, rivers to be channeled, or energy to be tamed by men.

Of course, women have also always been persons, linked to men as mothers, sisters, and wives, so that they have never been *only* resources to be manipulated. But as a result of these two attitudes toward women, women have occupied an ambiguous space in societies. Sometimes they are linked to men as controllers of nature, and at other times they are seen as part of nature to be controlled. In this latter role, they are not accorded intellect or judgment.

This history of patriarchy in religion has colored how religions have understood sexuality, because in patriarchal religions, women have not played leadership roles. They have had little if any voice in creating, selecting, or interpreting the canon of sacred texts, and little role in creating the theology or doctrine or officiating in rituals of the religions. The religious product produced in the absence of women then represents the perspective of men, and seldom that of women, even when the men involved in these decisions were well disposed toward women in general, or even devoted to the particular women in their lives.

Seeing women as Other. Because the foundations of most religious teaching on sexuality proceeded from a male perspective, there has been a tendency in that teaching to understand women as the Other, in terms of their differences from men, of which the principal one is the capacity to reproduce human life. Women were often defined in terms of their reproductive capacity rather than their cognition, a faculty shared with men. Reproductive capacity was so central to the ability of a society to flourish and survive that it seemed unavoidable, even imperative, to male leadership elites that women's reproduction be regulated.

When it came to sexual desire, men closely associated their own desire with the allure of women. Thus control of women—their dress, behavior, and movement—became seen as part and parcel of the social need to control reproduction and to control male desire, both of which if left unregulated could plunge a society into chaos and extinction.

Modern Changes in the Structure and Meaning of Marriage

Shifting from ancient and prehistoric to more recent history, over the last few centuries in the West marriage patterns have changed as the economy has broken up extended families and made nuclear families more mobile (see chapter 7). In 1800, almost 90 percent of American families were farm families, many of them multigenerational extended families. Following two centuries of rapid industrialization and consequent urbanization, which drastically changed prevailing gender roles, in 2000, more than 95 percent of American families lived in cities and towns, not on farms, and the majority were small nuclear or even single-parent families. Our workforce is mobile; corporations move workers from one city, even one country, to another. Industrial plants close in one state; and if workers, not to mention managers, want to keep their jobs, they move to the new plant in another state.

No longer do individuals live lives surrounded by extended family and lifelong friends and neighbors in the same location, where every human interaction is with someone who knows them and reflects back to them who they are, their history and relations. The rural mirrors that reflected back to humans who they were have been lost and replaced by urban strangers who surround us for much of our lives. This change has important implications for identity formation.

Today, due to both mobility and urbanization, our human interactions are increasingly anonymous and impersonal. Very often we fail to make intimate friends even of the persons we work with all day long, for when the office or factory closes, we all head for various neighborhoods of the city that may be hours from each other. The commute to work is so long that we hesitate to add to it into our leisure time. This change in the nature of our surrounding relationships over the past two centuries has put extreme pressure on marriage and other long-term sexual relationships. Increasingly, the sexual or marriage relationship bears the burden of providing all or almost all the interpersonal and intimacy needs of a person that in the past were satisfied by a variety of long-term relationships. This is a next-to-impossible load, for no individual can provide all these needs. Thus we see a high failure rate in contemporary marriage and marital-type relationships.

Shifts toward companionate marriage. But marital relationships do not always fail; many contemporary marriages do satisfy enough of the intimacy needs of husbands and wives to survive, even sometimes to flourish. They can do that because they have changed along with the nature of human work, and often because they have also developed a variety of supports, as we will see in the next chapter. The first and most basic change in marriage in response to modernity's impact on families and work is that it became more voluntary. Traditional arranged marriage has virtually disappeared in fully modern societies.

Historians have often noted that perhaps the first shift in the West from a model of arranged marriage to one of companionate marriage came with the merchant class in the early modern period of the seventeenth and eighteenth centuries, in which husbands and wives shared much of the same work in small family shops. While in agriculture the roles of husbands and wives were separate and complementary, among shopkeepers husbands and wives worked side by side, with common interests and skills. As women in the nineteenth century gradually moved into the same kinds of work as men in factories and then offices, and as universal coeducation of males and females became the rule in the West, the perceived differences between males and females further diminished, and the possibility of husbands and wives being companions and friends as well as sexual partners/ parents became more evident. Compatibility became more important when husbands and wives lived longer lifespans that extended the length of marriage, and became especially important when wives and husbands were to spend their working hours in shared work and/or close proximity.

Moves toward interpersonal intimacy. With all these changes, the nature of love in marriage changed, too. When marriage was largely an arranged affair, with spouses chosen for reasons involving land, money, power,

Fig. 5.2. A young Jewish couple is about to sign their ketubah, or marriage contract.

friendships within the parental generation, or simply convenience, love within marriage was understood to be something that one pledged in the ceremony and then committed oneself to developing within the resulting relationship. Marital love then consisted largely of respect, loyalty, and, especially for women, fidelity, as well as a limited partnership for the rearing of children. Marriage was an exchange, and like other forms of exchange, marriage involved a contract. While that contract was implicit in Christianity, some religious cultures, including both Judaism and Islam, have had formal written marriage contracts, often still used today.

Distrust of romantic love. Romantic alliances were almost universally distrusted within systems of arranged marriage, partly because they were thought to be shallow and short-lived, little more than infatuation, but largely because they could result in defiance of parental wishes and obstruction of more advantageous, appropriate alliances. In societies of arranged marriages and complementary rather than similar roles and responsibilities for husbands and wives, men were expected to find their friendships and associations among other men, and women with other women, because these were the people with whom one had common interests. Persons of the same sex (and class) were one's natural intimates, the people who shared the shape of one's life, training, and expectations. The spouse was a kind of foreign territory with whom one had an ongoing treaty under which the material needs of each could be met. Emotional intimacy was seldom thought possible, much less desirable, in such a marriage.

Acceptance of romantic love marriages. Of course, there have always been some love matches, no matter how out of fashion they were. As men and women began to share more of the same education and work, these changes began to raise the legal and social status of women to greater equality with men. It was in such a context that love matches gradually became the norm. As the twentieth century progressed, the marital relationship gradually came to take on more and more of the tasks that had in the past been shared with extended family, neighbors, and friends. For example, spouses increasingly shared complete responsibility for care of children, for often there were no grandparents, aunts, uncles, or cousins near enough to share their care. Grandparents became increasingly independent of their children's families with the institution of national retirement programs in the mid-twentieth century. Occasional childcare from grandparents, rather than live-in help from grandparents, became the rule. But intimacy was the chief function that devolved to the spousal relationship in the absence of other, usually same-sex, avenues in extended family and neighborhood. Gradually, especially in the middle class, it became assumed that social and cultural activities were to be attended and performed by husband and wife together. The husband who went out with the "guys" or the wife who went out with the "girls" too often was suspect—of selfishness, of disloyalty, even of infidelity. Love meant that the spouses were to be enough for one another. When a spouse felt he or she was not having all their personal intimacy needs met, the marriage was dissolved. Serial marriage became increasingly common; seldom did the spouses understand that it might not be that either of them had failed, but that the model of marriage they were living was doomed to failure because their expectations of spouses were too high.

Working wives and mothers. The most recent of the changes in marriage is the shift of married women into waged work. Poor women, widows, and many spinsters had always worked, but in many nations women worked only until they married or had children. This has been the pattern in Japan, for example, into the twenty-first century. But since the midtwentieth century, married women in western developed nations began working in growing numbers, in part because the median wage of men steadily shrank beginning in the 1960s, and in part because the aspirations of working- and lower-middle-class families began to include higher education for children. Two-career families added tremendous stress to many households. Childcare, eldercare, and cooking family dinner became difficult, and whole new industries rose to cater to those who could afford them. But the stresses continued: Who would stay home with sick children, or to let the repairmen in, or to handle children's doctor and dentist visits? How should housework and childcare be divided when both parents work? A third reason was, of course, that more and more women who received specialized training or higher education wanted to use that education in careers.

Western religions more or less ignored these momentous changes in human life happening in modernity, except to condemn their effects, repeating the traditional rules condemning fornication, adultery, and homosexuality, and for decades, divorce and working mothers. Religions insisted that contextual change did not matter; church teachings were God's teachings, and thus eternal. Religious focus on revelation as divine and eternal has often blinded religions to the varied interpretations of their tradition that have already prevailed in the past, as well as to new interpretations available in the present.

Finding the Useful Parts

As intimated above, much of traditional religious teaching and regulation concerning sexuality is both based in long-gone social arrangements and too tainted with a patriarchy that our society has been shedding for almost two centuries to be very useful in pointing us to helpful insights about sex within religions today. We will find very little in past religious sexual thought that supports the postmodern commitment to gender egalitarianism or is compatible with contemporary work organization. Religious revelation, except in those few religions with modern origins (e.g., Baha'i), not only understands sexuality in patriarchal ways, but also contains understandings of male and female that reflect patriarchal contexts. For these reasons, many feminist scholars today endorse Feuerbach's "hermeneutics of suspicion" in approaching religious texts. Some have suggested that the general exclusion of women from religious and social leadership for millennia has led to a necrophilic culture that prefers war to peace, death to birth, and anger to joy, which may be a direct result of the attempt to exclude "the mother" (women). It is interesting that while late-modern people have had few problems jettisoning earlier religious understandings of medicine, healing, and health, or of appropriate punishments for wrongdoing, they have clung to earlier religious understandings of sex and gender despite obvious problems within them. Nonetheless, despite all these reservations, the bulk of which is much greater in sexuality than in most other areas covered by sacred texts, there are some gems to be found within religious traditions.

Religious Treatment Concerning Sexuality and Marriage

Religion as a part of culture was subject to some of the same constraints regarding sexuality: committed to the continuation of the society, religion had to support sufficient fertility to maintain, if not grow, community size, and had to legitimate marital rules that would protect fertility and create a stable society. Within these very general constraints, religions could and did develop very different ways of dealing with human sexuality. Some religions have lifted up celibacy as the ideal state, but one that will be chosen by few, as we see in Buddhist and Christian monasticism. Others have enjoined fertility on all members, as has clearly been the case in Judaism and Hinduism. While Islam has not required marriage and fertility, it has a strong pronatalist history.

Yet even in religions that understand that marriage and reproduction are the duty of all, there has been strong suspicion of sexual desire and arousal as not easily controlled and capable of creating instability, conflict, and even violence in families and society. As we saw above, due to patriarchal structures that ensured that religious texts and practices were created and interpreted by men, the suspicion of sexual desire and arousal tended to take the form of suspicion of women. Women, it was felt, were the cause of men's desire and arousal, and were therefore responsible. Controlling sexual desire generally took the form of controlling women—what they wore, where they were allowed, and what company they were allowed to keep.

All the world religions have forbidden sex outside marriage, though there are differences in the seriousness with which offenses against these rules have been treated. There are also exceptions, in that ancient sacred texts sometimes took for granted rape in war, or sex with slaves, with no accounting for the marital status of either males or females.

But before moving on to thumbnail sketches of teachings of the world religions on sexuality, we will look at how religious concern about sex outside marriage influenced, and still continues to influence, some religious approaches to contraception. The early contraceptive movement in the West was condemned by religions in general through the midtwentieth century. All Christian denominations condemned contraception. Judaism allowed it only in marriage when there was sufficient reason to resort to contraception (a woman's health, for example). Only in 1933 did the Anglican Church begin a non-Catholic Christian opening to the use of contraception under special circumstances (mother's health, extreme poverty, etc.), which over the next decades broadened to general acceptance within marriage across Christian denominations and a variety of other religions.

In the second half of the twentieth century, modern contraception spread to developing nations, and religious opposition arose there also. A major reason for the reservations of all religious officials was that if pregnancy were no longer a risk of having sex, the religious prohibitions on sex outside marriage might be ignored. The Catholic Church has continued to resist the trend to allow any use of artificial contraception, affirming its traditional ban on artificial contraception in the 1968 encyclical *Humanae vitae*, which argued that artificial contraception was against natural law, and would encourage promiscuity inside and outside marriage.[3]

This fear of promiscuity seemed on target. Beginning about the time that the first contraceptive pill was released (1960), surveys began to record higher and higher numbers of youth reporting premarital sexual experience in both Europe and the United States (currently in the United States, over half of youth have had sex by age sixteen). But in hindsight it has become clear that contraceptive availability was not by any means the only reason for this increase. By 1960 a number of other demographic changes had been also going on in the West. For one, age at marriage had been increasing for some time, following the rising level of education in the general public. Additionally, in the 1950s and 1960s, huge numbers of persons whose parents had no high school education, or who had not even completed elementary school, graduated from high school and married significantly later than their parents. All around the world today, raising education levels, especially for girls, raises the age of marriage. By the late 1960s, larger percentages of people were going on to college and university after high school. In the United States, some of these university students were following older brothers or fathers who had taken advantage of the GI bill after the Second World War and the Korean War to become the first members of their extended families to attend university. University attendance not only further postponed marriage for many, but it also allowed single young people to live apart from families, relatively independently. At the same time, partly due to enhanced higher education opportunities for women, career opportunities for women were expanding into many fields that had previously only been occupied by men. The combination of these shifts meant that more and more youth were remaining unmarried for longer and longer periods, associating with the other sex in both academic and work environments while living independently, unsupervised by the parental generation.

As more and more education became necessary to obtain choice careers—in some professions, education did not end until age twenty-five or even thirty—the average age of marriage continued to rise until for the middle class, at least, it was ten or more years later than it had been in 1900. Chastity—waiting until marriage for sex—became more and more difficult as the age of marriage became later and later, and, with the availability of effective contraception, chastity seemed to many more and more unnecessary.

There were other factors as well in the rise of nonmarital sex. The steady rise in divorce throughout the twentieth century meant that there were always adults who had become accustomed to marital sex but were now without partners. Better health among the elderly meant that many widows and widowers were, like divorced persons, still interested in sexual intimacy but bereft of sexual partners. Dating and courtship in all age groups came to include more sexual activity than in the past. Increasingly, when persons looked for marital partners (for reasons we will shortly examine) they demanded a higher level of intimacy than in the past before committing, and sexual intimacy was regarded as a major constituent of the intimacy they sought.

"Fornication" flourished, but it took on a somewhat different character than in the past, becoming more open, less covert, and many times more likely to take place in ongoing relationships. Fornication today is complex. Before the midtwentieth century, the majority of nonmarital sex involved many, often most, unmarried men and a very small pool of females, most of them professional sex workers. Fornication today is much more relational, frequently taking the form of cohabitation, extended engagements, or other longstanding relationships. While most religious people see increases in nonmarital sex as negative, it is nevertheless positive that most of this nonmarital sex is within relationships, rather than commercial sex with prostitutes.

At the same time, contrary to the assumptions of many, there is some evidence that living together before marriage does not confer any advantages in avoiding divorce. Recent evidence suggests that the more practiced persons become at exiting sexual relationships, the more likely they are to exit new ones when problems develop. Thus, using cohabitation as a way of checking out a series of potential marriage partners may undermine the strength of commitment in an eventual marriage. This form of cohabitation is different from already-engaged couples cohabiting. The marital stability disadvantage comes from practice in exiting sexual relationships, not from cohabitation itself. The results appear to depend upon the level of commitment with which the couple entered cohabitation.

Now a brief survey of particular treatments of sexuality in world religions.

Buddhism

For Buddha, the issue of sex was simple. All desire is problematic in that it binds us to materiality, to the world of wanting and suffering. The ultimate goal for all humans in Buddhism is to release oneself from all forms of desire, even the desire for conscious individuality. Shedding sexual activity and overcoming sexual desire are relatively early stages in this process toward the full enlightenment of *nirvana*. This central teaching endures to this day. Buddhist laypeople marry and have children, hoping to earn enough merit in this life through good works, including the support of monks and nuns, to rise to a higher level in a future reincarnation, during which, usually as a monk or nun, they can aspire to *nirvana*. It is the celibate monks and nuns who have chosen what we might call the "fast track to *nirvana*," directly imitating the path of the Buddha.

For this reason, in Buddhist communities the customs around sex and marriage tend to be understood more as custom than religion. Buddhist religion has focused more on the celibates. As we saw in the Five Precepts, the initiation vows for lay Buddhists, only one refers to sexuality, and it merely pledges one to refrain from sexual misconduct. It was largely local custom that defined what constituted sexual misconduct. Though adultery and sex outside marriage were generally included under sexual misconduct, the norms did change from place to place. For example, though Buddhist scriptures are critical of polygamy in the few places it is mentioned and most Buddhist nations practice monogamy, both polygyny (multiple wives to a single husband) and polyandry (multiple husbands to a single wife) have long been practiced in Buddhist Tibet. Tibet is one of the very few places in the world to practice polyandry, of which the most common Tibetan form is fraternal polyandry. Marriage, while accepted in Buddhism, does not have any special status, and Buddhism did not develop particular marriage rituals. Divorce is allowed as sometimes necessary for individuals in their path toward enlightenment, and there is generally no religious or moral stigma attached to divorce.

Buddhism does not have much religious treatment of homosexuality. One reason is that all persons are expected to sooner or later renounce sexual activity and desire altogether. Additionally, since the religious ideal is to be celibate, there is no religious basis for banning non-procreative sex. Buddhist treatment of homosexuality, like that of other traditions, varies widely from place to place, but there is some evidence of acceptance of male homoerotic and even homosexual relationships within some Buddhist monasteries in the past. Significant numbers of Japanese Buddhist texts attest to acceptance of sexual relationships between an older and a younger male monk in Buddhist monasteries during a period of at least five to six centuries—a well-known and publicly accepted practice that scandalized early Christian missionaries to Japan.

Christianity

Christian treatment of sex has some similarities with Buddhism due to the presence of celibate clergy, though Christian theology and law were considerably more interested in regulating lay life, especially sexuality, than was the case in Buddhism. In the first few centuries of Christianity, there was a celibate minority that began as desert hermits and later developed formal monastic structures. Between the second and the sixth centuries, women were excluded from ministry, and the new supervisory position of bishop was reserved for upper-class married men. Over the following centuries, bishops became celibate and then waged and won a centuries-long battle with married priests over bishops' attempts to impose celibacy on secular priests (those who served lay communities, as opposed to religious priests who lived in monastic communities).

From the end of the first millennium until the Reformation, there were two classes of Christians, celibate priests and religious on the one hand, and laypeople who married on the other. Religious, and to a somewhat lesser degree secular priests, were considered to be full-time Christians who strove for sainthood in lives devoted to prayer and meditation. Laypeople had many other obligations—to make a living and fulfill their role in the family and community—around which they had to fit religious practice. Laypeople were not regarded as nearly so serious about gaining salvation. Thus sex was associated with a commitment to worldly endeavors, and celibacy with complete devotion to God and salvation.

Church law ordered couples to abstain from sex during menstruation, on various holy days, and before receiving communion—laws that celibate clergy enforced in the confessional. Many clergy advocated "Josephite" marriages, in which there was an agreement not to have sex at all. The only acceptable reasons to have sex were for reproduction and to prevent one's spouse from serious sin (adultery). Theologians were divided about the sinfulness of marital sex. Augustine considered even marital sex to involve minor sin, because it was so difficult, he said, to avoid pleasure in sex. But Thomas Aquinas considered that sexual pleasure as a result of sex for the purpose of either reproduction or saving the spouse from sin was not sinful. Nevertheless, there existed for most of the history of Christianity strong suspicion of sexual pleasure as sinful in itself, and as a gateway to sin because sexual pleasure was understood as undermining the ability of human reason to discern good from evil.

Divorce was prohibited until relatively recently in Christianity, based on statements of Jesus in the gospels of the New Testament. Today the Catholic Church still does not recognize divorce, though Protestant churches do.

In the sixteenth-century Reformation, Protestantism rejected mandatory clerical celibacy as unnatural but retained most of the previous reservations about sexual activity. Acceptance of sexual pleasure, even in marriage, grew slowly in the Protestantism that emerged from the Reformation, and it was not until the midtwentieth century that Protestant Christian churches accepted marital sex that was even temporarily deliberately nonprocreative. Though the Catholic Church has not officially accepted the use of contraception, the vast majority of Catholics globally utilize artificial contraception.

Christianity has generally not tolerated homosexuality. The Hebrew Scriptures (Christian Old Testament) are explicitly opposed to homosexual acts. Catholicism, which teaches that the unitive and the procreative aspects of sexuality cannot licitly be separated, additionally condemns homosexual acts because of its inability to be reproductive. Here again, Christian attitudes toward homosexuality have been changing, not only due to changes in the scientific understanding of homosexuality, but also as a result of the global acceptance of contraceptive heterosexual sex and western acceptance of romantic love as the basis for sexual relationships. The Anglican Church is in schism over the issue of ordaining and consecrating as bishops practicing homosexuals, and other Protestant denominations are internally divided over issues of gay marriage and ordaining gays and lesbians.

Judaism

Judaism has a strongly pronatalist tradition. As a small people that except for a very brief ancient period has not proselytized, Judaism has depended on reproduction to maintain its numbers. Beginning with the Babylonian conquest and continuing through Greek conquest and the final destruction of the Temple and dispersion of the Jews by the Romans in 70 CE, through periodic persecutions in Christian Europe culminating in the Holocaust, Jews have felt extreme pressure to reproduce in order to maintain their existence. All Jews have been expected to marry. But rabbis of the early Common Era decided that it was not fair to place the duty to reproduce on women, because reproduction entails significant risks for women. So the duty was placed on men. Women were granted the right to refuse sex to husbands, presumably for health reasons, though husbands who were refused for long periods of time had the right to divorce wives.

While placing the duty on men rather than women showed a sensitivity to the situation of women, the rabbis nevertheless insisted that the male duty to reproduce was so strong that a man in a childless marriage for ten years had a duty to divorce his wife and marry another who could give him children. Many discussions ensued over the centuries on how much reproduction satisfied this duty, and the eventual answer was that two children (replacement of the couple) was the minimum fulfillment of the duty.

Judaism (and Hinduism and Islam, as we will see) has understood sexual pleasure as a legitimate end for both husbands and wives. In Judaism, the rabbis of the Talmud specifically charged husbands with the duty to satisfy their wives' sexual needs. The rabbis not only understood women to have two kinds of legitimate sexual needs—sexual desire and a desire for children—but even more unusually, the rabbis also recognized women's right to have sexual desire satisfied in marriage.[4] At the same time, however, as in other world religions, Judaism has understood sexual desire and pleasure as powerful and problematic, as something that needed to be kept under careful control.

Islam

As mentioned above, Islam has been pronatalist for most of its history, though this is quickly changing today. Fertility rates have been dropping rapidly in virtually all Muslim nations, and clerical opposition to contraception has largely subsided. Muslims are still generally expected to marry and reproduce, and the marriage of the Prophet Mohammed to his first wife, Khadija, is considered the model for Muslim marriages. She is revered as the first hearer of the message given to Mohammed and was his principal support in accepting the revelation as real and divine. While he was married to Khadija, she was Mohammed's only wife, and all his children were born of her.

At the same time, the Qur'an allowed polygyny—up to four wives—and conservative Muslims have attempted to use the example of the Prophet's later polygyny (after the death of Khadija) to make a case for polygyny as central to Islam. While most Muslim-majority nations today allow polygyny, many have put a number of legal restrictions on it. Common restrictions are that a man may have no more than the Qur'anic four wives, that he must have the consent of his first wife to take a second or successive wife, that he must register all marriages, and that he must observe the Qur'anic obligation to treat all wives and their offspring equally. Scholars today increasingly interpret the Qur'anic permission for polygyny as a grudging one, even one possibly contingent on the existing circumstances referred to in the Qur'an, which were that warfare had created many widows and orphans who needed to

be cared for. In support of such an interpretation, they note that the Qur'an both says that one must treat one's wives equally, but also says that it is impossible to treat wives equally.

Islam understands adultery, homosexuality, and sex outside marriage as sinful, although, as in most religions, adultery and sex outside of marriage have always been seen as more serious offenses for women than men. Much of Islam resisted accommodation to modernity as part of its opposition to colonialism, and this has been especially true of modern gender equality. While seventh-century Islam granted to women a number of rights and privileges—especially economic ones—not previously available to them in Arabia, or to western women until the midnineteenth century, it did not by any means enjoin gender equality, particularly in sexuality. A husband could divorce his wife merely by speaking the words aloud, while a wife seeking divorce needed to state her case before Mohammed, or later before the religious courts. Some of the Muslim divorce provisions that were commonsensical at the time have become discriminatory, for example, child custody laws following divorce. In seventh-century Arabia, it made sense for custody of children to go to the father when the children were still relatively young, since only men could train young sons in an occupation or arrange apprenticeships, and it was men who arranged betrothal of daughters at puberty. But career training and marriage are much later today. Yet divorced women are commonly deprived of custody of sons about five or six, and of daughters by nine to eleven, because these ages were set centuries ago. If a woman remarries, she automatically loses custody of children, because in the ancient world, women did not have the authority to protect her children from a new husband, but it was assumed that a father could and would protect his children even from a bad stepmother.

In some parts of the Muslim world, local sexual and marital customs have continued after conversion to Islam and thus become understood as "Muslim," though not rooted in Islam. Examples include *purdah*, the seclusion of women in the home, and the requirement that when they must go into public they be veiled and accompanied by a male relative; the infamous *honor killings* of some North African nations, in which the honor of the family rests on the sexual integrity of its women, which when cast into doubt is purified by killing the woman; and female circumcision, a largely African Muslim (and African religions) custom not practiced by most Muslims in the rest of the world.

While Islam gave women a great many rights that women in other parts of the world would not gain until much later, its jurisprudence interpreted the Muslim regulation that husbands at marriage give wives a *mahr* (a payment that she controls and retains as insurance in case of divorce) as an act of exchange: his money for sexual access to her body. This traditional understanding has restricted the ability of Muslim jurisprudence to deal with many of the issues around sexual justice for women. For example, in this understanding, rape in marriage is impossible.

At the same time, Islam is not short of accounts of husbands and wives enjoying sexual pleasure together, and imposed no rules limiting sex in marriage. While there is more emphasis on male sexual pleasure, and wives' duty to accommodate husbands in this regard, there is also great appreciation of mutual sexual pleasure in marriage.

Hinduism

While all religions take on different flavors in different cultures, the diversity within Hinduism is such that we often speak of Hinduism as a system of related religions, rather than a single religion. This diversity extends to sexuality. In general, Hinduism has been historically pronatalist. The ancient laws of Manu obliged parents to arrange marriages for their children at very young ages. Marriage in Hinduism was regarded as shifting a woman from her own natal family to that of her husband, which was the reason why divorce was extremely rare and remarriage of widows forbidden in the upper castes.

At the same time that Hinduism has been pronatalist, however, it has also had a prominent place for celibacy. In its stages of life (*asramas*), Hinduism assigns great respect to the last, voluntary stage of *sannyasi* (*sadhu/ sadhvi*), in which persons renounce home and family and become celibate wandering beggars who pray and meditate. While the student stage prepares one for the householder's responsibilities to family, the third stage, the *vanaprastha* (hermit) stage, is preparation for committing to the fourth, celibate stage of *sannyasi*. These wandering, celibate, holy beggars have cut all ties to family and home in order to pray and meditate, and they subsist on the charity of others.

Westerners who know little about the theology, philosophy, or ritual of Hinduism often know of the *Kama Sutra*, a compendium of Hindu wisdom about sensual and sexual pleasure in relationships and family life that includes advice on obtaining and giving sexual pleasure. Westerners are also often fascinated by some ancient Hindu temples that have elaborate carvings of various gods and goddesses at sexual play. The phallus and vagina (*lingam* and *yoni*) are often depicted in religious scenes, for together they represent creation, the origin, and the oneness of imma-nent reality and transcendental possibility.

Tantric schools of Hinduism (and Vajray-ana or Tibetan Buddhism as well) have been more oriented to the married householder than the monastic or solitary renunciant. They include an acceptance of the world and of the unity of spiritual and material reality. Most forms include some transgressive acts, which often included the use of partnered sex to achieve new planes of spiritual con-sciousness. Though feminist authors are often leery of claims of complete sexual equality in Tantric history, it is clear that many women as well as men have been recognized as accom-plished Tantric practitioners and spiritual masters.

Sex and Mysticism

As we might infer from the above treatment of Tantric Hinduism, some of the most helpful insights into sexuality from within religions emerge more or less indirectly from mysti-cal elements within the various religions. The ecstasy of orgasm has frequently been com-pared to the ecstasy of mystic union with the Creator/unified cosmic reality. Women mys-tics across religions have often understood themselves as married to the Divine One, using the erotic language of spouses and lov-ers to describe each other.[5] Rabi'a al-Basri, a celebrated Muslim Sufi mystic, refused to marry for this reason, and often told others who wondered at her ascetic solitude, "My Beloved is with me."[6] It is no accident that Catholic nuns for many centuries have worn a wedding ring upon taking final vows and are said to be married to Christ.

One part of this association of orgasm with mystic union with the Divine is that in both experiences, the individual can feel as if

transported out of self, out of body, to another plane—one of total sensation—above the plane of rational thought.[7] Bernini's sculpture *The Ecstasy of St. Teresa* depicts the mystic nun in classic (post-)orgasmic pose: mouth open, eyes half-lidded and thrown up, body limp, corresponding to her description of her mystical experience (see below).

Just as mystics practice a particular disci-pline, a way of life that facilitates the mystic experience from which it proceeds, so mutual orgasm between long-time lovers proceeds from a particular discipline and way of life that feeds the experience of giving oneself and receiving back not only the gift of the other, but also oneself enhanced. Until recently within Christianity, mystics have largely been associated with monastic life,[8] and so many laypeople have not made the connection between their own "out of body" experiences in orgasmic sex with those of the mystics. In traditions such as Islam, which does not have monastic orders and yet which has his-torically both significant numbers of mystics (Sufis)[9] and recognition of the legitimacy of sexual pleasure in marriage, the association of ecstasy in sex and in mysticism is not quite so startling or unusual, and, of course, Tantrics in both Hinduism and Buddhism have also recognized sexual communion as a path to experience of ultimacy.

One of the clearest contemporary expli-cations of this connection in the West was perhaps the 1986 book commissioned by the United States Catholic (Bishops) Conference, *Embodied in Love: The Sacramental Spiritual-ity of Sexual Intimacy*, written by Charles A. Gallagher, George A. Maloney, S.J., Mary F. Rousseau, and Paul Wilczak.[10] This book pre-sented sexual intimacy in marriage as the closest human experience of the love that exists within the Trinity, and insisted that the

Fig. 5.3. An angel stands over St. Teresa in Bernini's sculpure, *The Ecstasy of St. Teresa*, in St. Peter's Basilica, Vatican City.

chief pastoral task of the church was to keep sexual desire alive and active within community—desire understood as the zest for life, the energy, the hope, and the commitment of lovers. Marital sexual love was presented as the furnace that kept the family, the church, and the larger community warm.

The authors of *Embodied in Love* understood sex in marriage, and most particularly orgasm, as the sacramental sign of marriage, that which expressed what marriage signified. They taught that sharing sexual love involved opening oneself to the other, becoming naked not only in body but in spirit, despite the risk of hurt involved. This risk, this trust, they taught, is rewarded in the pleasure of orgasm. Thus marital sex, by teaching spouses that risk in loving is rewarded, becomes a school

for love. A life of being rewarded for risking self with the spouse disposes us to risk opening ourselves in other ways to other people: to our children, to neighbors, in an ever-widening circle.

This is a spirituality of marriage, and it should be no surprise that it shares features with other spiritualities, such as that of the mystics. Intimacy is one, whether with the Divine Love, or our earthbound lover. Intimacy requires letting ourselves be known, drawing down the barricades that we erect to protect ourselves from hurt and disappointment, and opening ourselves to the love of God and to God's love flowing through others. How reasonable, the authors say, that the relationship that is the most like union with God is the marital relationship in which we have most fully opened ourselves to love. However, it is no secret that openings to such understandings of sexuality in religions have been rare, resisted, and usually retracted or disavowed soon after.

"**Sex and spirituality—really?**" This is clearly the response of many people today who understand sex as a mammalian appetite that needs to be satisfied. But for those who experience, or intuit, the potential for sexual union to be revelatory, to give some insight into ultimate reality, there is more to be explored. What kind of sex opens this revelatory experience to us? Here we get into questions about casual sex, serial monogamy, divorce, and civil unions/gay marriage. So let us proceed to some of the contemporary questions.

New Ethical Questions on Sexuality and Marriage

In many western societies today, persons experience more sexual freedom than at any time in recorded history. There are many ethical problems associated with that freedom. Unfortunately, in many religions, there is a tendency to recognize as moral/ethical problems only, and all, deviations from historic religious teachings. For these persons, all sex outside marriage is condemned, all extramarital sex is adultery and condemned; masturbation, oral sex, all sex that is not clearly heterosexual, and sometimes artificial contraception, are condemned. And there is silence about marital sex, as if it always satisfies moral requirements.

More progressive religions and religious authorities are attempting to sort through contemporary sexual practice and suggest avenues that could guide their believers to responsible sexual practice. They, too, are

clear that there are morally dangerous aspects of contemporary sexual practice, but they often see different aspects of contemporary sexual practice as dangerous.

Some young—and not so young—persons ask today whether there is any problem with a series of impermanent sexual relationships, with couples staying together so long as the relationship works for both of them, and splitting when it doesn't. Others suggest that casual sex—hooking up for the night—could also be ethical. But ethics is not about drawing or withdrawing lines between good acts and bad acts. Casual sex or hooking up cannot be approved en masse any more than marital sex can.

In our culture, sex is so personal—usually our most intimate relationship, close to the core of who we are as persons—that beginning our explorations with virtue ethics makes great sense. What should we understand as ideal? What should we teach our children to expect and to aspire to? What should we teach them are lesser aspirations? What kind of sexual acts and relationships have the greatest potential to make us just, compassionate, and responsible human beings? If we are to be responsible, then given that we have extensive evidence that serial relationships are not an ideal environment for raising children,[11] a bottom line for uncommitted sexual relationships should be contraceptive use.

Does it matter whether both persons think, or only one thinks, that there no longer is a relationship between them? In most relationships, at any given time one person is more willing to invest in the relationship, to work on it, and to stick with it through some suffering or discontent, than is the partner. Unless our ethical discourse treats an ongoing series of sexual partners as morally problematic, we do little to discourage sexual adventurism, relationship sloth, and ethical egoism from moving the less committed partner to a new relationship at the first sign of trouble. We should not make it too easy to move on.

On the other hand, contemporary life has become so complex that there are increasing numbers of serious reasons that relationships do not last. Some couples, among both married and unmarried, break up because one wants children and the other doesn't, or because the career aspirations and training of each lead them to different parts of the globe. Such differences are almost impossible to resolve if these commitments are strongly grounded, for when we marry, we are not only marrying a person, but a life, and that life includes certain roles. We can say, for example, that couples should discuss whether they want children before committing to cohabitation before marriage. But many a cohabitation or marriage begins in youth, when the details of later occupation and location are still unknown, and identities are not yet completely firm. It is not surprising that many break up when they face the practical decisions that come with greater age.

Analyzing Responsible Sexual Ethics

One of the most worrying aspects for religionists is sexual activity among children and adolescents. Some sexual activity involving children is clearly criminal exploitation by adults, whether in child pornography, child sex trafficking, or molestation of individual children in families, schools, churches, or other local institutions. Other child sexual activity is just as obviously imitation of adult behavior to which children have been inappropriately exposed, such as first graders imitating the movements of coitus. But all these,

or at least the incidence of these, seem to be related to a more general trend.

Sexualization of children. There is in our society a cultural push toward early sexualization of children, which almost certainly is responsible for some portion of what seems to be an explosion in child sexual molestation. This early sexualization can perhaps be most clearly seen in girls' clothing. Kindergarten and elementary school girls are now wearing heels, just like their mothers. It is difficult to shop for elementary school girls if one doesn't want to deck one's ten- to twelve-year-old in low-cut shirts, skirts made to display panties underneath, or logos blazoned across chest or butt. What else, other than pressing little girls to act overtly sexual and/or to be objects of

Fig. 5.4. This cartoon female functions as a model of stylish clothing for young girls.

sexual attention, could account for pants in a child's size 10 that say JUICY across the buttocks?[12] This problem extends far beyond child beauty pageants into the ranks of the majority.

What our society obviously needs with the age of marriage retreating ever higher is raising the age of sexual interest and activity, not lowering it, if for no other reason than controlling the spread of sexually transmitted diseases. This early sexualization of children and the earlier sexual activity that it leads to is a serious problem for a number of reasons. Young children are not mature enough to deal with the strong emotions that sexual relationships can evoke. The principal task of young adolescents is separation from parents and developing independent identity. These immature and not yet independent selves are capable of both inflicting and receiving great emotional injury and are often not capable of exercising responsibility in such things as contraception, protection from STDs, or even sexual abuse. The fact that adult engaged couples are frequently having sex before the marriage ceremony is not the same level of serious moral problem as eleven- or twelve-year-olds having sex, despite many churches' classifying them both as fornication.

There are of course limits to how much we can raise the age at which sexual interest and activity become common. We know that improved nutrition and healthcare have hastened sexual development. The average age at menarche is now five years younger than it was a century and a half ago.[13] Hormones, of course, dictate much about sexual interest and predispose many to sexual activity. But we should not be aggravating the situation by training early and even pre-adolescents to appear and act sexual. Much of what children learn, of course, is by imitating adults.

A divorced parent who is desperate to find another lover/spouse in effect sends a message to their child that individuals cannot flourish without a sexual partner, that the child should find one, too. The media is filled with this message, that singleness is lonely and unfulfilling, that a central purpose and need in life is to attract a sexual partner.

Controlling fertility. Because most religions have been pronatalist, they have found it difficult to take seriously the new environmental situation of the last century in which human fertility has become the single biggest danger to sustaining human life on our planet.[14] Obviously, we should also point the finger at obscene consumption levels in the rich countries, which need to be drastically reduced. But contemporary humans, especially those who live where consumption levels are highest, have a responsibility not to add to the human population.[15] This means only reproducing ourselves—normally two children per couple.

Adultery. Adultery is a traditional sexual sin that needs to be carefully examined. Though global cultures in general remain opposed to adultery, understanding it as serious sin/offense, there are two situations in which adultery in the West is becoming popularly defended. The first, a tragic situation that is increasingly common, occurs when one spouse moves beyond the initial phases of dementia, as in Alzheimer's disease, and no longer recognizes and responds to others. While it is clear that the optimal response is to remain faithful until the marriage is completely ended, in the case of dementia this could require many years, even decades, of sacrifice and solitude on the part of the well spouse. Pastorally, many clergy recognize that not everyone has the strength of character to look beyond the cultural norm of sexual intimacy to find nonsexual sources of intimacy to sustain him or her in fidelity in such a situation. At the very least, the well spouse, if divorcing the demented spouse, has an obligation to see that the sick spouse is well cared for.

This is one of the cases in which it becomes most clear that not everything that is legal is moral. Legally, one may divorce a demented spouse and have no further responsibility for him or her. But there can be no moral justification for renouncing one's duties to a spouse because he or she suffered the misfortune of illness, whether mental or physical. Do we not pledge fidelity in just that case when we marry ("in sickness and in health")? Fidelity is not just outmoded religious language; it is something that the vast majority of humans want in their marital relationships: we want to know that this person to whom we have revealed more of ourselves than to anyone else, with whom we have shared our life, to whom we have committed ourselves, also values us above all others, and will be true to marital promises. The failure to abide by the vows we take often worsens situations already saturated with suffering.

The second case in which adultery is sometimes defended is often referred to as "technical adultery." It occurs when a couple is separated and/or in the process of divorce and one of them engages in sex with someone else. Except in the case of some exceptionally long drawn-out divorce, which is rarer and rarer these days, new sexual relationships should wait until divorce is final. As many a second spouse has realized too late, "If he had sex with me when he was still married to her, I should have known he wouldn't be faithful to me, either." Today increasing numbers of persons think nothing of taking on new sexual partners when they are separated, even when

the ostensible purpose of the separation may be to reflect on whether the marriage can be saved. "We're separated" or "We're getting a divorce" have become the most common lies in offices and singles bars. The hurt that comes with disillusionment could be avoided if one had only responded, "Call me when the divorce is final."

All too often today, adultery has become a way of testing one's commitment to a marriage. It is a very poor test, much like the late medieval test for witches (throwing a bound woman in a pond; if she sank and drowned, she was innocent, and if she floated, she was a witch to be burned). If a marriage was in trouble but could have been saved, too often adultery is the final stressor that breaks the bond. Adultery destroys trust, undermines the ability of the betrayed partner to believe in the love of the adulterous one, and even raises doubts in the betrayed partner about their own worth. The wounds caused by adultery are very difficult to heal. Children who are aware of parental adultery often take it as a very personal injury, for the basic security of children, which allows them the self-centeredness that supports their exploration of the world, is based upon the stability of parents. When those parents are at odds, children are torn and often internalize blame.

Masturbation. Historically, emphasis on sex being for the purpose of reproduction led to condemnation of masturbation. Today medical science has demonstrated that masturbation in infants is instinctual; infants routinely manipulate their genitals for pleasure (for example during diaper changes) and infants of less than one year have been known to masturbate to orgasm.[16] Increasingly our society understands masturbation not as sinful, but as normal for children and adolescents. Sex therapists commonly prescribe masturbation for women as a way of their learning erotic touch and becoming comfortable with sexual arousal.[17] Even in marriage, when one spouse is unavailable for sex due to extended absence or illness, masturbation can be the preferred way of dealing with sexual desire. Masturbation is best understood as preparation, or second-best substitute, for mutually pleasurable sexual activity. Consequentially, it is not terribly difficult to justify the practice of masturbation, as the only harm known to follow from it comes in the rare case of a masturbator becoming fixated on self-stimulation and preferring it to a more mature interpersonal sexual relationship when this becomes possible. It is appropriate that masturbation is disappearing from religious categories of sexual sin in the West.

Homosexuality. Homosexuality is another sexual practice that has been extremely problematic in pronatalist religions and cultures, but which is now becoming more open and accepted in many western cultures. One reason is that as homosexuals in the West become more and more open, the general population comes to the same conclusion that researcher Dr. Evelyn Hooker did in the 1950s: instead of homosexuality being a practice of deviants, whose moral character and relationships were warped by their sexual deviance, skilled psychiatrists have been generally unable to discern homosexuals from heterosexuals based on their character and their quality of relationships.[18]

Research into sexual orientation and sexual identity is still relatively new. There is extensive research, and thus many conflicting results, concerning the "causes" of gay and lesbian, not to mention bisexual, transsexual, and transgender sexuality. All that is clear thus far is that the "causes" are complex, and interrelated. We know there can be some

genetic predisposition, but that environment also plays a part. The process of sexual identity formation appears different for gays and lesbians, and the process(es) for bisexual and trans-persons (who are not necessarily homosexual in the biological sense) may also be even more varied.

While religious conservatives across many different religions and denominations have historically rejected all nonheterosexual sexuality as deliberately chosen sin, more liberal approaches in modernity first understood homosexuality as a form of mental illness that mitigated moral responsibility. Then in the 1960s and 1970s, many liberal western understandings focused on new research among gays that showed homosexual orientation having formed in early childhood as evidence that it could not be morally chosen, but must be somehow natural and inevitable because it predated the "age of reason." When the first evidence of a genetic link to homosexual orientation was discovered, these two pieces of data became the foundation of a liberal religious defense of homosexuality: that it, like heterosexuality, was genetically based, and was God's decision, not the individual's. Following the statement in Genesis that said that God surveyed all he had made and found it good, many concluded that there was no human choice involved in either orientation, and thus homosexuality was as morally acceptable as heterosexuality or any other part of God's creation.

Today we know that neither heterosexuality nor homosexuality is a genetic "given." Continuing research, in which there are still many unanswered questions about all sexual orientations, even about the concept of orientation itself, has shown that this earlier liberal approach is not tenable. It never fit the majority of the evidence. This model of homosexual persons knowing from early childhood that they were sexually attracted to the same sex was true for many, but not nearly all, gay men, and for very few lesbians, many of whom did not realize a same-sex orientation until their twenties, thirties, or even later. And it did not explain bisexuality at all. Many persons who jumped to adopt this understanding of sexual orientation as given in biology and nature did so for political reasons: it seemed the strongest counterargument to the intolerance of religious conservatives who insisted that homosexuality was deliberate, sinful perversion of all human beings' natural heterosexuality.

Today virtually all sexuality researchers have adopted what is called a "constructionist" approach to the formation of sex, gender, and sexual orientation, which means that a number of factors, including genetic, hormonal, and other biological factors, and environmental factors, including social, cultural, religious, and personal experiential elements, are all bundled together, along with our personal preferences among these, to construct our sexual selves. This means that our individual choices—not completely open and free, but constrained by our biology and life environment—share some responsibility for who we are and who we become. But the fact that there is some degree of personal choice involved—the amount of which clearly varies tremendously from individual to individual—is not to be used as a stick for beating GLBTQ persons. There is simply no reason for understanding nonheterosexual orientations as inferior today. It is important for all of us to understand and accept the responsibility that we have for the persons we become. If the lack of reproductive capacity is no longer the basis for condemning sexual activity, then GLBTQ orientations and relationships

become analogous to heterosexual ones, and actions by GLBTQ persons can be evaluated in relation to the same values as heterosexual relationships. The argument that sacred texts condemning homosexuality have the final word has become less and less tenable as scholarship in sacred texts makes clear that in every tradition some parts of sacred texts have been lifted up as binding and other parts suppressed, depending on their compatibility with the current context. If other parts of sacred texts are ignored and not considered authoritative any longer—such as those accepting of slavery—then there is no compelling reason that heterosexist—or misogynist—texts should be.[19]

Qualities of Ethical Sexual Relationships

Ethical sexual relationships should be responsible, which at the very least means just, caring, compassionate, mutual, and (mutually) pleasurable.[20] Most religions insist that they be both exclusive and permanent, but increasingly, western culture insists at most that they be exclusive while they exist, and optimally but not necessarily permanent. Some groups insist that both exclusivity and permanence are outmoded values for heterosexual and homosexual persons alike. This latter rejection of exclusivity and/or permanence is common among some GLBTQ groups, though many other GLBTQ persons have vigorously campaigned for the right to marry in state after state. Here again, the historical context may play an important role.

Changing realities for GLBTQ persons. The rejection of exclusivity and permanence by some GLBTQ persons may be a remnant from the repression of homosexuality in the past, which still continues not only globally, but also in many parts of the United States.

When covertness was necessary for GLBTQ persons to survive, casual transient relationships were not only the safest, but were also often the only ones available. As GLBTQ persons in some places have come to experience more possibilities available to them, the GLBTQ community has consequently split over issues such as gay marriage, same-sex unions, dating and courtship relationships, and casual hooking up, with some but not all choosing options historically represented by heterosexual marriage. Whether this choice for marriage represents a throwing off of historical patterns of casual sex necessarily developed under persecution or ongoing cultural pressure to adapt to heterosexual norms is not yet clear.

There is some evidence that among some GLBTQ groups, perhaps especially among gay men, there exist social circles of friends in which all or virtually all have been the lovers of all the others. Some members of the circle may be paired presently, but physical intimacy and shared sexual knowledge of each other seem to be the basis of the friendships that hold the entire group together. This could be a different model of sexual interaction, with possibilities for supporting personal and group intimacy and moral responsibility. However, one must also consider that the historic lack of social tolerance for nonheterosexuals has encouraged covert, short-lived sexual liaisons as less risky than enduring ones. As society began, very unevenly, to open to gays and lesbians, the remaining intolerance required the construction of supportive social groups made up of other GLBTQ persons. Inevitably, since the GLBTQ community is a minority to begin with, the group of previous sexual partners and the persons available for a supportive community will overlap. Whether this or other present sexual patterns will still exist once societies have ensured equal justice for persons with all sexual identities and practices is open to question. It is not yet at all clear whether GLBTQ persons will continue segregated social groups when this is no longer necessary, and the issue of sexual norms will be greatly influenced by this decision.

Argument from dignity. The dismissal of exclusivity and permanence as valuable in sexual relationships is strongly rejected by many traditional western religions as not reconcilable with a religious view of the human person. They insist that human persons are not only inherently and essentially relational, but that they are ends in themselves. This is what Judaism and Christianity, for example, mean when they quote from the creation account in Genesis, "in His own image and likeness he created them, male and female he created them."[21] Human beings are not to be used as instruments toward other ends, such as for another's pleasure, as if they were a dildo or a blow-up doll. Humans are persons, ends in themselves, not to be made into objects. Created to be in communion with God, humans do not encounter God only in prayer and mysticism, but perhaps most often discover God mediated to them through relationships with other humans. In those parents who sacrificed to keep us safe, healthy, and educated, who enjoyed being with us and sent us prepared into the world, we experienced God's love for us. Because, in a religious view, we were made for some kind of ultimate union with/dissolution into God/oneness, whether we understand that union as Hindu *moksha*, Buddhist *nirvana*, or Christian heaven, we are relational: we need to be in relation to others, to achieve various degrees of intimacy with others.[22]

Thus, at least for most persons formed in religious environments, instrumental sexual interactions are the most problematic of all instrumental interactions. But one does not necessarily need to be religious to see the force of the argument. It is inevitable in late modernity that we have instrumental interactions. We lack the time and energy to establish any kind of intimacy with every grocery clerk, parking attendant, cashier, and salesperson that we must engage with on a daily basis. Respectful politeness is the most that we can manage. But to have this same kind of instrumental interaction in sex can invite miscommunication. Instrumental sex seems to many to involve a kind of deceit, to send two completely different messages. Even when either the circumstances or explicit verbal agreement between the participants indicates that the sexual act is casual, without commitment or any future expectation, as is often the case in hooking up, there is in the sexual act a physical intimacy that is frequently interpreted as inviting emotional intimacy—at least in the view of many representatives of traditional religions. This invitation to intimacy that so many find in sex is why authors and scriptwriters so often depict the postcoital interlude between just-met persons as uncomfortable and embarrassing. How is it possible, they implicitly ask, to move smoothly from the most physically intimate of embraces to the impersonal leave-taking of virtual strangers? The shift is awkward because it moves abruptly from what we instinctively know is intimate to what is clearly impersonal—from lovers to strangers. Or so many have thought and felt.

Why the priority for emotional intimacy over sexual intimacy? On the other hand, some GLBTQ theorists ask why it is normative for emotional intimacy to precede sexual intimacy and not follow it, why casual sex should be always understood as disrespectful of persons, as using them. They dispute the identification of casual sex with instrumental sex, arguing that it is a remnant of slaveholding patriarchy, which understands sex as inherently the use of one by another. If on a long intercontinental flight I disclose a great deal of intimate information about myself to the stranger in the next seat, have I instrumentalized that person for my own benefit? We generally assume that if the other person consented to hear my confidences, I did not "use" that person selfishly. Why should sexual intimacy be different here from emotional intimacy? In short, these theorists question why, when modernity deconstructed the traditional arranged marriage based in material factors and aimed at reproduction—why did emotional intimacy come to be understood as the common purpose and end of sex? Why could sex not have been equally well understood as a respectful and relatively casual activity that could lead to emotional intimacy and pairing but need not?[23] Their point is that history shows that sex can serve a variety of functions in different situations, and there was no need to fasten on this one function (emotional intimacy) to replace the previous one (reproduction), and then insist that morality requires at the very least that the degree of sexual intimacy be proportional to the degree of emotional/interpersonal intimacy already developed in the relationship.[24] It might be a historical accident that love marriages began around the same time that a socially mobile economy destroyed traditional village life and extended families.

Ironically, there is some support for this view from some long-married heterosexual couples, who note that the sexual intimacy of their youth helped to create the emotional intimacy that sustains their relationship once sex is no longer so possible. However, there is a need for caution, in that we cannot only look at those who were successful in moving from sexual intimacy to emotional intimacy, ignoring the numbers who never moved beyond the sex. Both sexual and emotional intimacy are valuable, but whether they are equally capable of being gateways to the other is still not clear.

Where to from Here?

These are some of the issues that societies are grappling with and will continue to grapple with in the coming decades. What social functions is sex best suited for? Clearly our contemporary choice of understanding sex in intimacy terms was a response to other trends in late-modern society that disrupted traditional forms of intimacy. Some would suggest that this contemporary association of sex with intimacy is also evidence of the greater social status and power of women today, since women's greater vulnerability both in sexual activity (rape and violence) and to the reproductive consequences of sex (pregnancy) had historically (through culture and/or genetics) caused women, much more than men, to be more interested in connecting sex with ongoing relationship. If that is so, then we might expect that as contraceptive control of fertility becomes universally available and women's social status and power become more nearly equal to men's, there will be a gradual lessening of the demand for linking sex to intimacy and ongoing relationship.

We do not know whether permanence and exclusivity will be retained by religions and civil societies as necessary moral conditions for sexual activity. Much will depend on to what extent the liberation movements of women and GLBTQ persons spread and

deepen. But that is not to say that liberation of women and GLBTQ persons necessarily leads to more casual sexual attitudes. Perhaps it will go in the opposite direction. At the present time, we simply cannot tell. In the meantime, whichever side of this issue one takes, there are some clear responsibilities in sex for both heterosexuals and GLBTQ persons. Respect for the other will mean that whether one believes that sex signals the existence of an ongoing relationship or just a casual friendly exchange, one has an obligation to ensure that one's prospective sexual partner *fully* understands this from the beginning. One should not assume that the other understands as one does, or that a casual remark in the midst of frenzied shedding of clothes is sufficient notice to the other of one's relationship expectations or lack of them.

Just as we have become more sensitive about our use of the masculine generic in language and now take care to use language that includes women as well as men, we need to become more sensitive to heterocentric language—which assumes that all sexual desire is heterosexual, that all couples are heterosexual, and that all sexual activity is heterosexual. The media, especially TV, have done much to begin the reconditioning process around heterocentric language in comedies of the last decade or so by using humor to remind us to make our categories more inclusive. But there is a long road ahead of us if we are to end exclusion of GLBTQ persons from ordinary sexual discourse.

Use of contraception where fertility is possible (unless committed couples are planning children), frequent testing for STDs and treatment of those when present, abstention from sex until treatment is completed, or at the very least full disclosure of one's disease status to a prospective partner—these are all lowest-common-denominator moral requirements for contemporary sex.

Regardless of whether one understands exclusivity and/or permanence as normative for sex, morality forbids using another's vulnerability to obtain sex. It is morally wrong to push for sex with someone who is inebriated/high, who is subordinate to one in any way (someone one supervises, employs, coaches, counsels), or who is indebted to one for any reason. It is similarly wrong to exploit a weakness in another to obtain sex, whether that weakness be due to mourning, fear, depression, or loneliness. And at the very least, sexual pleasure should always be mutual; it is not enough to assume that everyone should watch out for themselves.

Transitions and Forgiveness

There are a number of difficult transitions that most human persons must make in order to become mature adults. Religions have marked many of these life transitions with rituals. Some religious communities have many more rituals of transition than others, but virtually all have marked the transition to adulthood, which traditionally accompanied puberty. As adolescents, we must come to terms with our changing pubescent bodies. Girls need to learn to dress differently as they grow breasts and to prepare for menstrual periods. Boys need to deal with the awkwardness of sudden involuntary erections and embarrassing voice changes. Later both sexes will gradually shift from satisfying

Fig. 5.5. Statue of Mahavira in a Jain temple in Rajasthan, India.

sexual arousal with masturbation to part-nered sex. In contemporary western society, if they are very lucky in the partners they encounter and they mature relatively early, they may escape a series of painful—but educational—broken sexual relationships, and settle into mutually satisfying partnered relationships that help them become still more responsible and compassionate. Many, however, will only arrive at this state late and mangled, if at all.

One of the most valuable things to be gar-nered from the riches of world religions, in addition to the above-mentioned dignity of the human person, is the need to forgive not only each other, but ourselves. As the Jain founder, Mahavira, taught:

> By practicing *prayascitta* (repentance), a soul gets rid of sins, and commits no transgressions; he who correctly prac-tises *prayascitta* gains the road and the reward of the road, he wins the reward of good conduct. By begging forgiveness he obtains happiness of mind; thereby he acquires a kind disposition towards all kinds of living beings; by this kind dispo-sition he obtains purity of character and freedom from fear.[25]

We should all do our best to be as responsible, compassionate, and respectful as we can be in all our relationships with others. But inevita-bly as we look back—which we must do peri-odically in order to assess our moral progress and plan our future steps—we find that we have sometimes failed to do the best that we could. Some part of our past experience, or some one of our desires, blinded us to what we should have done, and we failed to be fully responsible, just, and compassionate to sexual partners, or to others we have encountered. Once we have recognized our mistake, asked forgiveness from those we have wronged (if possible and appropriate), and committed to doing better in the future, we need to for-give ourselves. Theistic religions tell us that God forgives us, and that in this, as in many other things, we should imitate God. This is practical advice that is also forthcoming from mental health professionals. Recognizing our own need to be forgiven our faults in sexual relationships should also make us more will-ing to forgive the faults of others by whom we may have been hurt, and to move on with our lives.

Case Study: Arranged Marriage

It was Dr. Hennessy's Contemporary Ethical Issues class, and as usual, the discussion was heated. The topic was sex and marriage. A small group of evangelical students had taken on what they saw as the hedonist group. A group, mostly male, accepted the hedonist label and defended hooking up. One of them, Tom, argued, "Look, I am twenty-two and headed to medical school, then an internship and residency. I really can't marry and start a family for another six to eight years, but you can't expect me to be celibate until I am thirty! It would not be fair to a woman for me to get into a relationship now—it's too long to wait, and I don't have enough time to put into a relationship. So casual sex is the best option. As long as we are both honest about that and use contraception, what is the harm in casual sex?"

Emily, one of the evangelical students, responded, "But sex is not like food and water. It is relational, meant to belong in a covenant. There is a potential for sacredness in sex. I think hook-up culture doesn't want to acknowledge that potential, and that is why sex is so tied to alcohol use in hook-up culture. If you are plastered, you don't have to think too much about what you are doing. One of my suite mates told me that at the beginning of her freshman year, she got involved in the hook-up party scene, but she got out in disgust. She has an allergic reaction to alcohol, and if you aren't drunk, she said, your whole take on the scene is different."

"That's very pretty and romantic, Emily, but what about the practical problem that Tom pointed out? Are you telling him he should be celibate for a decade?" asked Neil.

Neesha, a naturalized citizen from India, interjected, "What is it with you Americans that you think sex is the major form of protein needed to fuel the body? People go without sex for decades all the time. Celibacy is not fatal. In fact, it is rather practical—no worries about pregnancy, contraception, sexually transmitted diseases, even HIV/AIDS. Sex gives pleasure and babies, but there are other forms of pleasure, and you don't want babies now."

Katie looked back and forth between Tom and Emily and finally volunteered, "I'm not Christian, but I have some problems with the hook-up scene. If there were another alternative, I would take it. But how else am I going to meet someone whom I could love if I don't go out and party?" A number of other students nodded at Katie, underlining her question. There was a pause in the discussion.

Mita, an exchange student from Indonesia, raised her hand and spoke. "My parents' marriage was arranged by their parents, as were the marriages of almost all their peers in Indonesia. My generation does not want that kind of marriage, where you may only meet your spouse once or twice before the ceremony. We are marrying older, and we are much better educated than the older generation. But we do not want your western way of getting married, either. It is too hard! It takes too long! It leaves too much to chance. We want help in finding a marriage partner, and we get that help principally from parents, but also from other relatives and friends who know us and care for us.

"My parents think they have found me a husband. My sister says I will love him. We have begun getting to know each other by Skype and email. I will go home to meet him this summer. I expect we will meet a number of times, talk more about what we want in a marriage, our plans for careers, children, where we would live. If we like each other through all this, we will marry in a few months. If we don't, we won't. There is no force, no coercion, though there is some pressure to marry, if not him, then another relatively quickly. In my culture, once one is ready to marry, one should marry quickly.

"I know many Americans get very tired of looking for a partner and are trying to get help. But I think that the trend to online dating services, even paid matchmakers, is not so good as our system, because it is impersonal. Our matchmakers care; they are parts of our family. Sometimes we do find our own spouses, especially in university. But we must get approval. A cousin of mine has brought three different women to meet his mother, who is a widowed civil court judge, and she has vetoed each one of them as a wife for him. From your perspective, this may look autocratic. But all of them have been western exchange students, two Americans, one Brit. My aunt does not think that westerners will want to live in Indonesia, apart from all their family and friends, and she does not want her only child on the other side of the world, apart from his family. She knows he won't be happy there. She will not choose his wife for him, but in our culture, she must approve."

One of the quieter students in the class, David, looked at Mita and said, "That seems like a great system to me. I wish I could enlist help from my parents in finding me a wife. My parents accidentally did find my sister a husband—my dad brought the new architect in his firm home for dinner, and he and my sister hit it off and started dating. They are getting married next month."

Emily offered: "You know, in your system, Mita, there is no ambiguity. When someone is introduced to you as a potential spouse, you both know that the other is serious and has publicly declared to other people their intention to marry. Here, everything is ambiguous. The idea that you fall in love, that it is in some ways involuntary, means that the pool of people we search in contains many who are not looking for permanent relationships. So there are huge possibilities for confusion, mixed signals, and unintentional hurt."

Dr. Hennessy asked, "Are you suggesting that we should have two social pools, one of persons intent on marrying, and one of people only interested in recreational dating, which might involve various levels of sex?"

"No, not really, Dr. Hennessy. It would be nice, but I don't think that could work here. Look at the computer dating sites that are trying to match people up for marriage. They have a hard time weeding out the people, mostly guys, who aren't serious, who lie to their dates and may have multiple sexual relationships going at the same time, all with partners who think they are headed to marriage," Emily replied. "This happens so often that it's a joke in commercials."

Dr. Hennessy asked, "From the readings that you did for this class, what do you think are the principal causes for these divisions not only between national cultures, but within the same general culture?"

"Well," suggested Sarah, "you have some of the factors Mita mentioned—all over the world, people are getting more education and marrying later. So sexual desire and arousal become an issue for much longer in the average life than they were when people married at fourteen or fifteen. And then you add in effective contraception. It is one thing to control your sexual desire until marriage when you marry while still in puberty, and quite another when you marry at twenty-nine to thirty, especially when there is no threat from pregnancy."

Neil added, "And don't forget the change in living patterns. Single adults are living on their own, with many more opportunities for sex before marriage. We don't have chaperonage any more. Teens can have sex after school in their parents' home—the parents are at work, so who will know?"

"But are you saying this is good?" asked Emily.

Here are three very different follow-ups to the class discussion. How realistic are they? What others might be probable in the class? In what ways do these follow-ups make clear the advantages of open discussions about sexuality of the type that this class had?

1. That Friday night Tom was headed to an off-campus fraternity party, and remembered the class discussion. He decided that he would not drink for a while, just to test out what had been said about the role of alcohol in hooking up. Over the next hour he found that he was constantly urged to drink, which he had never noticed before, and the longer he waited to drink, the more people pushed drinks on him. Two hours after arriving, he realized that he was on the sidelines, bored, though when he drank he would be at the center of the action, dancing and getting it on with one of the most attractive women there.

2. Mita had a Skype date the next afternoon, and she detailed part of the class conversation to Ahmad, her Skype friend: "You know, I do not like the American dating system and think our system of enlisting family to help locate potential partners is much better. And I don't approve of casual sex, or even premarital sex for engaged couples. But I think it is a problem in our culture that when couples have met and are deciding if they are compatible, sexuality is something that is never talked about or experimented with. I think that when we meet next month, we need to try some forms of physical touching to see if we have positive reactions to each other, and talk about our sexual expectations. How do you feel about that?"

3. Katie was telling her roommate about the class discussion. "I wish there were somewhere that we could meet guys to just talk and hang out, someplace where nobody drank to get drunk, and where you don't go to get laid. When I was in high school in my small town, there were only the youth center dances and events, with no booze. We used to wish it were more exciting, but it was a place we all went for entertainment, and though a few kids hooked up there and left to have sex, most of us just talked and danced. Now I wish there were something like that for university." Lillian, her roommate, laughed and said, "That's easy for me, Katie—that place is my church. The young adult group has weekly events—hikes, dances, campouts. There are a few duds, but also some great guys there, many of them not particularly religious, but like you, looking for a place that you don't have to be drunk and naked to connect."

DISCUSSION QUESTIONS

1. In what ways has patriarchy contaminated much of religious treatment of marriage?

2. Why do you think so many couples who profess not to be religious want to be married in churches?

3. Should sexual relationships have different rules and values than nonsexual relationships? Why or why not?

4. Are there necessary differences between married couples and unmarried couples who have openly lived together for the same length of time? Are there any

advantages for couples in either being married or unmarried? What are they?

5. Most people obviously consider parenting a positive part of their marriage. Is there any reason that marriage necessarily requires parenting in order to be fulfilling? Does parenting require marriage in order to be fully competent?

6. Do couples have a right to have as many children as they can support? Why or why not?

7. Do you think there is a moral imperative to retrain ourselves to be inclusive of GLBTQ persons in our discussions of sex, abandoning traditional heterosexism, or not? Why or why not?

FOR FURTHER READING

Adler, Rachel. *Engendering Judaism: An Inclusive Theology and Ethics*. Boston: Beacon, 1998.

Ali, Kecia. "Slavery and Sexual Ethics in Islam." In Bernadette J. Brooten, ed., *Beyond Slavery: Overcoming Its Religious and Sexual Legacies*, 107–23. New York: Palgrave Macmillan.

Biale, Rachel. *Women and Jewish Law: An Exploration of Women's Issues in Halakhic Sources*. New York: Schocken, 1984.

Cahill, Lisa Sowle. *Sex, Gender and Christian Ethics*. New York: Cambridge University Press, 1996.

Farley, Margaret. *Just Love: A Framework for Christian Sexual Ethics*. New York: Continuum, 2006.

Gallagher, Charles A., George A. Maloney, S.J., Mary F. Rousseau, and Paul Wilczak. *Embodied in Love: The Sacramental Spirituality of Sexual Intimacy*. New York: Crossroad, 1985.

Gudorf, Christine E. *Body, Sex and Pleasure: Reconstructing Christian Sexual Ethics*. Cleveland: Pilgrim, 1994.

Jung, Patricia Beattie, Mary E. Hunt, and Radhika Balakrishnan, eds. *Good Sex: Feminist Perspectives from the World's Religions*. New Brunswick, NJ: Rutgers University Press, 2001.

Kamitsuka, Margaret D., ed. *The Embrace of Eros: Bodies, Desires and Sexuality in Christianity*. Minneapolis: Fortress, 2010.

Maguire, Daniel C., and Larry Rasmussen. *Ethics for a Small Planet*. Albany: State University of New York Press, 1998.

Mortimer-Sandilands, Catriona, and Bruce Erickson. *Queer Ecologies: Sex, Nature, Politics, Desire*. Bloomington: Indiana University Press, 2010.

Nelson, James. *Body Theology*. Louisville: Westminster John Knox, 1992.

Simon, Caroline J. *Bringing Sex into Focus: The Quest for Sexual Integrity*. Downers Grove, IL: InterVarsity, 2012.

Spade, Dean. *Normal Life: Administrative Violence, Critical Trans Politics and the Limits of Law*. Cambridge, MA: South End, 2011.

Traina, Cristina L. H. *Erotic Attunement: Parenthood and the Ethics of Sensuality between Unequals*. Chicago: University of Chicago Press, 2011.

FILMS

Asking for It, by Sut Jhally, 2010. Media Education Foundation.

Boys to Men? by Frederick Marx, 2004. Media Education Foundation.

Dreamworlds 3, by Sut Jhally, 2007. Media Education Foundation.

Further Off the Straight and Narrow: New Gay Visibility on Television, 1998–2006, by Katherine Sender. Media Education Foundation.

The Line, by Nancy Schwartzman, 2010. Media Education Foundation.

Understanding Hookup Culture: What's Really Happening on College Campuses, by Sut Jhally, 2011. Media Education Foundation.

NOTES

1. Demographic transition is the period between the drop of the death rate and the time when population equilibrium is reached by a matching drop in the birthrate. During the demographic transition, population size can increase very rapidly. Demographic transition took well over a century in western Europe, but many developing nations have achieved demographic transition much more quickly.

2. William Stacey Johnson, "The New Testament, Empire and Homoeroticism," in *The Embrace of Eros: Bodies, Desires and Sexuality in Christianity*, ed. Margaret D. Kamitsuka (Minneapolis: Fortress Press, 2010), 53, 55.

3. *Humanae vitae* also argued that moral legitimation of contraception would make poor populations vulnerable to abuse by tempting governments to violate basic human rights in order to meet population reduction targets. Later on, in fact, accusations were made that western governments and foundations, often in collusion with governments of developing nations, were forcing contraception on the people of developing nations. There were even charges that contraception campaigns aimed at genocide, rather than at stabilizing population growth in order to facilitate economic development, as governments claimed. Many interpreted the implementation of the Chinese one-child policy of 1979 as just this type of coercion and violation of basic human rights. A number of well-publicized heinous cases of involuntary late abortions forced on women by overzealous local Chinese officials supported such views. In the decades since the 1970s when these charges reached their zenith, however, contraception has become largely accepted globally not only for individual reasons but also for developmental and environmental reasons. Consequently, much of the globe has become increasingly appreciative of the Chinese one-child policy as climate-change and air-quality data accumulate.

4. Rachel Biale, *Women and Jewish Law: An Exploration of Women's Issues in Halakhic Sources* (New York: Schocken, 1984), ch. 5.

5. For example, among the many Beguines and monastic mystics of northern Europe see the works of Mechthild of Magdeburg, Beatrice of Nazareth, and Hadewijch of Antwerp in Emilie Zum Brunn and Georgette Epiney-Burgard, *Women Mystics in Medieval Europe*, trans. Sheila Hughes (St. Paul: Paragon House, 1989).

6. Widad El Sakkakini, *First among Sufis: The Life and Thought of Rabia al-Adawiyya*, trans. Nabil Safwat (London: Octagon, 1982).

7. One needs to be very careful to say that not every experience of physical orgasm has this element of rapture. Sometimes the experience of physical release in orgasm can leave the individual depressed, in tears, deeply aware of something missing, of fortune lost. This is most common when the relationship in which the

orgasm occurred was lacking, defective in some manner, and not supportive of the capacity of love-making to enhance both partners. While physical orgasm is involuntary, this mystic aspect of orgasm is an emotional, voluntary capacity, not simply a physical one.

8. The Beguines, and to a lesser extent their male counterparts, the Beghards, were a prominent group of Christian laywomen closely associated with mysticism in northern Europe during the medieval period and later. They were persecuted by church officials who believed women belonged under supervision either in marriage or cloistered convents; their vernacular accounts of their mystical experiences were popular but often suppressed or condemned.

9. There are Sufi orders, however, in which some minority of Sufi leaders have been celibate.

10. Charles A. Gallagher, George A. Maloney, S.J., Mary F. Rousseau, and Paul Wilczak, *Embodied in Love: The Sacramental Spirituality of Sexual Intimacy* (New York: Crossroad, 1985). Although commissioned by the American Catholic bishops, nothing was done to promote the book, probably because the episcopal conference was experiencing a tidal wave of change from new conservative papal appointments.

11. See, for example, A. J. Cherlin, F. F. Furstenberg Jr., L. Chase-Lansdale, K. E. Kiernan, P. K. Robins, D. R. Morrison, and J. O. Teitler, "Longitudinal studies of effects of divorce on children in Great Britain and the United States," *Science* 252, no. 5011 (June 7, 1991): 1386–89. There was a great deal of research on this subject in the late 1980s and early 1990s, but there was so much agreement in the findings that little research has been done since.

12. There was a public outcry at the placement of the Juicy logo on the seat of girls' pants some years ago, and since then Juicy has placed the logo elsewhere. But one must ask about the very choice of this logo for women's clothing, especially young girls' clothing, and not only about its placement on the clothing.

13. Charles A. Wood, "The Doctors' Dilemma: Sin, Salvation, and the Menstrual Cycle in Medieval Thought," *Speculum* 56, no. 4 (1981): 710.

14. For a glimpse at the support for contraception and abortion to be found within religions, see Daniel C. Maguire, ed., *Sacred Rights: The Case for Contraception and Abortion in World Religions* (Oxford/New York: Oxford University Press, 2003).

15. Daniel C. Maguire and Larry L. Rasmussen, *Ethics for a Small Planet* (Albany: State University of New York Press, 1998; Christine E. Gudorf, *Body, Sex and Pleasure: Reconstructing Christian Sexual Ethics* (Cleveland: Pilgrim, 1994), ch. 2; and Susan Power Bratton, *Six Billion and More: Human Population Regulation and Christian Ethics* (Louisville: Westminster John Knox, 1992).

16. Robert Crooks and Karla Baur, *Our Sexuality*, 11th ed. (Belmont, CA: Wadsworth, 2011), 345–47.

17. Ibid., 422–23.

18. Eric Marcus, "The Psychologist—Dr. Evelyn Hooker," in *The Columbia Reader on Lesbians and Gay Men in Media, Society and Politics*, ed. Larry P. Gross and James D. Woods (New York: Columbia University Press, 1999), 169–74.

19. Reformist Muslim scholars are publishing variants on these arguments, which are common among Christians and non-Orthodox Jews. Reformist Muslim scholars point out that many Muslim-majority nations have adopted a great deal of civil law based on *shari'a*, the divine law found in the Qur'an. Proposed changes to legislation regarding women is often, most notably in Saudi Arabia, rejected as counter to *shari'a*, though the reformers point to the areas in which *shari'a* law has not been implemented in civil legislation. Why should some of *shari'a* be completely left out of civil law and other parts absolutely unchangeable in civil law? In Islam generally there is much broader agreement on the inerrancy and eternal truth of Qur'an than exists in Christianity regarding the Bible, and greater resistance to liberal interpretation. Arguments by a minority of Muslim scholars that verses giving men management of women in the Qur'an should be treated like the verses allowing slavery, which was later renounced by the Muslim *umma*, are generally rejected.

20. Perhaps the best resource for examining justice in sexual relationships is Margaret A. Farley, *Just Love: A Framework for Christian Sexual Ethics* (New York and London: Continuum, 2006).

21. Genesis 1:27, *The Bible: New Revised Standard Version* (Glasgow/London/New York: Collins, 1989).

22. Admittedly, this is a very theist and western approach to Buddhism—Buddhists would not agree that dissolution of the self and union with the divine are the same thing, but in terms of the loss of self-consciousness—a big concern in the West—they are very similar.

23. I am especially indebted to colleagues Whitney Bauman and Lesley Northup, as well as to a variety of recent graduate students, for these arguments against proportionality between sexual intimacy and emotional intimacy as normative.

24. Many cultures have used this "proportional" standard. For example, in the United States in the 1950s, hand-holding accompanied initial exchanges of personal information, kissing accompanied the beginnings of commitment that could be discontinued at any time, petting signaled a stronger commitment, and intercourse was reserved for engagement or marriage. While there is some evidence, especially among teens, that fellatio is used as a way of postponing acquiescence to male demands for intercourse, the custom of proportional stages is largely gone.

25. Mahavīra in *Uttarādhyayana Sūtra* 29:17–18.

CHAPTER 6

RELIGIONS ON MAKING AND KEEPING FAMILIES

In every age and in every culture, there have been a variety of family structures. One basic reason for this is that humans did not, and still do not, control death, neither accidental death nor death from disease. We often tend to think that it is modern divorce that has produced variety in family structures, but this is not at all true. Some parents have always died, leaving orphan children. There have always been women who died in childbirth, and men in war; disease and work accidents took far higher tolls in the past than today. Sometimes the widow/er has raised children alone without remarrying. But the surviving spouse often remarried, creating a new or blended family. Often a new spouse brought his or her previous children into the new home. Or a maiden or widowed aunt would move in to raise the children. Aunts or uncles, grandparents or family friends have also taken orphans into their own homes and raised them as their own.

Religions have not had terribly much to say about families. They typically enjoined children to respect and obey parents, though many implicitly or explicitly placed limits on that obedience (both Buddha and Jesus, for example, left their homes and families to pursue an individual path). Religions largely took for granted that families constituted the major circle in which lives were lived. For many local religions, the family itself was a major focus of religions—the family consisting of the ancestors, the living, and those yet to be born. On the other hand, there were recognitions in some religions that there were loyalties that superseded that to family. A major aim for Mohammed was to make the Muslim community, the *umma*, rather than familial tribe, the source of identity and focus of loyalty. Jesus spoke often of bringing disruption to families and of the need to leave behind family in order to serve the kingdom of God that was breaking into the world. For Buddha, the path to *nirvana* lay outside family, in the community of the monastic *sangha*.

Because religions have been dependent upon families—for after all, it is families who produce children and teach them the stories, prayers, and rituals of religion—even those religions that grew out of messages that relativized families (Islam, Christianity, Buddhism) have not made reservations about families central to their teachings. Most have responded negatively to the late-modern changes in families, perhaps seeing their own dependence upon families as jeopardized by changes taking place in families. In this chapter we will begin with social analysis concerning shifts that have affected families over the last few centuries, and the role religion has played in some of those shifts, before moving on to look at religious themes that might be relevant to the current situation and developing trends within it.

Framing the Issues

Today some of the reasons for variety in family structures are different than in the past (divorce and serial marriage, drug or alcohol addiction, car accidents, plane crashes, terrorism), but the resulting patterns are not so different. There are, of course, changes in the incidence of different patterns. For example, until the last century or so families were large, with a great range in age between oldest and youngest child in the family. It was not uncommon for younger siblings to be orphaned and then raised by older married siblings. While it still does happen today that older siblings take formal guardianship of younger ones, this is rarer, and more often in our society it is a very young adult taking formal responsibility for a teen sibling not far from legal adulthood, or a stepbrother or -sister from an earlier marriage taking on the child of a parent's later marriage.

Changes in Family Structure

One significant change today is that in developed nations we have many children raised "by the system" than ever before. Many of those children are placed in good, loving, and permanent homes. But large numbers of children in the United States, and in many developed nations, are shuffled from one foster home to another, quickly losing any hope of security.[1] Worse yet, in many developing nations, there are thousands of "street children" who have either been abandoned to the streets by their families or else run from abusive homes or orphanages.[2] The life of these children is brutal and often short. This phenomenon is not new, of course; it has not significantly changed since Dickens acquainted many with the lives of mid-nineteenth-century street children in his portrait of Oliver Twist,[3] and the pattern long preexisted Dickens.

Families affected by disease. At the same time, the HIV/AIDS pandemic has left hundreds of thousands of children to be raised by grandparents in both the developed and developing world. Simultaneously, millions of otherwise healthy elderly are being struck down with Alzheimer's or other forms of dementia, sometimes of the early-onset type that may require decades of physically and emotionally exhaustive care on the part of family members. In many such cases where the elderly parent/grandparent can no longer live alone, a nuclear household becomes an extended family household for a time.

Late-modern shift from extended to nuclear households. The predominant form of family was, until late modernity, the extended family. In some cultures the extended family shared a single household, or a single compound, and in some they did not. In many tribal cultures there was a collective men's house in the village where young and unmarried men lived and from which husbands went back and forth to their marital home for meals, sex, and interaction with children.[4] Male society and ritual society usually centered around this shared space.

Fig. 6.1. Traditional extended families lived in the same house or in nearby homes, as depicted in this antique stereoptical photograph from the 1900s.

Some extended families were matrilineal; most were patrilineal. Some were matrilocal; most were patrilocal. In the matrilocal pattern, men married outside their village or clan (exogamy), and in matrilineal systems, ancestry and property descended through the female line (children inherited from maternal uncles, not fathers). Most cultures were the reverse, both patrilocal and patrilineal. Even when different generations of the family did not live in the same house, or when not even the nuclear family all lived together, it was expected that all able-bodied members of the family would take care of needy elderly members, whether these were their parents, aunts or uncles, or family orphans, often as distant as second or third cousins. Also, extended families were often responsible for contributing to dowries or bride prices (money, land, a cow, cloth, a pig, a radio) so that siblings and nieces and nephews could marry. Similarly, members of extended families often benefited individually when a member of the extended family obtained a large dowry or bride price from a wealthy family.[5]

Development of the Nuclear Family

In modernity, especially in the West, the nuclear family has replaced the extended family as the effective family unit. The reasons for this are many, some based in material life and some in ideology. At the ideological level, the Enlightenment spread ideas of the rights of man (much later interpreted as including women), and encouraged individualism, which militated against the authority of patriarchs over adult sons. The Enlightenment "man" was stripped of all that was peculiar to him, including family history and relations, and understood only in terms of what was universal among human citizens. Such an understanding, of course, took many decades to replace older understandings of humans as embedded in extended families but eventually served to relativize traditional responsibilities to extended families.

Dropping death rates and industrialization. At the material level, dropping death rates coincided with industrialization in modernity. Agricultural areas could no longer absorb all the workers who were born and survived within them, and new factories in the cities attracted large numbers of people from rural areas. As most of these laborers migrating to urban areas were young (some single men and some families), this mobility disrupted extended family households.

Colonization as family disrupter. During the early modern period, western nations (Spain, Portugal, England, France, and later Germany) extended their economic and political control over much of the earth's South in colonialism. Colonialism transported huge numbers of young European men—soldiers, sailors, merchants, administrators, and fortune-seekers—to distant parts of the world, for years at a time, even permanently. At the same time, many European families—mostly young—moved to settler colonies in North America, South and Central America, North, East, and South Africa, and Southeast Asia to set up homesteads, businesses, and religious communities. Within these colonial territories colonists attempted not only to reproduce European social patterns in their own colonial communities, but also to impose them on natives in the interests of introducing them to "civilization." The patriarchal nuclear family was one part of "civilization" that was spread by colonialism and later supported by industrialization in the colonies and former colonies.

Effects of demographic transition. The rural-to-urban mobility of industrialization and the international mobility of colonialism continued to grow throughout the modern period. As the *demographic transition* (a drop in the death rate before birthrates begin

to drop from contraception) began in the late-eighteenth-century West and gradually spread, family size increased, often at the same time that mobility increased. It became less and less possible for extended families to live near each other, much less together in a single compound or home. More often than not, one of the children would remain close to aging parents (either by chance or design) to care for them, or the parents would be regularly moved from the location of one child to another, a move that often involved shifting not only to other cities, but states. Due to the virtual ubiquity of social security systems for the elderly and better health among the aged over the last decades in the developed world,[6] elderly parents are now often independent physically and financially for many years. Thus adult children today, accustomed to the independence of retired parents, often find their parents' need for personal care or financial help at the end of life as not only a shock, but often as an imposition.

Move to the suburbs after World War II. The massive population shift to the U.S. suburbs in the years following World War II was yet a later step in the disruption of the extended family. Returning soldiers and sailors and their families made use of new government-sponsored mortgage loan programs to move their nuclear families from traditional ethnic areas in the cities to new suburbs, which were connected to the cities by a new system of highways.[7] The inner cities were, for the next three to four decades, made up of aging parents of suburbanites, new immigrants to the United States, and an urban underclass of poor, often minority, persons.

Changes in family size. So by late modernity, while there continued to be a great deal of variety in family structure, the central pattern was no longer extended family, but nuclear family. That nuclear family became smaller and smaller over time, all over the world, as we shall see.

At the same time, since at least the 1980s in the United States, the makeup of the nuclear family has itself become much more varied. Census records show that the "traditional" nuclear family, made up of husband and wife and their children (often his, hers, and theirs), today makes up only about a quarter of families in the United States.[8] There is no longer any clear majority household pattern. Almost equally as common are families composed of one parent and children, or one or two young adults with no children; not far behind is one nonparent relative (grandparent, aunt, older sibling) and children, two seniors married or unmarried, or two adult relatives of different generations (e.g., grandmother and mother), sometimes with children and sometimes not. In many large cities in the United States, the average number of household members is less than two, due to both large numbers of persons who live alone, and increasing numbers of second and third homes belonging to persons whose main residence is elsewhere.

The Changed Function of Family

It is impossible to describe all the many functions of family in the multitude of kinship systems that have existed in our world. Limiting our view to the West, there have been some major changes during modernity in the principal functions of the family. Probably the most important change is that the family today in the West is rarely ever the location of production.[9] Until industrialization created the factory system, farmers were not the only people working out of their homes. Blacksmiths, jewelers, millers, printers, makers of ale or beer and wine, tailors, hatmakers, and dressmakers/tailors all produced out of

home workshops. All members of the family worked in this shop, often along with hired laborers or apprentices. This pattern of work in the home was even true for retailers—most storeowners, whether in rural towns or large cities, lived above or behind their stores.

Today neither production nor retail sales are located in the home in developed nations. Even among American family farmers, wives or older children still living at home often hold down jobs outside the home, or the family farm gives way to agribusiness, in which none of the workers own the farm, but are only hired labor for a company. While some professionals and semiprofessionals in the West work from their homes through the Internet, this "production" is individual, not involving other members of the family, and usually virtual, not material.

Though the developing world does still contain a great deal of home production of material goods, the work is increasingly farmed out piecework from larger factories, involves unskilled work, and is very poorly paid. All over the world, factories have become the norm for production, and the home a major center of consumption. We have only to glance at the media to understand that virtually all advertisements urging consumption of yet another product are aimed at the home: everything from widescreen HD or 3D TVs to breakfast food to cleaning products. The only work tools that are mass advertised are those used for decorative hobbies, such as pretty lawns and flower gardens, or paint for repainting the family home.

Family effects of the shift in production. The shift from home production to factory production had profound implications for the family, regardless of its shape. It removed men from the home and from contact with children for most of the day (and sometimes mothers as well). This shift in the location of production not only removed children from the work they had done on the farm or around the family shop. It also ensured that those children who did work in factories were no longer under the protective supervision of parents, that they worked the same ten- to fourteen-hour workday as adults, and often, because they were the lowest-paid and most dispensable workers, they were given the most dangerous and onerous work.[10] Perhaps most important of all, the removal of production from the home weakened the authority of parents, who no longer were involved in the occupational training of their children and no longer had occupations/businesses to leave to their children.

Effects on women. Though some women have worked in factories from the beginning of factories—in the nineteenth and early twentieth centuries most often only until they married—the shift of production from home to factory removed most women from production. The spinning, weaving, dressmaking, canning, preserving, candle- and soap-making that they had done at home were all now removed to factories, whose products must be bought with currency. Women in general went from being producers—alongside men in the home—to consumers. Instead of adding to family wealth, wives increasingly became depicted as a drain on a man's resources. With no production of their own to exchange for money, women became dependent on men to pay for all personal and household expenses.[11]

While sacred religious texts across many traditions had lauded women whose productive and managerial talents as housewives added to their family's resources and comfort,[12] the modern function of women within the family, especially middle- and upper-class families, became that of consumer/decoration.

They were to be a credit to the earning power of their husbands by adorning their bodies and homes as attractively as possible. This was one of the trends that contributed to ending earlier Calvinist Christian support for capitalism that Max Weber described.[13] This new decorative function found for women when they were deprived of their former role of producers worked against the simple lifestyles that had allowed earlier Calvinists to save and invest in expanding their businesses. Calvinist men still worked hard, but their work served more and more to support the attractiveness—even ostentation—of wife and home.

Contemporary Functions of Family

The functions left to the family in developed nations today revolve around personal relationships. The family is still the primary institution for protecting the welfare of children and overseeing their general training for adult responsibilities. Yet no longer is the family able to supervise children's training for work in any serious way. Much of the power to enforce discipline that the family had when the family home was the site of production is now lost. There is no longer a home "factory" that can be bequeathed—or not—to children, and there is no longer a family "apprenticeship" responsible for training children in a profession that parents could threaten to withdraw to make rebellious children behave. Today the only relationships that tie families together are those of affection. If there is no affection, there is no tie.

Parents and children are no longer co-workers in any regular way. Each has their own set of companions, interests, and occupations outside the family home. The ties of affection binding family members together come under more and more pressure from these outside associations today. Because of this, families are more fragile. Many people spend more time, and have more in common, with friends or coworkers than with their families.

Effect of social security systems for the elderly. In the developed world, the institution of social security systems for the aged have also introduced significant changes into families. On the one hand, the elderly in nations with such systems are no longer destitute, totally dependent on their adult children for care and maintenance. This is a tremendous advance in recognizing the dignity of the elderly. It is one factor that has allowed some grandparents to raise children who have been effectively orphaned by the death, addiction, or abandonment of parents. On the other hand, many, perhaps most, grandparents are no longer in the home or near enough to assist in the rearing of children. No longer dependent upon children for their support, many elderly feel no obligation to assist adult children. They have moved to some sunny clime, go south each winter, or live in complexes that ban children. The expectation that retired parents are independent and self-sufficient has also eroded a sense of responsibility for our elders in much of our population, as well as made the elderly a popular target of scams and fraud by both relatives and strangers.

Fertility Decreases

In the shift of families from rural agriculture to urban settings, fertility drops with the aid of modern contraception. In the new urban settings (in which families do not produce their own food, children become removed from production altogether, and education becomes expensive and extended over many additional years), children became much more expensive. More and more couples limit the number of their children, aided by successive improvements in the effectiveness of contraception. Beginning with contraceptive practices as crude as *coitus interruptus* (withdrawal), through successive improvements in condoms, to the more scientific methods of oral contraceptives, diaphragms, IUDs, and injectables, family sizes have decreased, beginning in Western Europe in the late eighteenth century.

While the one-child policy introduced in China in 1979 has received the lion's share of attention regarding the sudden and precipitous drop in fertility, many other nations over the last few decades have achieved fertility rates (the average number of children born to a woman in a society) that are as low or lower than China's. Most nations of western Europe have fertility rates of 1.4–1.8 children per woman and are facing fast-declining populations. For over a decade following the collapse of the Soviet Union in 1991, Russia and most of the former Soviet states and satellites had average fertility rates of around 1.1, along with drastic drops in life expectancy, both of which have now improved some. Japan, with a longstanding fertility rate of under 1.5 children per woman, has the oldest population in the world, and the sharpest decreases in population size. The United States, though it too has an aging population, has largely managed to remain at or slightly above the replacement fertility rate of 2.1 children per woman, due almost exclusively to immigration.[14] (However, currently, as the chart on page 162 indicates, the U.S. fertility rate has dipped slightly below replacement as a result of the economic recession that began in 2007.)

Though the demographic transition began much earlier in the West than in other parts of the world, the spread of new, more effective means of contraception beginning in the 1960s caused birthrates to drop precipitously in the developing world, a drop that was as much as four to five times faster than had been seen in the West. The world fertility rate, after rising rapidly during the modern period as a whole, has in the last half century dropped sharply. In most of the world, with the great exception being some parts of Africa, the fertility rate has dropped in the last fifty years from well over six children per woman to a

world average of 2.47 children per woman, and is still dropping. For present fertility rates around the world, see the chart below.

The political and economic implications of this declining fertility are beyond the scope of our discussion here. The trend is uneven; a number of African and Middle Eastern nations, though reflecting the generally lowered trend, are still at rates of five to six children per woman. The lowered rates globally are the best news for the survival of

HIGHEST AND LOWEST FERTILITY RATES IN THE WORLD			
Lower Range		**Higher Range**	
Singapore	.78	Niger	7.52
Hong Kong	1.09	Uganda	6.65
South Korea	1.23	Somalia	6.26
Czech Republic	1.27	Mali	6.35
Poland	1.38	Burundi	6.10
Japan	1.39	Ethiopia	5.97
Italy	1.40	Afghanistan	5.64
Germany	1.41	Republic of Congo	5.59
China	1.55	Angola	5.54
Canada	1.59	Nigeria	5.38
United Kingdom	1.91	Malawi	5.35
Tunisia	2.02	Gaza Strip	4.97
United States	2.06	Chad	4.93
France	2.08	Senegal	4.69
Libya	2.09	Central African Republic	4.57
Turkey	2.13	Yemen	4.45
Indonesia	2.23	Mauritania	4.22
South Africa	2.28	Sudan	4.17
Argentina	2.29	Tanzania	4.02
India	2.58	Kenya	3.98
Egypt	2.94	Ivory Coast	3.82
Pakistan	3.07	Data from the 2012 figures posted by the U.S. CIA at https://www.cia.gov/library/publications/the-world-factbook/fields/2127.html.	

Fig. 6.2. Highest and lowest fertility rates in the world, 2012.

the biosphere that we have. But the sociological implications for families in this decline in fertility are immense.

Family impacts of decreasing fertility. Smaller family size at the replacement level (2.1) or lower means that the majority of children are only-children; few will have more than one sibling. Increasing numbers of children have no siblings, no aunts or uncles, and no cousins. In many nuclear families, there is thus no extended family safety net should a family member lose a job, a home, health, or the life of a parent. This also means that for a child, should his or her own family be abusive or dysfunctional, there is no other family refuge. There is not even another family model to use in relativizing one's own negative experience of family—which is a difficult task even when one has a number of healthier models to imitate.

This change in fertility levels has not only moved many nations beyond the extended family as a living unit and the focus of identity, but if continued would extinguish national communities altogether. This shift, however, is not necessarily final. We may, and should, attempt to stabilize population size at or near the replacement level where this is possible. Though the best solution ecologically is to allow immigration flows from the areas with high fertility to those with low fertility, which more or less continues to occur in the United States, culturally homogenous nations with low fertility such as those of Western Europe and Japan are resistant to inflows of Africans, Asians, and other cultural strangers. But the bottom line is that global population growth is not feasible for the many different ecological reasons explicated in earlier chapters. Fertility declines are a necessity; nations and families need to learn to better manage the impact of fertility declines, but supporting population growth above replacement level is not responsible.

Religious Treatment Concerning Making and Keeping Family

The phenomenon of adoption has been viewed very differently within religions.

Orphans in the Christian Roman Empire. The Romans felt strongly that abandonment of unwanted infants was morally superior to infanticide, which had been practiced by many of the peoples that they conquered while expanding their empire. Abandonment avoided direct killing by parents and left open the possibility that children would be rescued and reared. In early Christianity, the bulk of abandoned children who survived became servants in the families that took them up, though a significant percentage of abandoned children were not intended to, and did not, survive abandonment.[15] Those who survived and were adopted as servants were often not much more than slaves of the adopting family, their service being the reason for adopting them. Yet Roman and later Christian literature was full of stories of abandoned children later found by and restored to their wealthy and grieving families from whom they had been torn by mistake, fraud, or maliciousness.[16] There were, of course, some few children who were adopted by childless couples who later inherited status and wealth from adoptive parents. Tales of both restoration to lost families and adoptees fortunate in their new homes served the purpose of legitimating the system of abandonment and enslavement of adoptees by maintaining the hopes of the discarded children who survived abandonment and by providing the public a happier image of the practice than reality suggested.

Orphans in Christian monasteries and convents. In a similar way, the monasteries and convents of late Roman and medieval Europe accepted children, a process known as "donation," from families who had often lost a parent or had too many children to feed or too many children to provide with livings or dowries.[17] As in the Roman Empire, it was not only the poor who "donated" or abandoned children, but also the rich, those who were well able to feed their children but did not want to divide their estates among multiple sons, or could not provide suitable dowries for multiple daughters. Thus the communities of monks and nuns became families for these children, some of whom were allowed the choice of leaving or taking vows upon reaching majority, and some of whom were denied the option of leaving. During the late Renaissance, when death rates for infants and children first began to fall in the demographic transition, many monasteries and convents refused to accept children any longer for fear of being inundated with the excess children of all classes.

Orphans in Shaker communities. Many different patterns evolved to deal with the contingencies of human mortality. Sometimes religions played a large part in those patterns, and sometimes not. One reason the Shaker community, which embraced celibacy for all, lasted two hundred years in the United States, is that towns and counties in the eighteenth and nineteenth centuries often placed orphaned children with the Shakers, who raised them in community, taught them useful trades, and upon their reaching their majority gave the orphans the choice of whether to remain or to leave the community.[18] Many remained, as the Shaker community had become their family.

Family in Islam

Adoption. If among Christians the ideal for orphaned children was adoption into a new family as a member of that family (and until modernity no one looked too closely to see if the new member was truly treated as family), the situation was different in Islam.

Fig. 6.3. These children became a family through adoption.

Mohammed had himself been orphaned at an early age[19] and was taken in by relatives as was common in tribal societies. Orphans (as well as widows) were a persistent problem for Mohammed and his successors as Islam expanded in the vacuum left by the crumbling Byzantine Empire. More or less constant warfare created many widows and orphans. Both Qur'an and *hadith* made clear that orphans were to be well treated.[20] Specifically, they and their property were not to be absorbed into the family of their guardian. They were to be cared for, the name and lineage of their biological family retained, and their property protected and restored to them upon their majority. Thus for Muslims, adoption as it was understood in Christianity was regarded as dangerous to the child, because it robbed him or her of property and lineage, but especially of his or her essential identity.

In the "open adoption" option increasingly practiced within the United States today,[21] we see increasing concern for a perspective similar to that of traditional Islam. Some of the reasons for this shift of perspective in the United States are that we see more adoption of older children, who remember their original family and may still have relationships with members of that family. Also over the last decades we have seen more adoption of children of racial, ethnic, and religious origins different from that of the adoptive parents. That "differentness" cannot simply be ignored, but demands attention within the family, and by the family in dealing with others. More and more the adopted child is seen, not as a blank tablet, but rather as coming into the new family with some enduring strings—a relationship to a birth mother, or members of extended family who might have some visitation rights, another culture that needs to be learned and nurtured in the new family, or

a family heritage that needs to be respected (such as a birth parent killed in military service in Iraq or Afghanistan).

Polygamous families. Islam is not the only religious culture that has been polygynous, meaning that men were allowed to have more than one wife (as opposed to polyandry—a woman having more than one husband). But Islam is the predominant religion with which it is associated today. Polygyny increases population quickly, which was for most of human history desirable, while polyandry made for very slow growth and was much rarer around the world. Many western religions renounced polygyny; for example, the Church of Jesus Christ of Latter-day Saints (Mormons) officially renounced new polygynous marriages in 1890. European Jews renounced polygyny in the eleventh century; although that five-hundred-year ban has now run out, polygyny is virtually unknown among Jews of European descent. Sephardic/Mizrahi Jews who live in nations, mostly Muslim, where polygyny is legal do sometimes practice it.

Hindus in India are forbidden polygyny, though Muslims are allowed it. Christians are forbidden multiple spouses and have been since the time of Christ. It has been a difficult issue for Christian missionaries, especially those working in Africa, for the absolute ban on polygyny was a terrible obstacle to converting polygynous households: husbands were made to cast off all but one wife, regardless of wives' age or ability to support themselves.

Forty-nine nations of the world recognize polygyny as legal. Most of them are either in Africa, where polygyny has been both religiously legitimated and historically expected of chiefs/kings and the wealthy, and/or in nations with large Muslim populations. Though a very few Muslim-majority nations

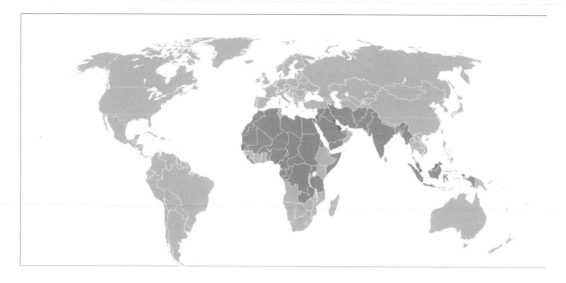

Fig. 6.4. World map showing where polygyny is legal, as indicated by darker shaded areas.

have banned polygyny (only Tunisia, Turkey, Bosnia, and Azerbaijan), the majority allow it, though usually with some attempts to regulate it in line with the Qur'anic requirements that a man can have no more than four wives, and that he must treat them equally, and sometimes a requirement for the permission of the first wife. While in some parts of Africa co-wives may live together with their husband, in Muslim communities it is more common for wives to have their own homes and live separate lives.

Because polygyny is expensive for a man, the number of polygynous families in Islam is and has always been relatively low (though much higher in rich nations like Kuwait than poor nations like Egypt). It has been largely associated with rural village life and not with urban life. In general, it is more often found in places where patriarchy is still strong and women are not well educated, though there are exceptions. Last year an academic friend of mine researching polygynous families in Indonesia spoke to the second wife of a

businessman. The second wife explained that she had proposed the marriage to him when she was thirty, and he and his first wife were some years older, with three children. She was a lecturer (professor) at a national university and found it increasingly uncomfortable to be single in a nation that expects all to marry. She had more and more social occasions where one was expected to bring a spouse, and felt that she was losing out on promotions and status in her job from her singleness. She did not want children, which an Indonesian man who did not have another wife would want, and she made a fine salary and so would not be an expense for him. For her, becoming a second wife seemed the most convenient and efficient solution to her problems. While this seems to westerners to be distressingly dry and void of love and romance, it is precisely the kind of practical grounds on which most (first) marriages were based everywhere before the late-modern period.

Thus alternative models of family have been common in history and are not new today. The varieties of family both now and in the past are legion.

Religious Communities as Family

Historically, many religious communities have presented themselves as families and tried to (re)create family ties between members. There have been varied explanations for such attempts.

Christianity. For example, early Christianity was considered very subversive in the Roman Empire. Its very baptismal formula (Gal. 3:28 ESV: "There is neither Jew nor Greek, there is neither slave nor free, there is neither male nor female, for you are all one in Christ Jesus") signified its rejection of the hierarchy that characterized the Roman household code, and its preference for egalitarian community. (The Roman household code ordered wives, children, servants, and slaves to obey their husbands/fathers/masters.) Because becoming a Christian for these first few centuries was understood as subversive and periodically put one in danger of persecution, conversion frequently cost the convert his or her family and entire social circle. Thus the church offered itself as brothers and sisters to the convert, understanding the convert as part of a community under the headship of God the Father and united with Jesus Christ as Brother (and in later centuries secure in the love of Mother Mary). Initiation into this new family took place at baptism, which was by immersion in water. The new initiate emerged from the waters of baptism as a child emerges from the amniotic waters of birth and received a new name, just as a newborn is named by its new family.

Local and new religions. Among some African tribes, the group of male age-mates who undergo the extensive and often harrowing ritual initiation into adulthood together are understood to constitute a kind of family. Through the extended preparation for initiation and the often dangerous and anxiety-ridden tests that are a part of initiation, these age-mates become brothers who are often closer, more trusted, and more relied on than members of their natal families for the rest of their lives.

Many cultures around the world include what is called fictive kinship: close social ties that resemble those of kin but between persons unrelated by blood or marriage. The *compadrazgo* system of patron/godparents in Latin America is one such example. *Compadrazgo* is an adaptation of pre-Christian customs to the baptismal ritual of Christianity in which an unrelated person, usually one of the most respected and prosperous members of the local community known to the parents, is asked to be godparent to a newborn in the baptism ceremony. It is an honor to be asked to be godparent, but the honor comes with serious responsibilities. The responsibilities of the godparent are to assist the child, providing both material and spiritual help when necessary.[22] These godparents often perform such functions as contributing to educational costs, giving help in obtaining a job, and making a large gift at the time the godchild marries.

There are numerous examples of fictive kin from Asia and Africa also.[23] There is a large literature on fictive kinship in African American communities, which seems to have roots in both Africa and in the hardships suffered by Africans in the Americas, first as slaves and later as freed people subject to severe discrimination.[24] Fictive kin serve a variety of functions, from providing safety networks for children and access to necessities in crises to allowing relationships between groups that would otherwise be forbidden. For example, in East Nepal, fictive kinship allows unrelated persons from superior and inferior castes to maintain relationships.[25]

It is no accident that members of monastic orders across religions call each other and are called by outsiders "brother" and "sister." Superiors are often called some version of "mother" or "father" to denote that their role is one of protective care for the "sisters" or "brothers." Today one of the most publicized New Religious Movements (NRMs) in the United States calls itself the Family [of Love—formerly the Children of God], and teaches familial relationships within the community.[26]

Thus religious cultures have long recognized that family ties are not limited to biological families. Perhaps never in human history has this awareness been more necessary than today, when biological families are under so many pressures. In addition to the pressures that arise from mobility and the loss of the family home as the center of production, occupational training, and employment, there is also a relatively new demographic pressure that has developed over the last generation or two.

New Ethical Questions on Making and Keeping Family

Today around the world, in both developing and developed nations, the changes outlined above, along with women's entry into wage labor, are causing big changes in family patterns. In different parts of the world, for a variety of reasons, more and more people are choosing not to marry, to marry but not have children, or to have children without marrying. Thus in much of the world as mentioned above, fertility rates are dropping. Marriage rates are also dropping and illegitimacy rates are rising, sometimes more among the poor,

and sometimes more among the comfortably-to-do. In Western Europe and parts of the United States, increasing numbers of couples are deciding not to have children. In countries such as Germany, one in five couples have deliberately chosen over the last half century to have no children.[27] Especially among the more educated in the United States, it can no longer be taken for granted that even couples who do marry desire to be parents.

The Work and Marriage Link

While there have always been men who did not marry, those numbers appear to be rising, though not nearly so steeply as the numbers of women refusing to marry in some parts of the world. For example, among well-educated working women in the United States, especially minority women, the pool of educated men in their respective groups is much smaller than the supply of women, indicating that many must either stay single or "marry down." Among U.S. cohabitors, studies show that among both black and white couples, transition to marriage depends upon the employment success of males but not females. Many men and women are uncomfortable when wives are better educated, especially when those wives out-earn their husbands.[28] Among the few marriages that do take place in these circumstances (women better educated with higher salaries), divorce rates are high.

Linking education and work. Poor populations generally have lower marriage rates (and higher cohabitation rates) than nonpoor populations. Thus up through the 1950s, black marriage rates in the U.S. had always trailed white marriage rates by a few degrees. But since the 1960s, though marriage rates have dropped for both whites and blacks, a huge gap has opened between white (53.5 percent) and black (30.6 percent) marriage rates, with

Hispanics (50.5 percent) only slightly below the white marriage rate. One significant factor in this gap is lower educational achievement for black males over both black females and whites of both sexes; the black male rate of high school graduation is only 2 percent lower than that of Hispanic males. (There is a question as to whether many Hispanics, first- and second-generation immigrants, will adopt the lower rate of marriage as time goes on, just as their fertility rates drop each generation.) But there are a number of other factors, including higher rates of death, addiction, and incarceration rates for black males over all other groups, and significantly higher unemployment rates among black males—especially young black males—than among all other groups.[29]

If we want people to be able to marry, then we need to look at these factors that seem to impede marriage. One interpretation might be that we need to induce more men, especially minority men, to complete their educations so that they can find steady and adequate employment and stay out of crime and jails. Another might be that we need to break down the racial barriers that prevent well-educated successful minority women from marrying into other racial groups. Yet another might be that we should not assume that people who are not marrying at the rates we were accustomed to in the past are prevented from marrying. Perhaps marriage simply does not appeal to them.

It is clear from data on various class and race groups in the United States and elsewhere that marriage is not equally attractive to all groups. We know that in many groups, marriage depends upon adequate male employment that is lacking. But we need further research to determine why people for whom male employment (and prior education)

is not a problem are still not marrying. Is it because they do not want domestic partners, or because they do not want the children that marriage is often thought to entail, or because they do not want the roles that are pressed on those who marry? It is clear among middle-class black single women that the majority do want to marry and have children, though some have reconciled themselves to the unlikelihood of that. Our ethical discussions about social policy should take these issues into account. Religious language and concepts need to be modified so as to be able to speak to these people who either do not desire, or cannot find, traditional family partners.

Women's New Demands around Marriage

In nations with significantly higher proportions of men than women (such as China and India), women are beginning to realize that the small supply of women relative to the supply of men wanting wives allows them to demand more—sometimes a working toilet among the rural poor of India,[30] or joint ownership of the home in China[31]—before agreeing to marry. Many millions of Chinese and Indian men will be unable to find spouses due to the use of sex-selective abortion in these nations over the last three to four decades. Though one may sympathize with some of the causes of son preference in these nations, such as the exorbitant cost of dowries needed to marry off daughters in India, or the need to have sons to conduct the ancestor rites for parents and other ancestors in China, sex-selective abortion clearly not only creates severe strains in a society, but also risks moral callousness in the society toward the destruction of (potential) human life.

Declining marriages rates in some parts of the world are not primarily due to an insufficient supply of brides, but more often to an increasing number of women no longer desiring to be brides. Many young women in wealthy Japan report that they find the dominant model of marriage oppressive and refuse to choose it. For many well-educated Japanese women, social custom around marriage forces them to choose between using their education in careers, or marrying and retiring to become mother, homemaker, and educational supervisor of a child expected to succeed. Increasing numbers reject this model of marriage for women as stultifying and choose careers instead.[32]

Young women in the developing world, such as those who work in Mexican *maquiladoras*, or other export platforms around the world, as well as more and more women in ordinary work situations, are also increasingly rejecting marriage because the marriage ideal is not realizable in their situation. Many fewer men are needed in agriculture everywhere due to mechanization. Yet many factories, especially in developing nations, prefer to hire women over men (for reasons of lower pay, smaller more dexterous hands, greater docility, higher reliability—usually related to less alcoholism—and less likelihood of unionizing). The women workers then complain that too many of the men in their communities do not have jobs and need to be supported by their wives but still expect the wives to keep house, cook, and raise the children for them. Moreover, because the men are without work, the women say, they are too involved in alcohol, gambling, and crime. Alcohol also raises the likelihood of domestic violence against women. Given this situation, the women argue, it does not make sense to marry. They take men as occasional lovers and raise their children either by themselves or with mothers, sisters, and friends. Thus marriage rates have gone down and illegitimacy rates have gone up in poor populations all over the world where women have more employment success than men. This pattern is only expected to increase where women's educational success outstrips men's—an educational pattern that is becoming disturbingly global.

There are great dangers in these varied patterns of both men and women, depending on the local situation, remaining outside traditional forms of family community, without necessarily having developed alternative forms of community.

Voluntary Families

We must look to "voluntary" families to replace the lost functions of extended families. In fact, this is happening all around us, of necessity. Family members far removed from their relatives are more and more often bestowing on close friends healthcare power of attorney in case they become incapacitated, or naming close friends as the guardians of their children in case of their deaths. The groups that gather around Christmas, Passover, or Eid-ul-Fitr dinner tables are more and more often composed of a mixture of friends and family, or only friends. There are a variety of reasons for this. One's family of origin may live thousands of miles away, may not approve of one's spouse/partner, or simply be uninterested in maintaining a relationship. For many GLBTQ (gay, lesbian, bisexual, transgender, and queer) persons, expulsion or estrangement from the family of origin has forced the creation of alternative family. Some only-children by middle age have no families of origin. And this will more and more often be the case: that the death of one's parents, only-children themselves, means the end of one's family unless one had produced children oneself.

Fig. 6.5. More and more people are assembling groups of close friends to fill the void left by shrinking, distant, or estranged families.

The amount of choice offered individuals today in forging personal identity also often makes families of origin much more difficult to navigate. The microchip engineer who lives in San Francisco and travels to Asia twice a month may have very little in common with a father with a grade school education who hangs wallboard and a mother who cooks in the school cafeteria in Alabama, or a brother who is a police officer in Atlanta. There may be love, but the extent of differences may strain that love. If the microchip engineer in San Francisco married a Korean and became a Buddhist, he may have even greater difficulties within his natal Southern Baptist family.

While, however, our families of origin may not be enough, we should be very wary of replacing them with voluntary alternative families. Supplementing them is wise; replacing them—unless absolutely necessary, which is sometimes the case—runs the risk of still ending up with less family than one needs.

Ethics and Voluntary Families

Many might respond, "How is this a question of ethics? It is a lifestyle issue!" This comment reflects a common understanding that ethics and morality are about law, about an issue that is already governed by law, or should be governed by law. But as the philosopher Zygmunt Bauman wrote in his *Postmodern Ethics*:

"Saints are saints because they did not hide behind the Law's broad shoulders."[33] Neither should we. Contrary to the common wisdom, everything that is legal—allowed under civil or religious law—is not moral. There are certainly *adiaphora*—things that are neither required or forbidden, but neutral, or morally indifferent. But this is a much smaller category than most people think. And some lifestyle choices that are legal are definitely immoral.

Lifestyle issues and *adiaphora*. Many, but not all, lifestyle issues are adiaphoric (morally neutral or indifferent). Whether a person exercises in the morning before work or in the evening after work, for example, is morally indifferent. But that a person exercise, both in general and especially if he or she has been told of a health condition that demands exercise to prevent illness or damage, is a moral requirement, because we all have duties to preserve our life and health. Of course, exercise must be fit into a lifestyle that contains a great many other obligations, which may take priority over exercise on any given day.

Smoking, for example, given what we know today about its health risks, is not a matter of *adiaphora*. It is a moral issue not only because of damage to health, but also because of the land and healthcare services it consumes, and because of the dangers to others of secondhand smoke. If smoking were simple to stop, continuing to smoke would seem to be a deliberate choice of evil. Since smoking is an addiction, we all have a moral obligation to attempt to be smoke-free, but those who have not yet quit are not to be condemned. The question of to what extent social programs and organizations such as life insurance or Medicare and Medicaid should provide incentives for not smoking, and/or penalties (lower levels of coverage) for continuing to smoke is debated with great heat in the United States and is increasingly an issue in the rest of the world. As is the case with many other lifestyle issues, the moral status of smoking changes rapidly as we have more and more certainty about its various consequences in our society.

Lifestyle issues as moral choices. Contrary to the common understanding, a great many lifestyle issues *are* moral ones also, and belong to the stuff of ethical discourse. Most of us have come to see that recycling, moderating energy and water use, and a host of other lifestyle practices around ecology are moral imperatives. Yet few of these can be legislated or otherwise mandated. For example, we all need to use less energy, both in heating and cooling our homes and in our vehicles. To bike to work is great, but some of us live at a distance. Some who live at a distance could perhaps move to within walking or biking distance of work, but not all, for some of these persons will have spouses whose commute to work would therefore be doubled, or whose children must then attend poor-quality schools.

As part of conserving energy, each car owner in the world should ideally get the smallest, most energy-efficient car that meets our needs and we can afford. But some of us transport kids' teams in our station wagons, and could not do that in a Prius, and others of us can only afford old clunkers, which do not tend to be the more energy-efficient cars. It is because all these different moral decisions must fit together in a single workable lifestyle that they cannot be legislated. For each of us, how much we can do in any one of these areas in which we have responsibilities depends on how much we are doing in another. The fact that someone who has dedicated forty years of her life to working as a nurse with refugees in poor and endangered refugee camps around the world does not now have the resources to insulate, or replace windows in, the house inherited from her parents in which she will retire does not mean that she will be guilty of an irresponsible waste of energy resources. We have responsibilities in multiple directions. We will not be able to satisfy them all. Often, we will not be able to satisfy any one of these responsibilities fully. We must do what we can.

Voluntary Families and Moral Choice

Like all these other choices, our choices of whether to marry, whether to have or raise children, and how many children to have or raise, as well as how tightly we stay connected to families of origin or create voluntary families, must be a matter of personal choice. These decisions cannot be legislated either by the state or by one's religion. One cannot be judged for such choices by anyone else. But these are nonetheless moral choices. We have obligations that are not reducible to law. Only the individual knows whether he or she could do more and should do more—or whether what one does will be "enough." Of course, the "enough" for each of us is almost always just out of reach.

It is our very diversity, which has become the hallmark of postmodernity, that has moved lifestyle issues, not only family and alternative family relationships, but all the varied lifestyle issues we have examined in this book, to the very center of personal morality upon which ethical discourse should be focused. We are too different, and our world is too fast-changing, for these things to be legislated in the way that many of them were in the past. This is the price of

our increased freedom: increased responsibility. In many ways, things are easier when these "small" lifestyle moral demands are legislated and violations punished, for then we do not have to think, analyze, or make difficult decisions. In areas where law demands that garbage trucks keep glass, metal, paper, and trash separated, for example, and garbage companies issue multiple labeled containers to each household, compliance is easy. We do not even have to think about whether or not to comply with the law, because if we do not separate, our trash will not be picked up, and we will live in a pigsty with the rats. The decisions we make about our lifestyles have everything to do with our moral selves and with the influence we exert upon the ethical discourse of our society. We will not find guidance for these in law.

Religious obligations to family. Religions and cultures have taught that humans have moral obligations to families, particularly to parents, but also to other family members. The law of the levirate practiced by ancient Jews and still today in parts of Africa requires male relatives of childless dead men (usually brothers) to raise up offspring with the widow, so that the dead brother would have posterity.[34] Those children inherit the dead "father's" share of family patrimony and share the father's lineage. As we have seen, many cultures have understood the living to have ongoing responsibilities to the dead, as in feeding and feasting them. The most common human obligations to the living have been to respect and to provide for one's parents in their old age and for all the needy among one's family.

Such obligations have functioned to provide social stability and cohesiveness in society, as well as to provide structure and discipline for individual moral life. These functions remain necessary today, despite the changes in families. The obligations that fulfill them are perhaps even more demanding than in the past. There are often fewer children to care for sick and dying parents, and fewer relatives to take in orphaned children or to care for other relatives (childless elderly or the disabled) who need care. Many of the obligations that in the past fell on adult children must increasingly fall on grandchildren, because so many adult children of needy elderly are now, due to extended lifespans, themselves elderly. In both developed and developing societies, individuals and organizations are now struggling to assume some of the burden for those who need care but whose much smaller circle of relatives than in the past is either not willing to care for them or are no longer able to care for them.

Institutional assumption of family responsibilities. But social assumption of these obligations by institutions exhibits numerous problems, as the scandals in nursing homes, orphanages, group homes, and foster care have multiplied around the world. As some family obligations devolve to social and governmental institutions, the responsibility we have for family members must be extended into the political arena, to ensure that institutional care meets the needs of the clients as well as of the families connected to them. Often we do not believe that concern for the quality of our institutions is any great priority for us until our own parent, or Down's syndrome sibling, becomes a client in a nursing home, group home, or workshop for the disabled. Families in the past "took care of their own." Increasingly today taking care of our own must mean creating national, state, and local governmental policies that provide the care that individual families no longer

can, and monitoring the resulting services to ensure the welfare of the clients.

Developing alternative or supplementary families. At the same time that obligations to family have in some ways become more individually burdensome due to the lengthening of old age, dwindling family size, and movement of women into the workforce (leaving no full-time caretaker in most homes), our families of origin are less and less the focus of our lives, interests, and development. Many of us have, in order to nurture intimacy and sociality as well as create near networks of care, developed alternative or supplementary families made up of friends. For some, these alternative or supplementary families augment our original family networks; for others, the new network replaces an original one that had disintegrated, was dysfunctional, or rejected us.

Both kinds of families are good, and most of us benefit from having both. Many find that relationships with family of origin change throughout our lives. When my husband and I began our family, our brothers and sisters were younger (some not yet teens), unmarried and without children, and lived hundreds to thousands of miles away. We came together with our siblings over long distances around our parents for celebrating holidays every other year or so. But in our own locale, we created a network of friends among whom all the adults were alternative parents to all the kids. This network functioned to provide ordinary sociality, because we enjoyed each other's company and gathered to share activities and stories, but also because we lacked the safety nets of local extended family.

The death of parents was not only traumatic in itself, but it constituted a crossroads: Would the families of the siblings continue to gather together or not? Factors influencing that answer differ in each family. If obligations to or affection for parents were the only reason for the previous gathering, the families of the siblings may go their separate ways. Children of the siblings may not feel connected to aunts, uncles, and cousins they have only seen a few times in their lives. However, it often happens that if the siblings have continued to keep in touch, they find that in middle to old age they have much more in common than they had earlier thought. Their children are grown, on their own or almost, and the siblings have more leisure. Often they find that their shared family of origin marked them more like each other than they realized when they were younger. Siblings of mine who were eight to fourteen when I married and moved far away are now good friends with my husband and me, despite the thousands-of-mile distances between our homes. We gather often and vacation together in small groups. This is also true of most of my husband's siblings. What made this possible, I think, was all of us demonstrating an interest in each other's children—asking to be reminded of graduations, showers, and birthdays, sending photos with news and messages, taking our vacation days to attend weddings, sending gifts at baby births.

Retaining longstanding friends. Relationships with siblings or neighborhood friends that we knew for years growing up are sources of readymade intimacy. When it is possible to reconnect or keep in touch with them, we find that they already know parts of us well and have many of the same memories and associations, which allows us to relax in their presence. We do not have to forge new bonds to other selves—the bonds are there; we only have to unearth them, which sometimes seems the easiest thing in the world. Today, to have both close-knit family and alternative

family is to be blessed. But just as maintaining kinship ties requires effort, so networks of friends do not just happen. They are made and maintained through a constant series of small choices.

Integrating families. When couples marry, they face the task of making two family networks, and usually some number of close friends, into a group that is comfortable with each other. Celebrations for birthdays, anniversaries, marriages, and graduations as well as funerals, religious holidays, or awards ceremonies are one way of integrating different sets of friends and family. Such integration, when it is possible, simplifies our lives. We do not have to constantly explain who this friend we mentioned is, or which sister is the one who is sick. We do not have to supervise the socializing at mixed family gatherings to make sure that no one was either left out or offended for some reason or other. There are no holes in the safety net that we have created for ourselves.

Of course, for some, such integration is not possible. The old saw about politics and religion being divisive, and so best left unmentioned, should probably today include sexuality. It can be as impossible to have one's brother, who insists on biblical authority that homosexuals and cohabitors will burn in hell, at the same picnic with a friend and her lesbian lover, as it is to have an uncle who insists that the president is a foreign-born monkey, at the dinner table with a friend who worked in the president's last campaign. Through trial and error, most of us eventually find a mix of people that works.

New couples often have to decide with which set of family to celebrate each holiday. For the few years when my husband and I lived within one hundred miles of both family homes, my husband, kids, and I ate two

Thanksgiving, Christmas, and Easter dinners. "Drive, eat, drive, eat, drive," my sons complained. It was only after the two sets of parents moved far apart from each other and we could alternate holidays between them that our stomachs could relax. Later, when we had graduations and both families came to our city, each side had enough in common through sharing grandchildren and from hearing news of each other for years, that they could deal well together, even if they would never become friends independent of us. The point here is that these things change and develop over time. Keeping the connections alive can be beneficial for later life.

Integrating one's network, integrating self. Integrating one's networks of friends and family has strong implications for integrating the different parts of our selves. Irving Goffman pointed out the different social "fronts" that individuals put up and perform in different settings and the various "teams" on which individuals understand themselves to be.[35] Goffman would point out that if in one's work one supervises a number of subordinate workers, one would generally not want to include them in a setting, such as a Sunday family picnic, where the front that one wears is not authoritative but egalitarian. Since it would be impossible to maintain both fronts simultaneously, the authoritative professional one and the egalitarian one for intimates, either one acts authoritatively at the picnic and irritates one's family, or egalitarian, and risks undermining one's authority with the subordinate workers upon returning to work on Monday.

At the same time, if our professional front is called for, even in an egalitarian family setting, there is no problem with a physician taking charge of a situation in which a sibling has collapsed, clutching his chest. But the authority granted the physician is clearly role

and situation specific; the doctor would not be allowed to order other family members around in other situations. Not all of our networks can be blended without blurring our roles in them. GLBTQ persons, for example, often do not come out simultaneously in all areas of their lives, and this can make the mixing of their relationship circles very complicated. But ideally, our family network and friends in our alternative family network see our same "front," for this is what allows us to develop an integrated self.

In many ways, the task of our younger years is to develop different parts of ourselves, and the task of adulthood is to integrate them, a task that for most of us lasts all our lives, since we continue to develop new parts, too. Once our authority on the job is no longer based on our office (and the front that represents it), but on the respect that our subordinates have for our greater expertise and experience, we can risk greater egalitarianism with them, just as once we have developed a mutual respect and attraction with the one we are dating, we can stop pretending, without risking the relationship, that our car is always spotless and our movie preference is always the same as the other's.

A moral component in integration. The integration process has a strong moral component, for in each of the different fronts we inhabit, we are adapting a script that is not ours, but is one that is given us by our culture. We all begin as plagiarists, because we are not born with scripts of our own. Our goal must be to develop our own scripts, thereby creating an integrated self to whom we can be true. We do this partly through integrating family/friends, and partly through working out our own personal moral code.

"Wait," you might be saying. "Why should I have to be the same person within each of my relationships? Why do I need to mix my circles? Why can't I be different in different situations? What's wrong with that if I don't commit any unethical acts?"

In fact, we *are* different in some situations. We act differently with our grandmothers than with our golf or bowling buddies. Our mannerisms and general decorum will vary a great deal in the different parts of our lives. And in fact, as noted above, we continue to develop new scripts as we make new friends and take on new interests throughout our lives. But the person—the values, commitments, and obligations—should be one. That one—the central I—is of course open to change, because human persons are historical, and historical beings in interacting with each other and the material world change themselves both intentionally and unintentionally. Having an integral self is essential if we are to know who we are and make choices congruent with the self that is us. The choices we make change the self that we are, and that new self makes new choices, in a never-ending yet relatively controlled spiral. Our choices should be based in the best knowledge we have of ourselves—our values, goals, and relationships—lest our lives take on the chaotic character of schizophrenia.

With regard to families and alternative families, our personal moral codes will of necessity differ and lead us in different directions. In general, though, we should attempt to stay connected with family, especially parents (because they are most likely to need us down the line, and because most of us usually owe them the most), but also siblings and extended family. Our ties to extended family will likely depend on what proximity they had to us growing up. My husband has close to a hundred cousins, many of them first cousins, due to large families on both maternal and paternal sides. But due to geography and age differences, he has only kept up with a few over the last decades. Not all relatives are equally apt for our family networks because not all of them have shared as much of our life experiences.

The value of reunions. It is a good idea to attend family reunions when possible. One advantage I have come to see in family reunions is that one's partner and children can often learn a different side of one from hearing accounts of one's childhood adventures and relationships. The more we know of our beloveds, the more we can love them. Sometimes also we may have uncomfortable childhood memories of relatives that we should at least test out, if not dismiss, for the sake of the advantages of family networks for our children.[36] One aunt who I had thought to be a witch when I was growing up became a good friend once I was married with kids of my own, and a third grandmother to my children. Through reunions and visits, children can learn to see themselves as securely embedded in this larger variegated community, and they also benefit from seeing this other side of us in our roles as child, sibling, niece, cousin.

Choosing Friends

Thus far I have spoken of networks of friends as alternative family but have not said much about friends themselves up until now. Religions have often recognized the importance of friends and the familial relationship that develops between close friends. In the Bible, Proverbs chapters 17 and 18 deal with friends: "Friends always show their love. What are brothers for if not to share troubles?" (Prov. 17:17), and "Some friendships do not last, but some friends are more loyal than brothers" (Prov. 18:24). Here the equation of friends and brothers—and I would add, sisters—is clear.

The Buddha's advice to Sigalo on friends pointed out some of the most important qualities of friends:

> "Young man, be aware of these four good-hearted friends: the helper, the friend who endures in good times and bad, the mentor, and the compassionate friend.
>
> "The helper can be identified by four things: by protecting you when you are vulnerable, and likewise your wealth, being a refuge when you are afraid, and in various tasks providing double what is requested.
>
> "The enduring friend can be identified by four things: by telling you secrets, guarding your own secrets closely, not abandoning you in misfortune, and even dying for you.
>
> "The mentor can be identified by four things: by restraining you from wrongdoing, guiding you towards good actions, telling you what you ought to know, and showing you the path to heaven.
>
> "The compassionate friend can be identified by four things: by not rejoicing in your misfortune, delighting in your good fortune, preventing others from speaking ill of you, and encouraging others who praise your good qualities."[37]

For most of us, having friends, and the quality of those friends, are two of the most important factors in our satisfaction with our lives. A friend, then, is someone we can trust to have our backs, to point us in the right moral direction when we falter, to whom we can express the thoughts that we are most uncomfortable with, our failings and fears. While we can sometimes meet someone and know that this or that person could be a friend, whether or not that person becomes a friend is a matter not only of the amount of effort we, and the other, put into it, but also of chance. If one of us moves before the friendship is well established, if the friendship began when both were single and the marriage of one changes shared interests or available time—various things prevent initial friendships from developing and becoming lifelong. Sometimes even well-established friendships erode. But there is something tremendously affirming about knowing that there is someone out there who is there for us, with whom we can, with no effort at all, pick up the friendship after months, even years of interruption—because we know each other.

Making time for friends and family, time to sustain the individual relationships that make up our network, is not easy. The pace of our lives is continually faster. We live with phones, however, and have access to email. Contemporary communication devices should make keeping in touch easier. Without a real effort, though, we find that we use the phone and email only for instrumental communication. We call to find out something, to give directions, to ask a favor. What we need to do is call just to talk, to check up on how things are going since our last conversation, or write an old-fashioned letter and send it by email. Sharing conversation around a televised ballgame, or the hoop at the park, over dinner or lunch—even if it is shared peanut butter sandwiches in a park over lunchtime—can keep friendships alive. Young men's friendships often form around doing things together—watching a ballgame, going to a concert, working on a car—with intimacy seeming an accidental consequence. And yet men as they get older often find that the shared activity becomes increasingly unnecessary, that they can communicate directly. The fronts come down. Women generally understand friends as being first and foremost for sharing their feelings and selves with. Shared activities are often less important.

Family and friends are essential for our development as moral persons. They support our development and make our lives enjoyable. Yet they entail obligations, too. They require us to care, which means to find time to sustain the relationships, to be open and loving, to be honest, to be responsible to and for the other.

Case Study: Family and Friends

"What are we going to do, Cam?" asked Lily, his wife. "We can't be in Spring Valley, eating Thanksgiving dinner with first your family and then mine (at the memory of these back-to-back feasts they both winced) and at the same time have James and Maria and Jill and Jaime and their families stay with us over the holidays."

Cameron and Lily had worked in Central America for eight years before returning to the States when their oldest son was ready to begin school. Lily was an engineer, and Cameron had grown up on a farm and earned a degree in agriculture. They had met in college and volunteered with a church program for Central America upon graduation. Neither set of their parents had understood their commitment to work with poor farmers in Nicaragua and El Salvador, helping them to dig wells, put plumbing in their houses, or improve their crop yields and raise healthier herds.

When they returned to the States, their families had expected them to put all those years in Central America behind them. Visits had been tense since they returned two years ago. All four grandparents adored Cam and Lily's two children but were appalled at what they saw as Cam and Lily's "radical" politics and their continuing contacts with the people they had worked with in Central America.

Now their parents expected them to return to Spring Valley, a three-hour drive away, for the long Thanksgiving holiday. But they had just learned that two of the people with whom they had become good friends over a number of years in Nicaragua, Americans James and Jill and their Nicaraguan spouses, Maria and Jaime, had finally gotten all the U.S. passports needed for the kids and spouses, and were coming to visit them. Neither James nor Jill had any close relatives still alive in the United States, so they were arriving the day before Thanksgiving, to spend a week with Cam and Lily in their large old farmhouse.

"I know what Mom will say if I tell her about their visit—she will say that we should lock up anything valuable and let them stay at our house while we come to Spring Valley. She won't be able to imagine our not being with the family for Thanksgiving. And I couldn't possibly suggest bringing them with us—I would be afraid of both deliberate and unintentional insults to them. My family is even worse than yours about what they would see as 'intermarriage' and 'mixed-race kids,' " said Lily.

"We know we'd rather be with friends," Cam said. "But do we have obligations to parents that should override our preferences? My parents would say, yes, we do. I know they would see this as our choosing other people over them—again."

"I don't see that we owe them this, Cam," insisted Lily. "Our obligations to parents are to care for them—but none of our parents are old or infirm enough to need our care yet, and you have two brothers and a sister who live close, anyway. If we thought that we had obligations to run our lives as they wanted, we would not have gone to Nicaragua in the first place. Our obligation is to love them. And we do—we just don't always agree with them, either set of them."

"So what are we going to do?" asked Cam. "It's such a little thing, but it could have major ramifications for our family and friends no matter what we choose."

There are a number of options Cam and Lily can choose. Which of the following do you think is the best option, and why? Are there others that might be as good or better?

1. Lily and Cam can call or visit their parents before the Thanksgiving holiday and explain that these are close friends they have not seen for two years, who have no one else with whom to celebrate Thanksgiving. Therefore, Lily and Cam will not be coming to Spring Valley for Thanksgiving but will spend a few extra days there over the Christmas holidays to make up for it.
2. Lily and Cam can call or visit their parents to tell them of the friends' upcoming visit and present their parents with a choice. Lily and Cam and their children can skip Thanksgiving in Spring Valley altogether, spending a few extra days at Christmas, or they can come for Thanksgiving Day only, bringing their guests with them—but only if their parents promise to be polite and hospitable and there are no derogatory remarks or embarrassing questions to their guests.
3. Cam and Lily can decide that peace in the family is so desirable that they will ask their friends to postpone the trip until the week after Thanksgiving and offer to pay the change fees on all seven airline tickets, using the money they had saved to remodel their antiquated kitchen.

DISCUSSION QUESTIONS

1. Variety in family structures has always existed. Why? What are some of the more common reasons for variety in families today?
2. Alternative families, sometimes religious and sometimes not, are not new. In what ways is the need for alternative families, those voluntarily chosen and assembled, greater today than in the past?
3. Keeping extended families connected strengthens society by providing support for individuals and nuclear families. What are some of the ways in which keeping extended families connected benefits individuals?

4. Thinking about your own extended family, how close is it? What or who is its center? How would the loss of that center affect the remaining family?

5. Do you have an alternative family—not just individual friends, but a network of friends that would support you through trials and tribulations, and last into the future? Do you see yourself assembling such a network?

6. What kind of moral obligations do we have toward families? Are these obligations limited, and if so by what? In what circumstances might one be justified in feeling relieved of moral obligations to family? In the case of estrangement, does it matter what the original cause of the estrangement was in deciding one's obligations?

7. Are the obligations toward alternative or voluntary family different from those to family of origin, and if so, why?

FOR FURTHER READING

Browning, Don S., Bonnie J. Miller-McLemore, Pamela D. Couture, K. Brynolf Lyon, and Robert M. Franklin. *From Culture Wars to Common Ground: Religion and the American Family Debate*. Louisville: Westminster John Knox, 1997.

Della Fave, Richard, and George A. Hillary Jr. "Status Inequality in a Trappist Monastery." *Social Forces* 59, no. 1 (September 1980): 62–84.

Farley, Margaret. *Personal Commitments: Beginning, Keeping, Changing*. San Francisco: Harper & Row, 1990.

Goodman, Ellen, and Patricia O'Brien. *I Know Just What You Mean: The Power of Friendship in Women's Lives*. New York: Simon & Schuster, 2000.

MacIntyre, Ferren. "Was Religion a Kinship Surrogate?" *Journal of the American Academy of Religion* 72, no. 3 (2004): 653–94.

Nelson, James. *The Intimate Connection: Male Sexuality, Male Spirituality*. Louisville: Westminster John Knox, 1988 (especially ch. 3, "Male Friendship").

Pahl, Raymond Edward. *On Friendship*. Malden, MA: Polity, 2000.

Rubin, Lillian. *Families on the Fault Line*. New York: HarperCollins, 1995.

Spencer, Liz, and Ray Pahl. *Rethinking Friendship: Hidden Solidarities Today*. Princeton: Princeton University Press, 2006.

United Nations. *Family: Challenges for the Future*. New York: United Nations Publications, 1996.

Velasquez, Eduardo A., Ed. *Love and Friendship: Rethinking Politics and Affection in Modern Times*. Lanham, MD: Lexington, 2003.

FILMS

Beyond the Nuclear Family. Cambridge Films, Item # 40310, 2008.

The End: Families Facing Death. Cambridge Films, Item # FMK33915, 2003.

Five Friends, by Erik Santiago. Media Education Foundation, 2010.

The Power of Family: Types of Families and Family Development. Cambridge Films, Item # 41239, 2008.

Remote Control: Children, Media Consumption & the Changing American Family, by Bob McKinnon. Media Education Foundation, 2007.

NOTES

1. See, for example, Jennifer Toth and Karolina Harris, *Orphans of the Living: Stories*

of America's Children in Foster Care (New York: Touchstone, 1998).

2. See, for example, Tobias Hecht's account in *At Home in the Street: Street Children of Northeast Brazil* (Cambridge: Cambridge University Press, 1998).

3. Charles Dickens, *Oliver Twist*, ed. Philip Horne (New York/London: Penguin, 2003 [1837]).

4. For a remarkably enduring description, see Hutton Webster, *Primitive Secret Societies: A Study in Early Politics and Religion* (New York: Macmillan, 1908), 1–3.

5. The Muslim *mahr* is often translated as "dowry," but it is actually neither dowry nor bride price. It is a payment from the groom (often helped by family) to the wife herself. Shari'a law dictates that it be given to her, not her family, as insurance in case of divorce. She is to both possess and manage it. In *fiqh* law, which developed later in different Muslim communities, the original intentions of the *mahr* were often eroded; for example, in Shi'a Iran, the *mahr* is not paid upon marriage, but only in a divorce, and only when the husband divorces the wife. Thus divorce cases often involve husbands and wives attempting to provoke each other into filing for divorce, in order not to forfeit the *mahr*, which usually amounts to the husband's annual income.

6. Herbert S. Klein, "The Changing American Family," *Hoover Digest* 2004, no. 3, July 30, 2004. http://www.hoover.org/publications/hoover-digest/article/6798.

7. Rosalyn Baxandall and Elizabeth Ewen, *Picture Windows: How the Suburbs Happened* (New York: Basic Books, 2000), 78–86.

8. In 1972, 45 percent of U.S. households consisted of married couples with their children. By 1998, that rate was 26 percent. See Peter Jenson, "The Changing Family," *Baltimore Sun*, January 2, 2000, http://articles.baltimoresun.com/2000-01-02/news/0001100316_1_divorced-married-raising-a-family.

9. Beverly Harrison, "The Effect of Industrialization on the Role of Women in Society," in *Making the Connections: Essays in Feminist Social Ethics*, ed. Carole Robb (Boston: Beacon, 1985), 44–46.

10. Of course, this was not only true in factories, where, for example, children were often designated because of their small size to crawl into the looms and other large machines to loosen jams, and were frequently injured in doing so, even losing limbs. It was also true in mines, where children, being the least skilled and of least importance, were sent in to check safety levels of dangerous gases. Alan Gallop, *Victoria's Children of the Dark* (Stroud, UK: History Press, 2003).

11. In the United States, farm women from the eighteenth to the twentieth centuries were considered to be advantaged over their urban sisters, in that they could sell excess egg production from their hens in order to have some independent disposable income.

12. See, for example, Proverbs 31:10-31, or the duties of a Buddhist wife in chapter 3.

13. Max Weber, *The Protestant Ethic and the Spirit of Capitalism*, trans. Stephen Kalberg (Malden, MA: Blackwell, 2002 [1905]).

14. The effect of immigration on fertility rates lasts one-half to one generation, meaning that the children of immigrants have fertility rates that more or less match those of nonimmigrant families.

15. Discussions of abandonment in the Roman Empire often distinguished between abandonment in the forest (where the

clear intention is the death of the child) and abandonment at a crossroads or on the steps of a house where there was some chance that a stranger would save the child. See John Boswell, *The Kindness of Strangers: The Abandonment of Children in Western Europe from Late Antiquity to the Renaissance* (New York: Vintage, 1990), chs. 1 and 2.

16. Ibid.

17. Susan Power Bratton, *Six Billion and More: Human Population Regulation and Christian Ethics* (Louisville: Westminster John Knox, 1992), 81–82.

18. Edward D. Andrews and Faith Andrews, "The Shaker Children's Order," *Winterthur Portfolio* 8 (1973): 201–14.

19. John Esposito, *Islam: The Straight Path*, 3rd ed. (New York: Oxford University Press, 1998), 5.

20. *Qur'an*, 93:3-12: "Allah has neither forsaken thee nor hates thee and the last shall be better for thee than the first. Allah shall give thee. And thee shall be satisfied. Did he not find thee an orphan and shelter thee? Did he not find thee erring, and guide thee? Did he not find thee needy, and suffice thee? As for the orphan, do not oppress him, and as for the beggar, scold him not; and as for the Lord's blessing, declare it." As for *hadith*, see *Al-Adab al-Mufrad Al Bukhari*, 7, 76:137: "Abu Hurayra reported that the Messenger of Allah, may Allah bless him and grant him peace, said, 'The best house among the Muslims is the house in which orphans are well treated. The worst house among the Muslims is the house in which orphans are ill treated. I and the guardian of the orphan will be in the Garden like that,' indicating his two fingers." Translated by Ustadha Aisha Bewley.

21. Micky Duxbury, *Making Room in Our Hearts: Keeping Family Ties through Open Adoption* (New York: Routledge, 2007).

22. M. Bloch and S. Guggenheim, "Compadrazgo, Baptism and the Symbolism of a Second Birth," *Man* (New Series) 16, no. 3 (September 1981): 376–86.

23. In Africa, see Conrad Phillip Kottak, "Kinship Modeling: Adaptation, Fosterage, and Fictive Kinship among the Betsileo," in *Madagascar: Society and History* (Durham, NC: Carolina Academic Press, 1986).

24. See, for example, Linda M. Chatters, Robert Joseph Taylor, and Rukmalie Jayakody, "Fictive Kinship Relations in Black Extended Families," *Journal of Comparative Family Studies* 25 (Autumn 1994): 297–312.

25. Peter H. Prindle, "Fictive Kinship (mit) in East Nepal," *Anthropos* 70, nos. 5–6 (1975): 877–82.

26. The Family is a high-demand faith group that emphasizes loyalty to the religious community over loyalties to one's family of origin, pointing to Jesus' teaching on the question. They stress Jesus' preaching in favor of poverty and a simple life, and live communally. The Family is known for its liberal sexual practices, but studies suggest that the child sexual abuse charged in the past has been rooted out and policed since. The Family, along with other NRMs, has been the object of both academic and government study, especially in Europe (e.g., Brigitte Schoen, "New Religions in Germany: The Publicity of the Public Square," in Philip Charles Lucas and Thomas Robbins, eds., *New Religious Movements in the Twenty-first Century: Legal, Political and Social Challenges in Global Perspective* [New York and London: Routledge, 2004]).

27. Michaela Kreyenfeld and Dirk Konietzka, "Education and Fertility in Germany," in *Demographic Change in Germany: The Economic and Fiscal Consequences*, ed. Ingrid Hamm, Helmut Seitz, and Martin Werding (Berlin: Springer, 2008), 79–131.

28. Pamela J. Smock and Wendy D. Manning, "Cohabiting Partners' Economic Circumstances and Marriage," *Demography* 34, no. 3 (August 1997), 331–41.

29. Linda Waite, "Does Marriage Matter?" *Demography* 32, no. 4 (November 1995): 483–507.

30. Emily Wax, "In India, More Women Demand Toilets Before Marriage," *Washington Post*, October 12, 2009, http://www.washingtonpost.com/wp-dyn/content/article/2009/10/11/AR2009101101934.html?wprss%3Drss_world&sub=AR.

31. David Eimer, "China's Divorce Rule Dubbed 'Law That Makes Men Laugh and Women Cry,'" *The Telegraph* (London), 11/11/11.

32. James Raymo, "Later Marriages or Fewer? Changes in the Marital Behavior of Japanese Women," *Journal of Marriage and Family* 60, no. 4 (November 1998): 1023–34; James M. Raymo, "Educational Attainment and the Transition to First Marriage among Japanese Women," *Demography* 40, no. 1 (2003): 83–103.

33. Zygmunt Bauman, *Postmodern Ethics* (Oxford: Blackwell, 1993), 81.

34. Michael C. Kirwen, *African Widows* (Maryknoll, NY: Orbis, 1979).

35. Irving Goffman, *The Presentation of Self in Everyday Life* (Garden City, NY: Doubleday, 1959), 22–30.

36. By uncomfortable memories, I am not referring here to abuse as uncomfortable memories. Obviously, we do not put our children in either emotional or physical danger from our parents or other relatives who have been abusers in the past. Nor do we put aside memories of abuse that have not been repented by the perpetrators, thus excusing the abuses. By "uncomfortable memories," I mean that sometimes we can be uncomfortable with families because we have not seen them in some time, or because our last meeting was acrimonious. In these cases, the water should be tested again. People can change.

37. Buddha, *Sigalovada Sutta: The Buddha's Advice to Sigalaka*, translated from the Pali by John Kelly, Sue Sawyer, and Victoria Yareham, verses 21–25, http://www.accesstoinsight.org/tipitaka/dn/dn.31.0.ksw0.html.

CHAPTER 7

RELIGIONS ON ANGER AND VIOLENCE

A generation ago some Americans, if asked what religions had to say about anger and violence, would have answered that anger was dangerous, evil, and led to aggression and violence. Some more discerning Christians would have distinguished righteous anger, as exhibited by Jesus, as an exception. Some Jews would have pointed out that anger even at God could be morally acceptable if it provoked one to engage with God in prayer. But most were almost certain that the religious response to anger was that it was a very negative emotion.

Today almost all Americans have become very aware that religions—any number of religions, including the Christianity and Judaism we are most familiar with—can be accused of justifying not only anger but even violence when they teach that humans sometimes act as the punishing hand of God. Given the violence that has attended much of the religious anger in the news over the last decades, some Americans have retained the predominant teaching of religions concerning anger, and think that anger, and religious justifications of it, are dangerous and to be avoided, while others have responded to

religious violence by pulling out those teachings in their own religions that justify the use of violence against evildoers. There is not as yet much clarity about what kind of anger is righteous anger, or whether, if recourse to violence is ever morally acceptable, anger is an acceptable emotion in carrying out that violence.

Framing the Issues

In the next pages, we will first discuss what we mean by anger and then distinguish different kinds of anger. We will then see that treatment of anger in world religions, and even of violence, has been like a river with a central stream, one that counsels against anger and violence, but with a number of sidestreams that deal with special, and normally rare, situations in which anger and even sometimes violence might be morally appropriate.

Most world religions have understood that anger is a normal emotion. Even the gods and saints of different religions have experienced anger. If we look at common human experience, we can see that among infants and toddlers, anger is the response to being denied immediate satisfaction of desires—desires for food, milk, toys, shiny objects, freedom of movement. Anger is an instinctual response to frustrated desires in humans. As humans mature, we learn, some of us more and some of us less, to moderate our desires and to accept frustration of desire with reason and not anger.

Anger can also be an immediate response to pain, whether it be the pain of a toothache or the pain of being rejected in love. But the expression of this kind of anger may be conditioned. For some, the anger that accompanies rejection will be directed outward, and for others it will be directed inward. Psychologists have noted that expressions of anger at being rejected in love are more common in males than females. It is not that females do not feel the pain of rejection, but that more of them tend to direct anger inward, into doubt about their own self-worth, even into self-hatred. This same distinction is true of responses to abuse—while both male and female responses are varied, many abused males tend to channel their anger into abusing others, and many abused females tend to channel their anger inward, becoming serial victims. Gender socialization in our culture has punished men for showing weakness or self-doubt but has been tolerant of male displays of anger. Many negative emotions in males have been expressed as anger. In females, socialization has encouraged women to accept subordinate roles in which displays of anger are prohibited and negative assessments of self-worth are encouraged. Because some kinds of anger are controlled and channeled by cultural socialization in both males and females, we know that anger is not an uncontrollable emotional response.

The possibility of controlling and channeling anger is central to religious treatments of anger. The primary message of world religions about anger is that it is dangerous—physically, emotionally, and morally. Whether we look at ethical decisions consequentially, deontologically, or in terms of virtue ethics, anger is dangerous. It is dangerous in that it frequently produces terrible consequences: innocent people are wounded, physically or emotionally, sometimes even killed; resources are wasted (our own property or that of others destroyed); and relationships are damaged or destroyed, all by anger. Anger is also dangerous deontologically, in that it can lead us to perform acts that are evil in themselves and always prohibited (think of Cain's murder of his brother Abel in the Bible).[1] But anger is also dangerous from the perspective of virtue ethics because of the damage it does to the angry person's own character. Virtue consists in exerting self-discipline over one's desires and emotions, in establishing good habits, but anger endangers self-discipline and tempts us to violate the good habits we have been learning.

Because anger wells up immediately, unbidden, it takes a great deal of practice for reason to interrogate and control it. Reason needs to interrogate anger in order to assess its root: What caused this anger? Only when we know the source of the anger can we then decide the appropriate way to deal with it. When we do not interrogate the anger we feel to discover what caused it, we are likely to respond inappropriately, to mistarget our anger. The husband who comes home from a long, frustrating day at work and finds no dinner waiting may explode at the slightest provocation from his wife, though the principal source of his anger is the work situation. A teenager just cut from the starting lineup may come home and take out his or her anger on a younger sibling or on the family pet.

Anger is not only individual. Among religious or ethnic groups, the mistreatment of one of "ours" by one of "theirs" can be an excuse to take out a myriad of individual and group frustrations (with the economy, with prejudice against one's group, with the hardships of immigration, with the dangers of assimilation) on all members of the offender's group. Mistargeted anger has the potential to cause violent retaliation, which can lead to a never-ending cycle of violence of the "eye for an eye" type that leaves everyone blind.

Some religions, such as Christianity, have seen the primary danger in anger to be in its temptation to immoral acts, especially violence, and to the creation of negative social consequences. Judaism has a singular and interesting teaching on anger vented at God, which can be individually and socially useful. Buddhism and Hinduism have seen the primary danger in anger as undermining the path to virtue of the individual. When anger persists, it can cloud our perception of reality, erode our relationships, rob our lives of the capacity for joy, and distort our personalities. When anger is shared within a community, the anger of each person is reinforced by the anger of others, and it is more likely to persist, with all the damaging results of persistent anger on all involved.

Anger in the Contemporary World

While humans have always had a capacity for anger, many believe that modern conditions of life have increased our experience of anger. In the West, and increasingly also in the developing nations of the South, anger has been recognized, for example, as linked to the experience of driving on traffic-clogged roadways. Road-rage, as it is typically named, sometimes moves beyond anger to physical violence, including fistfights and even

shootings. Road-rage can target other drivers for not driving as fast as we would like or driving too fast; not moving out of parking spaces fast enough, or for darting into a space that we intended to take; turning without signaling or signaling and slowing a mile in advance. It is difficult to avoid thinking that some of what we term road-rage has nothing to do with the road or drivers but has been simmering within, waiting for some relatively minor irritation to set it off.

Bullying is another form of anger outlet that is increasingly pointed to not only as a form of victimization, but in some cases, such as school bullying, has been seen to escalate into widespread killing violence, as in the school shootings that have become periodic in the United States.

Psychologists have posited that modern urban life, and the close quarters it forces humans to live in, is a major cause of irritation. Our apartment neighbors are too loud or park in our space, leave their garbage outside the containers, or hold the elevators, forcing us to take the stairs. There is an accident on the highway on our way to work; we are late for a meeting, and the boss complains. When we get home, we have a headache, and our roommate is booming his fusion rock at top volume, and the neighbor lady complains to us as we get the mail. The little irritations add up more and more, and then some little thing—like a slow driver ahead of us—lights our fuse.

Religious Treatment Concerning Anger and Violence

This is the kind of anger that most religious teachings are aimed at. While we may have additional stressors from living in close quarters

Fig. 7.1. Bullying is an increasing problem even among young schoolchildren.

that many of our long-ago human ancestors did not have, the fact is that even thousands of years ago when most world religions were forming their teachings, humans experienced stress. Rainy springs that prevented planting crops until late raised the specter of hunger in the winter from less-than-bountiful fall harvests. During harsh winters people not only

Fig. 7.2. Lord Krishna.

froze to death, but the constant cold weakened human health, making populations vulnerable to disease. Pregnancy was dangerous, and a third of all women died in one of their many childbirths. Natural disaster, war, raiding—the stressors were different but very real, many of them more serious than the bulk of our irritations. Religions tried to help people deal with these varied stressors that caused anger. Later we will look at some of the specialized religious treatments of anger and violence that are still relevant today.

Hinduism

Different religions focus on slightly different causes of anger. In Hinduism, anger is most often treated as the result of unfulfilled desire. Anger is a form of frustration: our will has been thwarted. Krishna, in the Hindu classic the *Bhagavad Gita*,[2] says that lust, greed, and anger are due to ignorance and lead one into perpetual bondage. The general message of Hinduism on anger is that we need to train ourselves not to be angry. Often our anger is at least partially constructed on an exaggerated sense of our own importance. Hindus strive to reach *moksha*, which entails escaping from illusion, including the illusion that we are an individual self. In Hinduism, learning humility is one medicine for anger. For example, when we are kept waiting for an hour after our appointment with a doctor or dentist, it makes a great deal of difference whether we focus on the inconvenience to us and our schedule, or we assume that there has been an unforeseen emergency that is causing the delay.

Buddhism

In Buddhism, anger is regarded as strong aversion, or even as intention to do harm to another. While everyone sometimes feels anger, Buddhism, like Hinduism, teaches that one should learn to recognize one's anger and its causes as the first step in moving beyond anger through transforming it. The Dalai Lama, asked whether anger is ever acceptable in Buddhism, answered:

Buddhism in general teaches that anger is a destructive emotion and although anger might have some positive effects in terms of survival or moral outrage, I do not accept anger of any kind as a virtuous emotion nor aggression as constructive behavior. The Gautama Buddha has taught that there are three basic *kleshas*[3] at the root of *samsara*[4] and the vicious cycle of rebirth. These are greed, hatred and delusion—also translatable as attachment, anger and ignorance. They bring us confusion and misery rather than peace, happiness and fulfillment. It is in our own interest to purify and transform them.[5]

Gautama Buddha was very descriptive in his treatment of anger, depicting angry persons as ugly and sleeping poorly. He taught that people in general lose respect for angry persons. Of the angry person, he says:

Fig. 7.3. The Dalai Lama, leader of Tibetan Buddhists.

Relatives, friends and colleagues avoid him. Anger brings loss. Anger inflames the mind. He doesn't realize that his danger is born from within. . . . A man conquered by anger is in a mass of darkness. He takes pleasure in bad deeds as if they were good, but later, when his anger is gone, he suffers as if burned with fire. He is spoiled, blotted out, like fire enveloped in smoke. When anger spreads, when a man becomes angry, he has no shame, no fear of evil, is not respectful in speech. For a person overcome with anger, nothing gives light.[6]

Many of us have known people who were consumed by anger. Some of that anger may have been originally righteous anger triggered by an injustice. But some people have obsessed about this injustice. They are not interested in any other topic and seem to resent any attempt to distract them. We do avoid them, not only because their single interest soon bores us, but also, and perhaps even more, because their failure to control their anger makes us afraid, and suggests to us a potential for uncontrolled violence.

In the above we see a common connection made in eastern religions between character and conduct. The angry man not only commits evil deeds, but his very personality becomes deformed. There is no light in his life. In both Hinduism and Buddhism, the primary ethical concern is for virtuous character, and only secondarily for virtuous acts. This is not because virtuous acts are not seen as important, but because these religions assume that if one has a virtuous character, one will as a consequence perform virtuous acts. In dealing with anger, one can see the sense in this approach. For even if one believes that the primary moral concern should be for virtuous acts, in the presence of great anger, the

only way to ensure that one's acts would be virtuous would be to transform the anger that possesses one, lest it lead one to committing evil acts.

Judaism

Jewish tradition on anger largely parallels that of other religions. In the biblical book of Proverbs (16:12) we find: "He who is slow to anger is better than a strong man, and he who masters his passions is better than one who conquers a city." The Jewish philosopher Maimonides wrote that one who becomes angry is as though that person had worshipped idols.[7] But there is one Jewish treatment of anger that is generally seen as unique, and that concerns anger at God. Most theistic religions treat God or gods as being angry—usually angry at humans, but in polytheistic religions sometimes angry at other gods. In most religions, for a human being or beings to be angry at a God or gods is to court disaster. It is regarded as irreverent, inappropriate, and dangerous in that it tempts the wrath of God/gods. Sometimes anger at God/gods is considered inappropriate because God is good and perfect; in other traditions anger at God/gods is inappropriate principally because the God/god is powerful and therefore to be treated very carefully.

Judaic religion is based upon the ancient covenant between God and the Jewish people, a covenant begun by Noah and Yhwh, ratified between Abraham and Yhwh, and finalized in the Mosaic covenant on Mount Sinai. That covenant relationship consisted of fidelity and obedience to Yhwh on the part of the Jewish people, and special status for and protection of the Jews on the part of Yhwh. Judaic tradition has always understood this covenant relationship to allow questioning, even complaints, addressed to God when the experience of Jews did not seem to correspond to Yhwh's obligations in the covenant. Thus Jewish speech/prayer addressed to God has sometimes included angry reprimands, perhaps the classic ones being those of Job in the Hebrew Bible. As a result of a bet between God and the devil, God has allowed the devil to test Job's loyalty to God by taking away his riches, his flocks, his children, and even his health, leaving him poor, sick, childless, and sitting on a dung heap. Job's friends come to see him, and assuming that such disaster could only be punishment for sin, urge him to admit his sin and be forgiven, lest his suffering continue. But Job insists he has not sinned, and addresses God:

> I loathe my life;
>> I will give free utterance to my complaint;
> I will speak in the bitterness of my soul.
>> I will say to God: Do not condemn me;
> let me know why you contend against me.
> Does it seem good to you to oppress,
>> to despise the work of your hands
>> and favor the schemes of the wicked?
> Do you have eyes of flesh?
>> Do you see as humans see?
> Are your days like the days of mortals,
>> or your years like human years,
> that you seek out my iniquity
>> and search for my sin
> although you know I am not guilty,
>> and there is no one to deliver out of your hand?
> Your hands fashioned and made me;
>> and now you turn and destroy me.
> Remember that you fashioned me like clay;
>> and will you turn me to dust again?
> Did you not pour me out like milk
>> and curdle me like cheese?
> You clothed me with skin and flesh,
>> and knit me together with bones and sinews.

> You have granted me life and steadfast love,
>> and your care has preserved my spirit.
> Yet these things you hid in your heart;
>> I know this was your purpose.
> If I sin you watch me,
>> and do not acquit me of my iniquity.
> If I am wicked, woe to me!
>> If I am righteous, I cannot life up my head,
> for I am filled with disgrace
>> and look upon my affliction.
> Bold as a lion you hunt me;
>> you repeat your exploits against me.
> You renew your witnesses against me,
>> and increase your vexation toward me;
>> you bring fresh troops against me.

> Why did you bring me forth from the womb?
>> Would that I had died before any eye had seen me,
> and were as though I had not been,
>> carried from the womb to the grave.
> Are not the days of my life few?
>> Let me alone, that I may find a little comfort
> before I go, never to return,
>> to the land of gloom and deep darkness,
> where light is like darkness.[8]

In Christianity and Islam, the very idea of prayer as complaint and accusation against God is shocking. Prayer is to consist of praise of the greatness of God and gratitude for God's goodness and mercy. But for Jews, part of what it means to be God's chosen people is that there is a relationship that binds Jews to their God and allows them to speak their mind. There is a cathartic element in the expression of anger at God, in questioning what God allows to happen to us. For example, a person who has lived a good life but learns that she has inoperable cancer of the brain at thirty-six is very likely to feel initial anger at God: Why me? Like Job, she has lived a good life, but has still been afflicted, and it feels unjust. Better to cry out to God with anger than take it out on one's family or friends. God will, after all, understand.

But while such anger at God is normal in the beginning, it, too, should give way to the reason and control that other religions urge. Jewish thinkers over the ages have suggested that in order to move past anger at God, one might consider that the situation may look very different from God's perspective and even have some good end; the suffering may be a test before an eternity of reward; or the suffering may have a spiritually constructive consequence. A very popular recent book by Rabbi Harold Kushner, *When Bad Things Happen to Good People*,[9] suggests that the source of much anger against God is the belief that God chooses and controls everything that happens. If God is compassionate but has limited power to intervene in the world once he created it and set it in motion, then holding on to anger against God becomes less reasonable and more problematic.

Christianity

Similar theological currents exist in Christianity, notably in process theology, which insists that God has limited God's self through both the gift of free will to human beings and by the patterns that God placed in nature while creating it. Thus, while anger at God may be a normal and acceptable initial emotion in some situations of suffering, and expressing that anger may be cathartic, holding on to that anger can still be dangerous. A group of psychologists studied people harboring anger at God and discovered that they scored higher than the norm on measures of

depression and anxiety.[10] It would be difficult to see one's world as supportive, as inviting one's trust, when one harbors anger at God.

There is, however, another Christian approach to anger that at first glance seems to contradict all the above. In a very influential essay that has been republished in dozens of languages, feminist Christian social ethicist Beverley Harrison laid out an argument for the value of anger for women and other marginalized groups. She begins by emphasizing that there is not just one Christian tradition. "It's always multi-cultural, pluralistic, and multi-layered. The theologian is to discern what in the tradition in the past is to be highlighted for living in the present, what has to be either repudiated actively or let go for a time. . . ," she continues. "My theological hope? God is with us; this I know. . . . As [Peruvian theologian Gustavo] Gutierrez says: 'Justice is the face of God.' And if you lose the longing for justice, you can't see God."[11]

In her essay titled "The Power of Anger in the Work of Love: An Ethic for Women and Other Strangers," Harrison argued that the personal energy of persons engaged in the struggle for justice arises from anger, anger at injustice suffered by ourselves or those we love. She thus presents anger not as something that should be suppressed—suppressed anger eventually erupts, often in uncontrolled violence—but rather as something that should be consciously drawn on to support ongoing efforts to redress the injustice.

Harrison is right that if we look at the struggles for justice such as the civil rights movement, the Gandhian independence movement, or the struggle of women and gays for civil rights, it is clear that the energy that kept people going despite great hardship and risks was anger at the denial of dignity, the infliction of suffering and death. Anger can be a source of energy for good, but only when it is transformed into reasoned commitment. Successful, effective movements for justice are not led by demagogues who stir up anger until it explodes into violence, but by responsible persons who are able to channel anger into long-term commitment to a social process aimed at justice.

Perhaps one of the most important implications of Harrison's groundbreaking article is that not to feel anger at injury done to ourselves or to those we care about is not to be fully human, not to know either justice or God. But a second important implication is that anger should neither be suppressed nor unchecked. It needs to be channeled in the direction of achieving justice.

Islam

In Islam, the Qur'an mentions anger a number of times—the anger of prophets such as Moses and Noah at the people, for example. But it also speaks familiar words of wisdom:

> The good deed and the evil deed cannot be equal. Repel (the evil) with one which is better (i.e., Allah ordered the faithful believers to be patient at the time of anger, and to excuse those who treat them badly), then verily! he, between whom and you there was enmity, (will become) as though he was a close friend. (Qur'an 41:34)

In a related manner, the Qur'an also tells of how Allah intervenes after the believers have defeated their enemies:

> [9:11] If they repent and observe the Contact Prayers (*salat*) and give the obligatory charity (*zakat*), then they are your brethren in religion. We thus explain the revelations for people who know.

> [9:12] If they violate their oaths after pledging to keep their covenants, and attack your religion, you may fight the leaders of paganism—you are no longer bound by your covenant with them—that they may refrain.

> [9:13] Would you not fight people who violated their treaties, tried to banish the messenger, and they are the ones who started the war in the first place? Are you afraid of them? GOD is the One you are supposed to fear, if you are believers.

> [9:14] You shall fight them, for GOD will punish them at your hands, humiliate them, grant you victory over them, and cool the chests of the believers.

> [9:15] He will also remove the rage from the believers' hearts. GOD redeems whomever He wills. GOD is Omniscient, Most Wise.[12]

The verses "and [He will] cool the chests of the believers. He will also remove the rage from believers' hearts" speak to God cooling the anger of the victorious Muslims after battle, lest they take vengeance against the defeated, and are a good example of the Qur'an's understanding of the dangers of anger in war and the virtue of controlling it. Clearly Allah does not support vengeance, even against those who were in the wrong, once they are defeated.

In the *hadith*, the stories of events and teachings in the life of Mohammed, there are many treatments of anger attesting to its need to be controlled. One such *hadith* reports Mohammed saying: "Power resides not in being able to strike another, but in being able to keep the self under control when anger arises."[13] In another *hadith*, when Mohammed was asked for wise advice, he replied, "Not to be angry." Asked again, he replied a second time, "Not to be angry." Asked yet a third time, he replied, "Not to be angry—heaven is your reward."[14] In yet another *hadith*, Mohammed said, "Some are swift to anger and swift to cool down, the one characteristic making up for the other; some are slow to anger and slow to cool down, the one characteristic making up for the other; but the best of you are those who are slow to anger and swift to cool down, and the worst of you are those who are swift to anger and slow to cool down." He continued, "Beware of anger, for it is a live coal on the heart of the descendant of Adam. Do you not notice the swelling of the veins of his neck and the redness of his eyes? So when anyone experiences anything of that nature he should lie down and cleave to the earth."[15] In a variation of this last *hadith*, Mohammed advises an angry person to first sit down to cool anger, and if that is not sufficient, to then lie down on the ground.

The teachings of Islam on anger are on the one hand less concerned than in some other religions to delve into the causes of anger (the one exception being anger at groups that attack the Prophet or his teachings or break their bond with his community). On the other hand, the advice in Islam for controlling anger is somewhat more physical than we see in other religions: If you have trouble controlling anger, sit down. If you still have trouble, lie down. If anger overwhelms you, perform the washing before prayer and then pray. This practical advice has the immediate effect of distracting us from complete focus on our anger, of helping us to cool down and allow reason a chance.

As we have seen, there are very limited differences in the teachings of the world religions on anger. In general, they provide practical wisdom learned through experience in human communities, wisdom concerning the danger of anger for the character of the individual actor, and danger to the community in which anger is loosed. Violence is clearly a major danger to the community from anger, and, as we will see, there are some differences in how religions treat the connections between anger and violence.

When Anger Erupts into Violence

We will not here delve into the specific religious regulations regarding violence within the family, among neighbors, or collective violence against other nations. We will restrict ourselves to how religions have seen the relationship between anger and violence. We need to be very careful in approaching the topic of violence in religions, for while it is often condemned in ancient religious texts, the word *violence* had a narrower meaning in earlier cultures than it does today in the West. We understand spanking our child or a child in our care, or beating a spouse or servant as acts of violence—lesser violence than knifing or shooting someone to death, but still violence. In the ancient world, such beatings were part of discipline, which was a responsibility of the heads of households. Severer acts of what would be called violence today—whipping, flogging, amputation of hands or feet, and various types of execution (hanging, beheading, burning at the stake, drawing and quartering) were also accepted as necessary discipline in the civil community. At the same time that religions accepted that violence was necessary to disciplined households and communities, they often counseled moderation and mercy on the part of those meting out discipline. Heads of households were urged to control their anger in punishing subordinates—for example, in Ephesians 6, after urging children to obey their parents, fathers are told: "And fathers, do not provoke your children to anger [by violence], but bring them up in the discipline and instruction of the Lord" (Eph. 6:4 NRSV).

At the same time, the right to use corporal punishment was not denied; see, as an extreme example, the Deuteronomy verse from the Jewish Torah/Christian Old Testament:

> If someone has a stubborn and rebellious son who will not obey his father and mother, who does not heed them when they discipline him, then his father and his mother shall take hold of him and bring him out to the elders of his town at the gate of that place. They shall say to the elders of his town, "This son of ours is stubborn and rebellious. He will not obey us. He is a glutton and a drunkard." Then all the men of the town shall stone him to death. So you shall purge the evil from your midst; and all Israel will hear, and be afraid. (Deut. 21:18-21 NRSV)

A great deal of what we view as violence today was seen as necessary discipline in the past. Many religions tried to soften that discipline a little, but their primary concern with violence was about the collective violence of war and the one-on-one violence that led to murder. In ancient societies, murderers were treated to execution or exile; religion either left those sentences to civil law, accepting its judgments, or sometimes, as in Israel, where religious and civil law were the same, pronounced the sentence directly. War, however, was more complex.

Hinduism. War is not a major theme in the religions of the East, but where it was treated there is some complexity. In Hinduism, for example, in the popular religious classic the *Bhagavad Gita*, Krishna advises the warrior Arjuna, who is having doubts about following his lord into a major battle when he also has relatives and friends in the opposing army. Krishna's advice is simple: Do your duty. You have pledged your loyalty to your lord—carry out that duty. It is not your worry what the

Fig. 7.4. This Japanese statue of Buddha demonstrates the serenity that is the best defense against anger.

consequences of these actions are. The right thing to do is to carry out your duty. This is one of the clearest cases of deontological (rule-based) ethics we have.

At the same time in Hinduism, we have the revered teaching of *ahimsa* (nonviolence, or doing no harm), which the Hindus long ago adopted from the Jains (who have a much clearer record of adhering to *ahimsa*). In Mahatma Gandhi's movement for Indian independence from Britain in the late 1940s, the combination of active resistance with *ahimsa* proved a very potent tool for the Hindus he led. Yet, when the former colony was partitioned in 1947 into contemporary India and Pakistan as part of the move toward 1950 independence from Britain, more than a million people were killed—Hindus killed Muslims and Muslims killed Hindus.

Buddhism. Like Hinduism, Buddhism's history is not devoid of violence, despite the centrality of Buddhism's teaching of nonviolence. It is well known that the initial spread of Buddhism was due to the emperor Asoka sending out Buddhist missionaries to the corners of his extensive kingdom only after he had conquered it in bloody warfare. Asoka thought that the peace teaching of Buddhism would discourage rebellion in the new empire. Nor has war been unknown in Buddhist-majority nations to the present. One reason for this seeming discrepancy is that the bulk of Buddhist teaching was created for and directed to the monks and nuns of the Buddhist *sangha*, who followed the teachings of the Buddha in a commitment to reach *nirvana* as quickly as possible in this life. Living in monastic community supported dedication to the path, but the path to perfection is an individual one with many stages. While Buddhism directed some practical teachings at the lay masses, they were not assumed to be

yet capable of the higher stages of the path, and so were seen to be liable to both anger and violence. The Buddhist cure for this was to join a monastic community; those who did not were in some ways considered simply liable to the illusions that led to violence.

At the same time, laity were also supposed to be responsible to central Buddhist teaching. The first precept accepted by lay Buddhists and monastics alike is: "I undertake to refrain from taking life." This precept was restated by the Vietnamese Buddhist monk, Thich Nhat Hanh, in 1966 during the American/Vietnamese war:

> Aware of the suffering caused by the destruction of life, I am committed to cultivate compassion and learn ways to protect the lives of people, animals, plants, and minerals. I am determined not to kill, not to let others kill, and not to condone any act of killing in the world, in my thinking, and in my way of life.

For Buddhists, then, this commitment should not only rule personal life, but also political and social life. Despite the clarity of Buddhist teaching on anger, violence, and their destructiveness and interconnection, war has been no stranger to Buddhist lands, though there are also some notable nonviolent political movements, often led by monastics, such as those in Myanmar and Tibet over the last decades.

Abrahamic religions. Unlike Buddhism, western religions have not simply denounced both anger and mortal violence, but have attempted to distinguish between just and unjust anger, and just and unjust wars. All three Abrahamic religions have understood wars on behalf of religion itself to be morally acceptable, even obligatory. Today many Jews understand not only the defense of Israel, but

Fig. 7.5. Thich Nhat Hanh, Vietnamese Buddhist monk and peace advocate.

even preemptive war in defense of Israel, to be moral, while most Christian authorities—though not all—have denounced preemptive wars as immoral. The biblical war of conquest against the Canaanites is cited in defense of the Israeli position; because Yhwh gave the ancient Israelites the land of Canaan, violence is understood as acceptable in conquering it then and retaining it now.

The Qur'an similarly understands Allah to have directed warring against those who opposed Islam, though as we have seen, anger that arose in the cause of the war was to be quenched upon victory; there was to be no vengeance against the defeated.

In Christianity, the scriptural argument is conflicted. The New Testament does have Jesus telling his disciples that he came not to bring peace, but a sword, but the context can be read to suggest that it is the followers who will be expelled from families and persecuted,[16] rather than about followers using the sword themselves. The New Testament also includes verses in which Jesus tells his disciples to put down their swords when he is being arrested, and adding that "he who lives by the sword dies by the sword."[17] On the whole, the message is pacifistic. Yet the Old Testament is also revelatory for Christians, and the supports for war are many and varied in the Old Testament.

While the first two to three centuries of Christianity enforced pacifism, often to an extreme degree such as not allowing self-defense, by the time of Augustine in the early fourth century, it was argued that defense of the Roman Empire against the "barbarians" required Christians (by then the majority in the empire) to take up arms against the pagans. While modern historians have shown that most of the "barbarian" tribes had already been converted to Christianity, the assumption that the invaders on so many borders of the empire were pagans helped shift Christian teaching on war from pacifism to just war theory.

The just war theory that developed attempted to lay out conditions that must be satisfied in order for a just war to be declared (*jus ad bellum*) as well as criteria for fighting a just war (*jus in bello*). At times these regulations were very restrictive—they forbade fighting around churches, cemeteries, monasteries, and convents, impeding movement of people and products to weekly markets, as well as fighting during Lent, Advent, holy days, and Fridays.[18] Today the basic criteria of just war theory are still being debated in relation to wars fought in the West, though today, as throughout history, it is doubtful that just war theory has ever prevented Christians from waging war, either offensively or defensively, and only fitfully has it affected the way that Christians have waged war. The most recent updating of just war theory in Christianity was the 1983 U.S. Catholic Bishops' document "The Challenge of Peace," which dealt primarily with nuclear war and found any use of strategic nuclear weapons indefensible.[19] The primary reason for this decision was that under the proportionality condition, it was impossible to find any cause that could justify the destructiveness of launching a strategic nuclear weapon. Second-strike launches were similarly seen as indefensible, since the consequences would certainly risk the destruction of all life on earth. The inability of strategic nuclear weapons to spare noncombatants was an important element in this decision. Yet this document, and the many discussions of it that followed, were not taken seriously by any nuclear power, all of which still have nuclear arsenals—which, although weapons numbers are being decreased among the major powers aware of their superfluity, are still being built up in nations such as North Korea and Iran, as well as Pakistan, India, and Israel.

A number of just war criteria would limit the possibility of anger escalating to the collective violence of war. Just wars must only be defensive, in response to great injustice done to one. The just war to be waged must be proportional to the original injustice. If a neighboring state has seized an airport of ours with virtually no loss of life, it would be wrong to begin a bloody war to regain it. At any rate, war must always be a last resort—peaceful means of resolving the problem must have been exhausted first. The goal of the war cannot be vengeance, or gain of any kind. And among the *jus in bello* conditions is again proportionality, which forbids escalation in the destructiveness of the war. All of these conditions militate against anger as the emotion

promoting the war, and demand careful reasoning both in deciding to go to war, and in waging the war itself.

Religions are made up of human beings, who are parts of communities and cultures that find themselves in conflict. So it is not surprising that religious teachings have only been marginally successful in preventing collective anger from leading to war, or in dictating how wars are fought. Yet the warnings and practical advice of religions about the dangers of anger both to self and others, and its connection to violence, remain some of the most hopeful resources we have.

New Ethical Questions on Anger and Violence

New ethical questions include those raised in debates about whether suicide is always to be understood as unjustified violence (which will be treated last), to what extent popular culture is promoting irritation and anger as normal modes of being, how such anger is used to control others, and how media are involved in making us more and more callous in the face of violence.

Normalizing Anger

In our late-modern society, perhaps for some of the reasons suggested above, the perpetually irritated person on the brink of anger has become a stock character in much of our entertainment media. On the one hand, these characters are held up to ridicule as being impossible to live with. On the other hand, they are represented as common in our lives, and therefore as possible models for us. Certainly they garner a great deal of attention from the persons around them and stand out as individuals, and this attention-getting potential seems to make them attractive models to many persons. Much of the contemporary media depends upon the masses of persons seemingly eager to reveal their banality, ignorance, egoism, and even innermost secrets to the world.

Most of these irritable, angry characters are male, because as explained earlier, anger has been one of the few negative emotions allowed to "manly" men—manly men have not been allowed to express self-doubt, suffering, emotional hurt, or other feelings considered incompatible with power and authority. Yet today we do see a few female characters who also seem perpetually irritated and quick to anger. Sometimes we laugh at the outrageous antics of such characters, grateful for relief from what seems the triteness of ordinary life.

We need to be very careful about accepting constant irritation or periodic bursts of anger as "just the way people are," as one of the variations of normal. We do not need to be perpetually cheerful; Pollyannas can be irritating, too. But when we see every little thing that happens as justifying expressions of anger and irritation on our part, we become a depressing burden to the people around us, leading both us and them to be more likely to respond to new obstacles or frustrations with angry violence.

Use of Anger as a Tool for Controlling Others

Expressions of irritation and anger, like other aspects of human behavior, can be learned, and unlearning them can be a part of our moral self-discipline. We need to query our expressions of anger, to ask to what extent we are using expressions of irritation and anger as threats to intimidate other persons, either so that they will not make demands on us, or so that they will accept the demands we make on them. We cannot avoid some feelings of

anger, but those feelings should never be allowed either to choose our actions for us or to be used as a threat against others.

Express or repress? At both popular and professional levels there have been mental health debates for half a century now concerning whether it is better to express hurt and anger or repress them. One theory is that repressing anger can either allow it to build until it blows up in random violence or turn it inward, into self-hatred; the other theory is that regularly expressing anger increases feelings of anger and therefore expressions of anger. There seems to be some evidence for both. It is here that religious treatments of anger can be helpful, because they neither urge us to express anger nor repress it, but instead tell us how to deal with it when we feel it. Muslim advice is to calm the anger so that it can be dealt with rationally and interrogated: when it is burning hot, therefore, we should sit down or lie down, and then if still necessary, wash our hands and pray. These are necessary, practical first steps in managing strong anger so that it does not escalate and turn into violence.

Transforming entitlement-based anger. Psychologists report increases in the need for anger management over the last decade or so, some of it court-ordered, resulting from cases of anger turning into violence. But the majority of the increase seems to involve irritation, sarcasm, resentment, annoyance—more low-grade, but difficult to evade, anger. Some psychologists suggest that many people seem to feel entitled not just to pursue happiness, or even to achieve a general happiness. They feel entitled to feel good all the time. If they don't, then something or somebody must be to blame, and anger at that someone or something is to be expected. This is, in effect, the Hindu diagnosis in more contemporary language. Hinduism teaches us that inflated egos can lead to perceptions of being slighted that arouse anger on a regular basis. Cultivating humility can help us avoid anger. Part of cultivating humility is not expecting to be happy all the time. Perhaps more interest in being virtuous—developing self-control and taking pride in growing it—could help us avoid feeling so much anger and irritation in the first place.

But from a Christian perspective, even when anger is justified, as when some serious injustice is perpetrated on us or someone we love, and that anger is the source of energy to right the wrong, we need to be careful to transform the anger. As we act to right the wrong, we should not be motivated by revenge against the perpetrator, but by a love of justice. Anger always needs to be transformed, because, otherwise, it corrupts us from the inside by eroding our self-control, which is at the heart of all virtue.

Anger at God. We learn from Judaism that we may feel anger at God in a variety of situations, and expressing that anger is okay. When we see wanton destruction of life, especially on a large scale, our hearts cry out, "Where were you, Lord; why did you let this happen?" The suffering is incomprehensible; there is no other place to refer it than to God. But usually, at least one part of this anger at God is being transferred from us to God. We were also, and perhaps more centrally, asking ourselves: "Where were we, and why did we let this happen?" At some level we know this. Our friend has a few drinks with us but seems fine and leaves to drive home and is killed in a car accident. We may well demand of God why this happened, but we also continue to ask ourselves what we could have done to avert this death. When we realize the transference, we can move beyond anger at God.

But transference is not the only thing going on when we complain about God. When faced with pain, suffering, and destruction, we want to know why and how this happened, because we want to be able to prevent similar things from happening in the future. We want to believe that human life can be safe and secure and predictable. We resist the understanding that suffering is random in our world. We want to believe that bad things happen to bad people, and good things to good people: that people whose houses are washed away in floods should have known better than to build in floodplains, that women who are raped should have known better than to go to that area at night, or to go out with someone they had just met. We want to believe that if we don't do these things, we will be safe. We do not want to accept that even if we exercise most precautions, we and those we love may still be subject to violence, disease, and death. But we will. Accepting this fact of human existence is a part of the humility that both Hinduism and Buddhism see as the key to overcoming anger. Overcoming anger, both anger at God and everyday anger, requires accepting reality as it is.

Violence Surrounds Us

Today when we listen to the news, we often feel surrounded by violence. The local news is full of crime—drive-by shootings that kill toddlers, drunken car accidents that kill whole families, school shootings—and the national news is full of riots, violent uprisings, and threats of war. Yesterday (as I write), for example, in Colorado, twelve were killed and fifty-nine wounded by a university student in a theater showing a Batman movie, while in Syria the death toll in the uprising against the Assad regime rose to 27,000 dead, and in my city a mother and infant were both wounded and a toddler killed when a drive-by shooter shot the wrong house. These events seem so far beyond our control—are we completely helpless in the face of such violence?

Media focus on violence. There are a number of ethical issues here. One is that news media have become almost totally focused on violence. Local news programs in particular have seemingly decided over the last two or three decades that local news consists of killings; shootings; serious car accidents; fires; crime sprees by burglars, robbers, or rapists; child molesters; spouse killers; and political scandals or controversies. Aside from local weather and national and local sports, "if it bleeds, it leads." There is evidence that this slanted portrayal of local reality has made many people live in fear. In those neighborhoods that catch the brunt of shootings, robberies, and rapes, fear and caution are probably necessary survival skills, and most residents do not need the media to tell them this. But the media presentation of local reality in general as characterized by violence has a particularly chilling effect on the elderly, who become more isolated and sedentary as a result of fearing violence if they leave their homes. Yet violent crime has not increased in the last century; proportionately, violent crime is slightly lower than it was fifty to seventy-five years ago. Yet our fear of violence is much higher.

Fear of violence heightens racism, for violence haunts the neighborhoods of the poor, who are disproportionately of minority groups. Afraid of violence, many whites and even many minority persons stereotype minority persons, especially males, as violent. This distances racial groups and makes for misunderstandings and tension when they do come together. What can we do?

News organizations need to have more pressure put on them to reduce the coverage of crime, and increase coverage of more positive parts of local news. If media covered community efforts to turn unused railroad lines into bike paths, or local efforts to create summer or afterschool jobs for minority youth, or some of the other newsworthy stories that are not covered because of the focus on violence, there would be some reduction in fear. But what typically happens is that increases in crime and violence are headlined, and reductions in crime and violence often do not make the news at all, though they happen just as often.

Perhaps the most important thing for media to do is to reduce attempts to elicit emotional responses to crime. This would involve not only presenting fewer details about crimes, but also not shoving a microphone and camera in the face of the mother whose ten-year-old was just killed by a hit-and-run driver, or not interviewing crying child survivors of school shootings. The media should tell us what we need to know to be both as safe and as involved as necessary in our community. We do not need our hearts to bleed every time we turn on the news.

Creating callousness. The overall effect of such coverage is not only to make us feel unsafe in our communities, but also to make us increasingly callous to suffering. A callus is a thickening of the skin that builds up to protect a spot that has been worn. In self-defense, faced with these attempts to make us bleed for strangers all over the world, our hearts become calloused, become inured to depictions of the suffering of others and sometimes even to our own suffering. As we become increasingly callous, the efforts of the media to make us care, to make us bleed, become ever-more blatant. We become ever-more callous in the face of everyday suffering. This vicious cycle must stop.

The Violence of War

It has often been observed that wars are promoted by politicians who want to turn popular anger and irritation at lack of employment, rising food prices, or other current problems to external targets. One reason they can do this is precisely because we have become inured to hearing about violence as an everyday occurrence in the media. Only in the midst of a war that involves our brothers and sisters, sons and daughters, even us, do we realize the magnitude of the violence in war: not only the deaths, but the amputees and brain-injured, the suicides, and those afflicted for years with post-traumatic stress disorder (PTSD), to say nothing of the civilian effects in the battleground nation. Those effects include the shattering of families, loss of homes, loss of employment, the fears and nightmares of children that will pursue them for decades, in addition to the deaths, amputations, and other injuries inflicted on civilians and fighters alike.

We need to be suspicious of either individuals or institutions who attempt to channel the energy generated by anger toward targets that were not the source of the anger, whether that be racial or sexual minorities, an economic class, a religion, or a foreign nation. Making a habit of interrogating our irritation and anger, so that we know its cause, is the best way of ensuring that neither we nor others are able to utilize our anger for violence or other illegitimate purposes.

For the U.S., this interrogation is an increasingly important moral discipline, because it is no longer the case that the burden of fighting foreign wars falls evenly on our citizenry. We no longer have a military draft, which guaranteed that at least every extended family felt the risk of sending off a loved one to war. We no longer even have war taxes, an additional payment to remind us in a small way of the cost of war. For over a decade our nation has been waging one or more wars, and the majority of the population has not been affected in any way. The bulk of the costs are felt by the poor and working class, whose children accepted the risk of war because of a lack of employment, or in hope of government help in paying for an education after exiting the military. It is too easy to acquiesce to war when one is secured against feeling any of the suffering of that war. The same self-control that is necessary to virtue in other fields is necessary with regard to interrogating our motives in regard to war, lest we be acculturated into saying a too-easy yes to initiating mass violence.

Suicide as Violence

Suicide, because it involves the taking of a life, is generally considered a form of violence. But there are in every society exceptions to such understandings. In a number of Asian societies, persons who have been disgraced—whether there is or is not a clear moral shame in that disgrace—are considered to have done the honorable thing when they commit suicide, because their death is understood to lift the disgrace, and clear the family, or even national, name. Thus a number of Japanese military figures committed suicide at the end of World War II rather than expose their families and nation to the scandal of their being tried for war crimes by the victorious allies, and they are celebrated in the military museum in the Shinto shrine at Yushukan in Tokyo.

In some Inuit communities until the last few generations, sick elders no longer able to contribute to the work of the community would deliberately walk out onto ice floes and freeze to death, to spare the community the expense of feeding them scarce food. There have been persons who volunteered to die in order to save others whom they thought more valuable to the community. There are captains who have gone down with their ships when they could have been saved; soldiers who decided to die with their wounded comrades rather than leave them to die alone. We have tended not to think of these as suicides, though of course they are.

Distinctions among suicides. But these are not the only distinctions to be made between suicides. Today it seems to many that there are important distinctions to be made between the suicides of fifteen-year-olds and ninety-five-year-olds, between suicides of the healthy and those of persons who are dying and try to escape the last painful weeks or months of the dying process, perhaps even between those who fulfilled all their responsibilities to others and prepared their community for their deaths, and those who left others to clean up the messes in their lives and their deaths. Many of these distinctions seem clear because of the changes in human life over the last centuries.

Suicide as sin. Western religions have largely understood suicide as a sin because it usurps God's control over life and death. Only God, who is responsible for life, should have the authority to decide when it should end, religious officials in Judaism, Christianity, and Islam have repeated. It was long regarded as *hubris* (pride; arrogance) for human beings to abrogate to themselves this clearly divine right.

There were other reasons given for why suicide was a serious sin. Christians pointed out that it was a sin to defy God's control over life and death, and a mortal one because it deprived a person of any opportunity to repent this sin. Suicide caused suffering for loved ones and deprived our communities of the contributions we could have made had we lived.

Contemporary people bring new questions, however, due to relatively new situations. Diseases that used to kill their victims relatively rapidly are now often treated with drugs that allow people to live, but often with severe disabilities and pain, for many years. The dying process itself has been extended, sometimes interminably. While there were in the past always a few individuals so unlucky as to suffer protracted painful deaths, this has become the rule. More and more do we envy those who die of heart attacks in their sleep, especially if they have had no previous health problems.

When many elders in the past lived with their children, and most mothers worked only in the home, there was full-time care of disabled and dying elderly in the home. Today, disabled and dying elderly end up in sterile nursing homes, surrounded by other suffering, dying persons, because there is no one in the family home to care for them. Suicide among the elderly takes a variety of forms, including stopping life-extending treatments such as drugs, dialysis, or transfusions, or, more traditionally, simply ceasing to eat or drink. Are these wrong? In response to traditional religious arguments about the obligation to preserve life, the elderly person can say, "Yes, God is in charge of my life, and God has taken away my appetite, signaling that it is time for me to die."

Suicide by cop. Television has made us all aware of the phenomenon of suicide-by-cop, in which a suspected felon refuses to lay down a weapon or begins to run toward a police officer who is pointing a gun at them. Sometimes the suspected felon is guilty of a shameful crime, such as child sexual abuse, and a trial will destroy their good name and put them at the mercy of other criminals in prison who abuse and kill child predators. For them, suicide-by-cop is a rational decision, and it spares both their family and the community the anguish of trial. Other times, the prospect of prison invokes panic, which brings on suicidal acts.

Suicide by the young. Suicide of the young is almost never rational, but takes place in the midst of terrific emotional stress and depression. Teen suicide has been on the rise and has a number of different precipitators: bullying, exclusion, sexual victimization, drug and alcohol addiction, as well as excessive thrill-seeking. Youth are particularly vulnerable to suicide because their selves and their rational processes are still relatively unformed. They have not developed as much self-control over their feelings and actions as adults and so commit acts that are not well thought out and would be later regretted—if they survived. Adults often find suicide by youth incomprehensible: they say, "But he had everything to live for—he was healthy, attractive, smart, with a whole life ahead! Why would he do this?" But to teens who have just lost their lover, been eliminated from the team, been ridiculed one too many times, been sexually used then abandoned, or discovered that they owe thousands on a credit card they cannot pay, suicide may look like the answer to all their problems.

While we need to become more discriminating in the way we understand and discuss suicide—we need to be less judgmental in assigning moral blame—there is no excuse for

simply "accepting" all suicide within a social ethic. We need to be active in spotting people, especially the young, who are at risk, and doing whatever can be done to make their lives seem worth living to them. Sometimes that will be more than we can do, but often it will be amazing how little it will take to "solve" their mortal problem.

One thing that will help us get straight about suicide is to go back and examine the traditional concept of a good death. The good death is not the sudden death that hits us in our prime, but rather the death preceded by a long life full of interesting work, loving family, and good friends. It is death for which we have prepared, making peace with those from whom we were estranged or had injured, paying our debts, making our will and funeral arrangements, perhaps planning a funeral service with our family. It is a death we die having said good-bye to all our loved ones and blessing their lives. It is a death to which we have become reconciled, and which in at least some ways, we will welcome, if only for the cessation of pain. It is a death in which we come to peace with our Creator. This good death may be reconcilable with some forms of suicide but not with others.

Not all of us will be able to have this good death, because we cannot all choose how we will die. But even while we hold up this death as the ideal death in our society, we need to be generous in our assessment of others who choose differently, at the same time that we try to save the misguided who would stumble into suicidal acts out of emotional blindness.

Case Study: Anger and Violence

"What the —— is the matter with women?" Harry cursed as he threw his jacket at the coat rack by his parents' front door. Stomping through the hall, he found his mother in the kitchen, and opened the refrigerator, gulping milk from the carton.

"Harry!" reprimanded his mother. There was a note of resignation in Alice's protest—she knew that Harry and his brothers, even sometimes their father, drank from the carton, despite her protests over the last twenty-five years. "What has you upset today?" she asked.

"What else? It's Julie. She got mad at me and doesn't want to see me tonight. Here we're supposed to be getting engaged as soon as we graduate next month, and she still gets on her high horse and cancels our dates. I'm beginning to think she's nuts," said Harry.

"What's she mad at you about?" asked his mother.

"I have no idea!" he said. "We were just driving back from our five p.m. class, and after getting stuck in thirty minutes of traffic, we had finally gotten to our apartment, when she turns to me and says she doesn't want to go to the barbeque at Tom and Dan's, and suggests that I go without her, as she really needs a night alone. Meaning I should get lost!"

"So there was no fight, no disagreements?" asked Alice.

"No, nothing," insisted Harry.

"What did you talk about on the way home?"

"The traffic was so bad that we didn't talk much."

"Harry, were you shouting and cursing?" demanded his mother.

"Not at Julie! Just at the *#%%** drivers, all trying to squeeze into the front of the line from the emergency lane, and the stupid traffic officials that close off lanes and paint lines during rush hour."

"Harry, did you ever know that I left your dad for two months when you were two years old?" Alice inquired.

"No, why? And what does that have to do with Julie and me?" Harry asked.

"Well, I'm not sure, and you need to get Julie to tell you what distressed her. Maybe I'm wrong, but I suspect it might be your temper. Maybe she's afraid of it."

"That's absurd. I have never touched her in anger, or even come near it, and I never would. She must know that. I never even shout at her, no matter how mad I am," protested Harry.

"You may know that, but it may not seem like that to her. When you were driving, did you have the windows closed and the A/C running?"

"Of course—it's hot today. So what?"

"So when you were cursing at the drivers and road maintenance people, only Julie could hear you?" asked Alice.

"Yeah, I guess."

"So who would you say got the brunt of your anger?"

"You think she got mad over that little thing?"

"Harry, lots of women are afraid of male anger. Lots of women get beat up, even killed by husbands, boyfriends, and fathers. We live in a culture of stories of such anger and abuse—none of us is immune from it. And displays of anger are also often deliberate control mechanisms—they say to the people around that you have a temper that is only barely controlled, so they better be careful not to upset you, or they might feel your anger. Displays of anger are often a threat of violence. If they weren't, they wouldn't happen only where there is an audience."

"That's absurd, Mom. Julie knows I would never, ever hurt her. And my shouting and cursing are just letting off steam so I can get rid of the anger. It would be more uncontrollable if I simply bottled it up."

"So you say, Harry. But I suggest that you find another way to let off steam. Take up running again, or boxing—some activity that doesn't entail making someone else witness your anger and stress and wonder if it is meant as a threat. You got your father's temper—you need to learn how to control it, like he did."

"Is that why you left him?" Harry asked.

"It is. I put up with the cursing and yelling at other drivers, even his following a couple of obnoxious and dangerous drivers off the road and offering to duke it out with them—thank heavens they all saw his size and fled. But one day he had had a bad day at the office and was going to have to cancel our vacation—his parents were going to be so disappointed. He was dreading having to tell them, and when he did, his mother didn't take it well. He got off the phone, came into the kitchen and began crashing dishes on the floor. You were terrified, sitting in your highchair, and I was, too. A splinter of ceramic from the plates flew and cut your cheek. That was it. I grabbed you and went to a hotel and didn't come back till he was in anger counseling."

"But you knew why he was upset—why couldn't you just understand? I wasn't really hurt, was I? I don't even have a scar," said Harry.

"I wasn't willing for you or me, or Billy—I was pregnant at the time with Billy—to live in fear of his anger, even if such things didn't happen often. Marriage requires trust in the partner, Harry, and it is very hard to trust someone you have to fear."

"But Mom, I can promise all I like that I will never hurt Julie, but how can I promise not to ever be angry? I can't control that," insisted Harry.

"You can't control the feeling, but you can control the expression of it. You know you can—I bet you don't blow up in front of your professors, do you, even when they make you mad. And I can think of many times that you waited until you got home to express your anger at some team member that got away with hits to other players in practice, because you knew your coach wouldn't put up with displays of anger," Alice reminded him. "You need to consider why you evidently think that you don't have to control anger around Julie, why you think she should just ignore it rather than feeling insulted or maybe even threatened."

Two days later Harry came back to his parents' house with Julie for dinner, and Harry volunteered to help his mother serve dinner.

This case could have a number of next steps. Of the following possibilities, which is the most appealing to you? The most likely? The most helpful? Why? Can you suggest another that might be more helpful than these?

1. Back in the kitchen, Harry said, "Mom, I talked to Julie. She said she is not scared of me at all, that she had had a bad day, and my cursing upset her. Everything is fine. I'll try to watch the cursing in the future, and she promised to be more understanding."

2. In the dining room, Julie turned to Harry's dad, Evan, and said, "I am so grateful to Alice for talking to Harry about his anger, Evan, and you, too, for your example. I don't know if he would have listened to what she said if she hadn't told him about leaving you until you began to control your anger. His anger makes me so uncomfortable. I don't think I feel physically threatened, but I don't want to be around it."

3. Harry said to his mother, "Mom, we did talk about why she was mad, and it was my anger. She wants me to talk to her pastor and pray over it. I'm not that keen on this religious approach, but I am in the doghouse right now and want to get out. What can I do?"

   "Talk to the pastor and ask him to suggest a counselor experienced in anger issues—then maybe you can get some practical help, and only report progress to the pastor and pray over it every once in a while. Praying certainly won't hurt, Harry."

DISCUSSION QUESTIONS

1. Is there anyone in your family or circle of friends who seems to be angry often? How do you and others treat him/her? What effect does it have on your family, friends, or you?

2. Have you ever been so angry that you might consider sitting or lying down or washing your hands and praying as helpful in calming down? What kind of event made you so angry? Did you interrogate your anger?

3. Do you think that most of us are more accepting of male anger than female anger? Why? Do angry females get treated differently from angry males? How?

4. Watch the evening news for a night or two. Do you see a focus on violence? Is that focus sustained in order to elicit emotional response in viewers? How could it be better treated? Did watching the news make you feel more at risk from violence?

5. Can you think of an incident where anger at some injustice against you or someone you cared about gave you the energy to act to redress the situation? If so, could you transform the anger so that you were not pursuing vengeance on the perpetrator but justice for the victim? Did it make a difference whether you were able to transform the anger or not?

6. Has anyone you know committed suicide? How did it affect those closest to them? Do you think that suicide can be selfish? Are there kinds of suicide that are more selfish than others? What makes them so?

FOR FURTHER READING

Carter, Frank, and Frank Minirth. *The Anger Workbook*. Nashville: Thomas Nelson, 1993.

Dalai Lama, His Holiness. *Healing Anger*. Ithaca, NY: Snow Lion, 1997.

Diamond, Stephen A., and Rollo May. *Anger, Madness and the Daimonic: The Psychological Genesis of Anger, Violence and Creativity*. Albany: State University of New York Press, 1996.

Edmiston, Susan, and Leonard Scheff. *The Cow in the Parking Lot: A Zen Approach to Overcoming Anger*. New York: Workman, 2010.

Hanh, Thich Nhat. *Anger: Wisdom for Cooling the Flames*. New York: Berkley, 2001.

Harrison, Beverly Wildung. "The Work of Anger in the Power of Love: An Ethic for Women and Other Strangers." In Beverly W. Harrison, *Making the Connections: Essays in Feminist Social Ethics*, Carol Robb, ed. Boston: Beacon, 1985.

Milhaven, J. Giles. *Good Anger*. Lanham, MD: Rowman & Littlefield, 1989.

Whitehead, James D., and Evelyn Eaton Whitehead. *Transforming Our Painful Emotions: Spiritual Resources in Anger, Shame, Grief, Fear and Loneliness*. Maryknoll, NY: Orbis, 2010.

FILMS

Killing Screens: Media and the Culture of Violence. Media Education Foundation, 1999.

The Mean World Syndrome: Media Violence and the Cultivation of Fear. Media Education Foundation, 2010.

Touch Guise: Violent Media and the Crisis in Masculinity (unabridged). Media Education Foundation, 1999.

Wrestling with Manhood: Boys, Bullying and Battering. Media Education Foundation, 2003.

NOTES

1. Genesis 4:8. *The Bible: New Revised Standard Version* (Glasgow/London/New York: Collins, 1989).

2. *Bhagavad Gita* (Berkeley, CA: Blue Mountain Center of Meditation, 1985), ch. 3.

3. In Buddhism, *kleshas* are mental states that cloud the mind and result in problematic actions; they are regarded as afflictions.

4. In Buddhism, *samsara* is the wheel of rebirth, on which persons are born, die, and are rebirthed to die again, on and on until one achieves *nirvana*—release from rebirth and the illusion of self and merger into True Oneness.

5. Dalai Lama, *The Urban Dharma Newsletter*, March 9, 2004, http://www.urban dharma.org/udnl2/nl030904.html.

6. Gautama Buddha, *Kodhana Sutta: An Angry Person* (AN 7.60 Pts A iv 94), translated from the Pali by Thanissaro Bhikkhu. Access to Insight: Readings from Theravada Buddhism, http://www.access toinsight.org/tipitaka/an/an07/an07.060 .than.html.

7. Rambam (Maimonides), Hilchot de'ot 2.

8. Job 10:1-32. *The Bible: Revised Standard Version*.

9. Harold Kushner, *When Bad Things Happen to Good People* (New York: Macmillan, 1981).

10. Julia J. Exline, Ann Marie Yalie, and Marcia Lobel, "When God Disappoints: Difficulty Forgiving God and Its Role in

Negative Emotion," *Journal of Health Psychology* 4, no. 3 (1999): 365–79.

11. Harrison retired from the faculty of Union Theological Seminary in New York City. This quote comes from the Union website biography of Harrison.

12. Qur'an 9:11-15, Translation: Dr. Muhammad Taqi-ud-Din Al-Hilali, Ph.D., and Dr. Muhammad Muhsin Khan.

13. *Sahih al-Bukhari* 8, bk. 73, no. 135.

14. *Sahih al-Bukhari* 8, bk. 73, no. 137.

15. *Al-Tirmidhi* # 5145.

16. Matthew 10:34.

17. Matthew 26:52.

18. "Peace of God, Pax Dei" in Richard Landes, ed., *Encyclopedia of Millennialism and Millennial Movements* (New York: Routledge, 2000), 529–33.

19. United States Bishops' Conference, "The Challenge of Peace: God's Promise and Our Response," May 1983, http://old.usccb.org/sdwp/international/TheChallengeofPeace.pdf

CHAPTER 8

RELIGIONS ON CHARITY AND BEGGARS

Every morning when I drive out of the walled complex around my high-rise apartment building downtown on my way to the expressway to go to work, there are one or two homeless men standing on the street corners, holding paper cups into which they hope drivers stopped for the traffic light will toss money. They are white, black and Hispanic, old and young. Some have tattered signs that say, "Hungry," or "Please look at me," or simply "Please." Every day I feel torn as I approach these traffic stops. Often, like most other drivers, I ignore their presence or simply shake my head as they approach my car. Sometimes I open the window and give them something. But when I don't, I find I cannot meet their eyes, and it bothers me. My crisis of conscience has been building now for four years, ever since we moved to this area.

My husband, a developer of affordable housing, works with a coalition for the homeless in Miami. He refuses to open the window for any of these men (there use to be a tall, skeletal blonde woman, with obvious tracks in her arm, but she disappeared two years ago, and is probably dead). The homeless are numerous in our neighborhood because we are near where the Catholic Church operates Camillus House, a large facility that feeds seven to nine hundred homeless men, women, and sometimes children daily meals. Theirs is only one of many such centers in Miami. Miami is one of few cities that has a tax (one-half cent on all hotel bills and restaurant tabs) that is exclusively dedicated to the Homeless Trust. My husband insists that there is no need for the homeless to beg, except for alcohol, drugs, and cigarettes, because the services offered to the homeless are legion. They include food, temporary housing, medical care, job training and placement, and assistance in finding permanent low-cost housing. When I have volunteered at Camillus House or other shelters and feeding stations, the staff have been clear that almost all of their clients come for food, but only a minority are willing to enter these other programs. Most do not want to leave the streets.

It is relatively easy to look the other way when young, healthy-looking men smoking cigarettes (now almost seven dollars a pack in Miami) hold up the "Hungry" sign. Maybe it shouldn't be easy to ignore them.

Fig. 8.1. A homeless American man.

But children, old men and women, legless or armless people, mothers with children—it really doesn't matter that they may also be addicts or drunkards—are impossible to ignore. Faced with them, when the light changes and the cars behind me honk before I can find my wallet in my purse and get the window down, I feel that I have failed. But I never turn around and go around the block to find them.

Framing the Issues

More and more I have been comparing attitudes toward beggars in the United States with those in Indonesia, where I have spent many months teaching and researching, and still return for several weeks a few times a year. In Indonesia, I have never driven with a driver—including hundreds of taxi drivers—who did not keep in a compartment on the dash a stash of coins for beggars. At every stoplight or stopsign in the denser areas of the cities, anywhere from one to twenty

beggars will surround cars.[1] These beggars are not only the numerous homeless and unemployed. In university cities, many students also approach cars carrying small crude mandolins, and will play and sing the first line of some popular song and then quickly extend a hand to beg. These are often not musicians—many of them cannot play more than the six to ten notes they play for motorists. But there is more pride in being poor buskers—street performers—than in simply begging like the homeless. Both student buskers, and the sick, homeless, jobless poor, are omnipresent.

When I first went to Indonesia ten years ago, I was appalled by the numbers of beggars. When I had first worked and traveled in the Andean regions of Latin America, there were always hordes of beggar children in tourist spots, and cathedral steps were dotted with begging adults and children, often with gross deformities. (With declining poverty over the last two decades, there are clearly fewer beggars, though they still haunt tourist sites.) I learned to look around cautiously before giving coins, lest I be trapped by scores of children pulling on me, which is a terrifying experience. In the Andes it was clear that I was a target because I was taller than most and blonde, clearly a foreigner, a tourist. But in Indonesia, beggars solicit from everyone, and virtually all classes of persons give. Housewives, taxi drivers, teachers, and workers of all sorts routinely give coins and even bills to beggars. I had to learn never to pay any charges with exact change, but to keep the small bills and coins and hold them ready for the outstretched hands. (I should explain that there are about 9000 rupiah to the U.S. dollar, and the smallest and most common bill is a 1000-rupiah note, worth about eleven cents. However, food is very, very cheap in Indonesia.)

Fig. 8.2. Girl begging at a metro railway station in New Delhi, India.

These very different experiences of beggars and their benefactors have left a number of questions in my mind. While it is clear that the number of beggars varies with the poverty of the region, why the differences in response to beggars? Religions have long histories of teaching believers to respond to the needs of the poor. How different are those teachings between religions, and how relevant are these teachings today? Are humans in general under moral obligation to give to beggars? Is it appropriate to draw distinctions between worthy and unworthy beggars? If so, on what grounds? In well-off societies that have accepted collective responsibility for the poor, and tax their citizens to provide for the poor do there remain any personal obligations to give aid?

Religious Treatment of Charity and Beggars

Because poverty has been a more or less constant part of human civilizations, religions around the world tend to have developed stances on giving charity to the needy, often connected to sacrifices to the gods.

Judaism

The original Jewish tithe, a donation of 10 percent of agricultural produce to two different classes of Temple priests, was a part of the Mosaic law. The tithe was used to support the priestly class, but also for various Temple programs that benefited the poor. Following the final destruction of the Temple in 70 CE and the accompanying diaspora of Jews, the tithe fell into disuse, but its presence in the Torah has supported a great deal of Jewish philanthropy through the ages. In postbiblical Hebrew, *tzedakah* refers to charity: giving to those in need. The term *tzedakah* is also translated as "justice." Judaism has tended to understand charity as an act of justice, of sharing the fruits of the earth. The Jewish tradition understands all persons to have a right to the necessities of life: food, clothing, and shelter. It is an obligation of those who have to share with those who lack. To give charity under Jewish law and tradition is not viewed as a voluntary donation that is supererogatory, but is rather seen as obligatory self-taxation. In the prayers for the High Holidays, it is mentioned that God has inscribed a judgment against all who have sinned, but *teshuvah* (repentance), *tefilah* (prayer), and *tzedakah* (charity) can reverse the decree.

Until Jewish Emancipation in the nineteenth century, Jewish communities in Europe were often separate from the non-Jewish majority and often even ruled internally. Structures and officials internal to the ghettos tended to care for their own Jewish poor, orphans, and sick. Over the last century, the Jewish community in North America has not only continued to care for its own orphans, elderly, sick, and poor through establishment of Jewish hospitals, schools, nursing homes, social services for the poor, and adoption agencies, but its philanthropy has also spilled over into the larger society in all these areas, as well as in the arts. Jewish support for the civil rights movement of the 1950s and 1960s, both in terms of monetary donations and involvement, was also disproportionately strong. North American Jews have also been an important source of funding for institutions that serve the poor in Israel.

Christianity

Within Christianity, the Gospels made very clear that for Jesus, it was impossible to be virtuous without responding to the needy—to those who were sick, hungry, thirsty, or cold. In the Gospel of Matthew in the New Testament, we read:

> "When the Son of Man comes in his glory, and all the angels with him, then he will sit on his glorious throne. . . . Then he will say to those on his left, 'Depart from me, you cursed, into the eternal fire prepared for the devil and his angels. For I was hungry and you gave me no food, I was thirsty and you gave me no drink, I was a stranger and you did not welcome me, naked and you did not clothe me, sick and in prison and you did not visit me.' Then they also will answer saying, 'Lord, when did we see you hungry or thirsty or a stranger or naked or sick or in prison and did not minister to you?' Then he will answer them saying, 'Truly, I say to you, as you did not do it to one of the least of these, you did not do it to me.' " (Matt. 25:31-45 ESV)

Gospel stories abound in which Jesus not only personally intervened to help the sick, the poor, the handicapped, and children, but also scolded the Pharisees for focusing on obedience to the law, rather than on concern for persons.

By the second Christian century, there were ascetics, desert anchorites for the most part, who took on voluntary poverty in lives of prayer and meditation. They became the basis for later religious orders, communities of ascetic monks and nuns, who took vows of poverty, chastity, and obedience to the rule of their order. Because many of the monasteries and convents were gifted by the wealthy over the centuries, temptations against the practice of poverty abounded among monks and nuns, and reforms were periodically necessary.[2] Yet the many Christian monasteries and convents became a symbol both of the virtue of voluntary poverty and of the need to alleviate involuntary poverty. By the early medieval period, the Christian church had established a network of institutions to aid the needy, beginning with the monasteries and convents, which commonly offered not only safe lodging and meals to travelers, but also often provided simple meals to the nearby poor and sometimes medical care for the sick. Monasteries and convents also took in abandoned or orphan children, usually raising them to become monks and nuns.[3]

Foundling homes, orphanages, and hospitals were also established by the church to care for the poor. Wealthy Christians confessing their sins were often given penances that included donations to these institutions. Within these institutions there were sometimes distinctions made between worthy and unworthy recipients of charity. For example, many, if not most, of the children abandoned to Christian foundling hospitals over the centuries were born to married couples who could not support more children.[4] To enable such couples to keep children safe and still avoid shame in abandoning excess children, foundling hospitals, which began in Italy and gradually spread north in Europe, incorporated an ingenious horizontal wheel in the exterior corner of the hospital.[5] Parents could deposit the child in the space between the spokes of the wheel and turn the wheel so that the child disappeared into the building without disclosing to those inside the identity of the parents. Yet provisions for unwed mothers were punitive. They were often incarcerated in foundling hospitals, separated from their children, and made to nurse for many months, sometimes even years, other infant foundlings, but never their own.

Within Christianity in the late-modern period, attention turned from both institutional and personal charity toward the poor to social justice for the poor. This occurred in conjunction with the civil shift to global democracy beginning with the French Revolution, with its emphasis on citizenship and the rights of citizens. Today many Christian churches are still involved in charitable outreach to the needy of all kinds, but are also active in promoting social justice through political and economic reforms. As Christian churches in many areas lost their state establishment, some have attempted to revive the tithe. Because the earliest Christians were Jews who tithed to the Temple priests, a practice resembling tithing is mentioned in the New Testament. In the epistles of Paul, for example, there is frequent mention of a collection that was gathered from gentile Christians outside Palestine to relieve the poverty of Christians in Jerusalem and nearby. There is some debate within Christian churches today about whether the tithe and the support of the church are one and the same, or whether one's tithe should be split between support of the church and personal charity in the community.

Islam

While Jesus inspired the creation of the Christian church but did not live to establish a church or give any systematic rules for a community, in Islam, Mohammed was not only the source of inspiration and channel for revelation but also the founder of Islam. He led his religious community for many years before his death, establishing innumerable precedents for later Muslim institutions. Within Islam, Mohammed understood and taught from the beginning that care for the needy was a collective responsibility, which he arranged to be collectively discharged. *Zakat*, the alms tax, is one of the five pillars of Islam, along with the profession of faith, daily prayer, fasting for Ramadan, and the *hadj* pilgrimage to Mecca. *Zakat* is a tax on wealth, computed in different ways, but usually equal to about 2.5 percent of wealth. In Muslim nations, it is normally collected by the state and is used to support hospitals, schools, mosques, debt relief, ransom of prisoners of war (in the past), and for programs for the poor.

Though *zakat*, as one of the five pillars of Islam, is obligatory, there is also a Muslim tradition of voluntary almsgiving, called *sadaqah*, which is also traced back to Mohammed and to the Qur'an. Mohammed taught that Allah will take into account the charity that individuals have shown to the needy. The Qur'an urges *sadaqah* in a number of places, including: "That which you give in usury for increase through the property of (other) people, will have no increase with Allah: but that which you give for charity, seeking the Countenance of Allah (will increase); it is those who will get a recompense multiplied" (Qur'an, 30:39).

Today *zakat* in many Muslim-majority nations and elsewhere is utilized for free or reduced-price rice programs, in providing popular clinics, education for the poor, mosque-building in poor neighborhoods, and many more public programs for the relief of poverty. *Sadaqah* can take the form of individual donations to these programs or others but may also take the form of personal gifts or loans (without interest, forbidden in Islam) to those in need, including street beggars.

Buddhism and Hinduism

In all three of these religions with western origins, the historical record includes both a recognition of the collective obligation to institutionalize care for the poor and strong encouragement to believers to give personal charity. Both of these are also present in religions of Asian origin, but complete renunciation of material possessions is in both Hinduism and Buddhism more closely connected to salvation (*moksha/nirvana*) than in western religions. Voluntary poverty in western religions is associated with Christian religious orders and some Muslim Sufi orders but has not historically been urged on the general laity. While this division between the spiritual elites and the ordinary believers, and the varying standards of material renunciation associated with them, also exists in Hinduism and Buddhism, there is a difference.

Hinduism. In Hinduism, the connection between ascetic *sannyasin* (*sadhu/sadhvi*) beggars and householders is closer because all male—and today female—householders are potential *sannyasin*. Normally those who choose to become *sannyasin* have discharged all their householder duties (their children are adults) before they take up the *sannyasin* life. All are potential beggars as *sannyasin*.

In Hinduism, as early as the *Rig Veda* (II, 28, 9), human virtue was described as always giving out help and never asking for help. This emphasis on giving charity to the needy continued in the Upanishads:

Taittiriya Upanishad III, 3, x: Like in a well the more you fetch, more water oozes, the more you give the more you get. Such generosity is mandatory for every individual. Hurry to promise or vow to help.

Mahanarayana Upanishad IV, 78: The Divinities rejoice when somebody's happiness is owed to another's sacrifice given voluntarily.

Manusmriti III, 15–19: The Creator God (Prajapati) gave His injunction to human beings, demons and divinities as: Datta =

Give away; Damyata = Curb your desires; and Dayadhvam = Be kind, respectively.[6] It is people's obligation always to share with others whatever they possess, and without fail on festive days, sacrifices, marriage, and funerals etc. which are especially marked for acquiring virtues. The best help is the one which is given to strangers where there is no reciprocation (of getting help in return). Even a beggar, a forest dweller, a monk must search for giving [to another] the help at his reach. Money is not the only thing one can part with. Every one shall always keep searching [for] one's own help, and [for] those who require help.[7]

In addition to these injunctions in sacred texts to give to the needy, as far back as the Vedic period in Hinduism, various kinds of ascetics who begged their food were venerated for the advanced meditative states they achieved, for their progress toward *moksha*, the goal of no-self, of being a part of pure being. Within the *asramas*, the four stages of life and disciplined virtue in Hinduism (student, householder, forest dweller/retirement, and finally, *sannyasin*, a renunciation of the life-affirming prior stages), renouncing material possessions and begging one's food from householders is central to the final stage of *sannyasin*. Begging and renunciation are signs of the detachment from the material world that *sannyasin* make, along with breaking ties to previous lives (to family, friends, and even sacred traditions) and becoming wandering beggars devoted to meditation and mysticism. As *sannyasin* they could hope to

Fig. 8.3. Holy *sadhu* men at stairs of Varanasi ghats in Benares, India.

either attain *moksha*, or at least to improve their karma sufficiently to be reborn in a higher caste, closer to possible attainment of *moksha*. *Sannyasin* are without caste; even a *shudra* can become a *sannyasin* and thereby overcome caste associations and limitations.

While the Hindu tradition taught that the ideal (male) Hindu would decide to become *sannyasin*, it also taught that as a householder one earned merit by feeding the *sannyasin*. This pattern of the majority earning merit by supporting the minority of elite religious practitioners passed into Buddhism.

Buddhism. In Buddhism, the path to *nirvana* for all runs through detachment. Though it is theoretically possible for householders to reach *nirvana* (there are historical examples), the monastic path is the normal fast track. Householders who settle for achieving merit toward their next life instead of choosing the monastic life, which could significantly advance their progress to *nirvana*, know that they are only postponing the task of complete detachment from the material world that is necessary for reaching *nirvana*.

Buddha proclaimed that he was about the elimination of suffering; this is the entire point of the Four Noble Truths, the central Buddhist teaching. In the *Ina Sutta* (*Anguttara Nikaya* 6.45), Buddha stated that "poverty is suffering."[8] The section goes on to describe the series of misfortunes that accompany poverty: debt, interest payments, being hounded by creditors, and even debt bondage, by which a person becomes more and more dependent, and more and more isolated from others.

But ultimately, this passage goes on to say that even poverty is, at base, about inattention to reality, about being taken in by illusion. The inattention may not be on the part of the poor person himself or herself. For example, many slaves have suffered the most extreme poverty, but their poverty was due not to their own, but to their owner's—and his society's—inattention to the interdependence of all things. People who view material things as ultimately real and important, and therefore covet them, are responsible for denying others the basic necessities for maintaining life. Poverty as lack is suffering. But poverty as simplicity, as acceptance of dependence, is liberating.

Voluntary poverty is at the heart of the Buddha's message, for his message was that to avoid suffering, one must avoid attachment to this world and all its objects. Therefore, those who desire to seriously pursue the goal of enlightenment, no-self, of *nirvana*, should normally become monks (*bhikkhus*) and nuns

Fig. 8.4. Zen Buddhist monk begging on a street in Kyoto, Japan.

(*bhikkhunis*) and follow the path laid out by Buddha as their full-time occupation.

Within Buddhism, the *bhikkhus* and *bhikkhunis* of the *sangha* (Buddhist community) were also, like the Hindu *sannyasin*, dependent upon food donated by householders for their daily meals. Buddha taught that it was not necessary to be serially reborn within the caste system until one achieved the status of male Brahmin before aspiring to *moksha* (*nirvana* in Buddhism) as had been the case in Hinduism; instead, any person, male or female from any caste, could, by completely devoting oneself to the path to *nirvana* as a *bhikkhu* or *bhikkhuni*, aspire to reaching *nirvana* within a given lifespan. Begging one's daily meal was both evidence of one's nonattachment to material things and a help in attaining the humility called for on the path to *nirvana*.

In both Hinduism and Buddhism, begging by religiously revered figures was facilitated by the teaching that householders earned spiritual merit by giving to *sannyasin*, *bhikkhus*, and *bhikkhunis*. Householders who were generous with those pursuing detachment improved their own karma by demonstrating some degree of nonattachment to material things, and moved closer to the possibility of reaching their ultimate spiritual goal. Thus in Hinduism and Buddhism, as in western religions, one has a duty to share with the poor, to give to beggars. Ordinary charity, that given to the nonreligious poor, was meritorious but generally considered not so meritorious as giving to the recognized religious elites. Not only the donation itself, but also the interaction with *sannyasin*, *bhikkhus*, and *bhikkhunis*, understood to be holy persons, was often considered to bestow a blessing on the donor. The donation given a lay beggar and a holy person might be the same, but the difference in spiritual status between them often made the donation to the holy person be regarded as weightier.

This distinction between religious and nonreligious beggars was sometimes sharper within Buddhism than in Hinduism. As Buddhism grew and spread, Buddhist monks and nuns were less and less solitary, but lived in well-organized communities, in monasteries and convents that kept histories of their communities and of the donors who gifted them. Even in the accounts of the *sangha* during the life of the Buddha, there are mentions of householders, both men and women, who were especially generous to the *bhikkhus* and *bhikkhunis*. The Buddhist *sangha* was able to publicly acknowledge generous donors in ways that neither *sannyasin* nor ordinary, isolated lay beggars, no matter how holy, could ever hope to match. Despite religious injunctions to give without any hope of reward or recognition for one's generosity, as development officers today know well, public recognition of donors is a sure way to ensure larger and repeat donations.

New Ethical Questions on Charity and Beggars

There are perhaps two questions that have arisen in late modernity concerning charity and beggars that do not seem to have been directly addressed in the religious teachings on charity. The first is to what extent personal obligations to give charity still exist in modern societies where taxes are collected to support a variety of programs to alleviate poverty, including providing housing, food, disability income, unemployment payments, worker's compensation, Medicare, Medicaid, Social Security, and others. The second is to what extent the existence of beggar scams, which are much more possible in modern anonymous society than in earlier societies in which strangers were rarer, alters our responsibility to give to beggars. We will return to this second question later.

Public Programs Do Not Erase Personal Obligations to Charity

There are a number of things to be learned from even this quick survey on charity to the poor in world religions that is relevant to my dilemma of how to respond to homeless in my neighborhood. Perhaps most importantly, there is some form of *both* collective and personal charity to the poor advocated and practiced in each religion, though Islam is perhaps the clearest on the need for believers to practice both. While the scale of modern government programs for the poor greatly exceeds those of the past, the religious imperative to give has never been exhausted by involuntary public taxation, because public programs have never eliminated involuntary poverty. In fact, it is well known that a majority of those who are poor in the United States are those already on public programs. For example, monthly income to the disabled under the Social Security program in 2012 averaged $700, in addition to $150–200/month of food stamps. In many urban centers in the United States, it is impossible to rent an efficiency apartment for less than $1000/month. Elderly who receive minimum Social Security payments often run out of food by the last week of the month, and are dependent upon privately funded soup kitchens.

We can only speculate on why religions have thought that neither collective, institutional care for the poor nor personal charity toward the needy was sufficient. Usually individuals organize institutional support for the poor in periods of increased social awareness

of the suffering of the poor. Sometimes this awareness is caused by a real increase in the number of those suffering, as in economic recessions, natural disasters, or wars. The worldwide recession that began in 2007–2008, one of the longest in modern history, has greatly increased the ranks of the poor and needy.

At other times, increased public awareness might not reflect actual increases in poverty, but only increased attention to longstanding situations, as was the case in the United States in the mid-1960s when Senator Robert Kennedy led a congressional delegation (and many reporters) to the rural South to expose the poverty there, which increased public support for new Great Society programs for the poor under President Johnson.[9]

How Many Poor? One might think that people would find it easiest to be charitable to the poor when there are many nonpoor householders and relatively few poor. But in fact this tends to be true only in very small communities, where both the poor and the nonpoor are known to each other and recognize each other as neighbors. Such was often the case in the eighteenth and nineteenth centuries among urban European Jews, who were generally restricted to Jewish ghetto communities in which they administered their own law as well as social services.

Villages and small towns in many cultures and religions functioned in this way, because as many theologians have noted, it is easier to love persons you know, who are connected to you in some way, than to love anonymous strangers. Also, when we personally know persons who are poor, we know better the reasons they are poor. But when the poor are not personally known to us and constitute an anonymous minority in our midst, we tend to dismiss their appeals: "Everyone else manages to find work and support themselves; why haven't you?"

Today in the West, and particularly in the United States, severe poverty is relatively rare. That does not mean that poverty does not exist in the United States, nor that people in the United States never starve to death. It does not mean that there are no nations where the proportion of poor is even lower. It only means that the proportion of the U.S. population afflicted by hunger, homelessness, and/or lack of medical care is lower than in most other nations.

Are the Poor Really Deserving?

There is a popular ideological explanation for why fewer persons in the United States are poor by global standards. The national story in the United States has been that American freedom allowed immigrants from other countries to escape poverty and even gain riches once they arrived. Economic success in America, the ideology went, was open to anyone willing to work hard. And for people coming to the U.S. from many nationalities over a period of four centuries, this national ideology was a more or less accurate predictor because America had, until the last half century, a chronic labor shortage and abundant natural resources. Nevertheless, not all who came to America experienced this economic freedom and opportunity. For enslaved Africans, the Chinese, Irish, Japanese, Italians, and other later immigrants, it was and is often left to their children, grandchildren, or even later descendants to escape poverty and injustice in America and find the freedom to succeed. But the real downside of this ideology, even for the many for whom it proved true, was that it has been, and continues to be, so often misinterpreted to mean that anyone who is poor is responsible for

their own poverty, that they were not willing to work hard or were not ambitious enough to succeed.

Since the economic downturn that began in 2008 in the United States, more Americans are becoming aware that poverty and even homelessness in the United States are closely related to factors that have little or nothing to do with willingness to work hard. The most obvious of those factors is economic recession itself and the massive layoffs that it produces. At the peak of unemployment in this recession, over 15 million Americans had lost their jobs, and four years later, the unemployment rate was still over 8 percent, at about 12 million. The ranks of the unemployed have contained both low-skilled workers in fields such as construction, and well-educated banking and finance officers, as well as myriad others.

Another factor, which, aside from economic recessions, is a very common cause for poverty is poor health. Over 50 million Americans lack healthcare insurance (at least until full coverage kicks in under the Obama administration's 2010 healthcare bill). For those without health insurance, any serious accident, surgery, or disease could make it impossible to keep up mortgage, rent, utility, or car payments, and threaten individuals and families with homelessness and/or hunger. It remains to be seen, after the nation recovers from this economic trouble and the number of poor decreases again, to what extent Americans will later remember that poverty should not automatically be assumed to indicate faulty moral character.

While few would blame the poor who were plunged into poverty by the loss of jobs in 2008–2009, or those who lost jobs and businesses in the Gulf of Mexico following the massive Deepwater Horizon explosion and oil spill, many do point a finger of blame at the housing foreclosure debacle. Because material success within the American ideology is often interpreted as the fruit of hard work and initiative, and thus the proof of virtue and worth, many sought the signs of success, such as large houses, before they had earned the level of material success that could safely support such signs. Many Americans have lived beyond their means not only in terms of houses, but also in terms of cars, vacations, and credit card expenditures. Any economic disruption, either personal or systemic, could bring them down. Such spending patterns are seen by many as irresponsible, both personally and for the larger society.

A Buddhist approach to spending beyond one's means would be to see one as taken in by the illusions associated with material things. In a peculiarly American twist, those who fell victim to outsize spending are also looked down on as having been deceitful—as having erected an image of success and claimed a level of worth that they had not earned. But while many Americans feel sympathy for victims of some kinds of scams—think of those who lost thousands, even millions, in the Ponzi scheme of Bernie Madoff[10]—these same people are often critical of those who are taken in by realtors or car salesmen who convince them that they can afford the new house or car. Perhaps we are more generous to the rich who are scammed, because we think them less likely to need to be bailed out by public tax dollars (though the big banks were among the first to be bailed out following the collapse of the mortgage securities market).

But our national ideology is not the only reason why so many nonpoor blame poverty on the poor. As we saw in the previous chapter on anger, many of us resist the idea that there is any randomness at all to suffering and evil, because if these are random, then we are

all at risk. We want to believe that the victims of suffering, those upon whom evil is visited, have invited such suffering upon themselves, have deserved it in some manner. Because if the victims of suffering deserved it, then we who are not yet victims can assure ourselves that it will not happen to us, the deserving. Our need to feel secure from poverty or other forms of victimization seems to almost demand that we blame the victims. Only when the victims include those we know and care for, those close to us, are we forced to admit the randomness of suffering—that it strikes the good and the bad. Only then do we look at the victims and recognize that it could be us, that our comparative good fortune is the result of chance as much or more than it is to our hard work and virtue.

Resisting Victim-Blaming

Sometimes, of course, humans resist the tendency to blame the victim and instead respond with our more generous side to the victims of suffering—to those who lose family or homes to hurricanes, floods, crime, job loss, and other calamitous events. But not always. Sometimes, especially if the victims are different from us, not perceived as part of our intimate community, we look for reasons to blame their victimization on them. Also, the more threatened we are by what happened to them, the more likely we are to blame them. Women, for example, are more likely to blame rape victims than are men, because they are more at risk. Women more often than men want to believe that the protective measures they have learned and their avoidance of "dangerous" places and activities actually protect them, that rape victims failed to implement these measures, and that this is why they were raped.[11]

This kind of reaction—blaming the victim—to the facts of poverty is much less possible in very poor nations. In Indonesia, for example, despite its surge in development, most take it for granted that the bulk of the population is poor, that the most common path to comfort and riches is not hard work but being related to a powerful politician or general, engaging in such activities as illegal logging of government land, or demanding bribes from businesses, foreign and national, as part of one's government job. The common wisdom is that the hardest work is done by those paid the least, that those paid the most often do the least to earn it. Thus being poor is not at all cause for moral blame. The ordinary person in Indonesia passing a beggar is much more likely to think, *There but for the grace of God go I*, than to think that the beggar is a scam artist too lazy to work, which would be common in the States. Many Indonesians to whom I have put the question why they are so generous with beggars tell me that it is their hope that by their giving to beggars regularly, Allah will see that they are grateful for the benefits given to them and are willing to share those benefits with others—lest Allah decide that their benefits should be taken away. It will be interesting to see whether the increasingly successful economy of Indonesia, which is steadily growing the middle class, will eventually change this attitude toward beggars. Will those who have been successful in escaping poverty credit only their own efforts for that success and blame those who have not had similar success? Or will they acknowledge whatever assistance they had, including sheer good luck, and see themselves as having obligations to the unlucky?

Efficiency and Virtue

We Americans both respect efficiency and expect it. Many Americans will support taxes that support the poor, as voter passage of the Miami tax for the Homeless Coalition demonstrates. But voters who support such a tax expect the money to be administered efficiently, which to most of us not only means that it is not stolen or wasted, but also that it is used to benefit those who are in need and, so far as is possible, also serves to move those needy out of poverty into self-sufficiency. In many ways our expectations around efficiency reflect an assumption that self-sufficiency is possible for everyone. But our poor include the chronically ill, the mentally retarded, schizophrenics, the senile demented, and other disabled persons, as well as drug and alcohol addicts. The poor are more than merely the momentarily jobless.

No reform of our economy is going to make all parts of our present poor population self-sufficient. There will always be some who need aid; some will need aid simply in locating and applying for the programs that can give them the material aid they need. So if there will always be some "poor," we must ask: What is the effect on us as moral agents of passing by begging poor in our communities? When I drive past the ragged man with the sign that says, "Meet my eyes," I am very aware that I am not meeting his eyes, and I feel guilty that I do not meet his eyes. Many of us tell ourselves as we pass the beggars in the street that we pay taxes to support the poor, and we give donations to United Way. We might even occasionally volunteer in soup kitchens or with Habitat for Humanity. What more could be demanded of us?

When I pass the street beggar without stopping, I have judged him as not worthy of help, for I could always and easily part with some change. I have judged him as an alcoholic or drug addict, as lazy, or as a scam artist, and I have done that without ever looking at him or listening to him. Why have I done this? Often, it would take no time, for he approaches while I am already stopped at the light. Is it the loss of the money? Not really, for even at a dollar a day, five or six dollars a week, this is what I spend in tolls to take the more convenient route to my office, rather than the side street. Why do I pass him by? The real reason, I think, is that I do not want to be pulled into his suffering, into the tragedy that his life seems to be. If I give him a dollar, will he ask me if I can give him a bed or find him a doctor? I am afraid to become involved. Even as I try to tease out the fears that underlie my passing him by, there is a screaming in my mind: "You are already too busy, with too many people to take care of! There is enough pain and hurt in your life without opening yourself to more! Be rational about this!"

The problem with this screamed message is that while there are undoubtedly some persons for whom it is true—for example, my sister, who has adopted over twenty abused or high-needs children over the last twenty-five years—for most of us it is not true. And if we are truthful, it is those like my sister who have already overburdened themselves with the needy who are the most likely to stop and offer help. Most of us are not overburdened by our charity. And the majority of the time, giving a dollar will not be followed by a larger request, but only by a polite expression of gratitude. Giving a dollar to a homeless beggar will not lead to opening our home as a homeless shelter. It will only mean giving a dollar.

I must ask, what is the effect on *me* of passing him by three or four times a week, week after week? It is hard for me not to think that closing my heart to this appeal for help makes it easier to close my heart to other appeals for help, that I risk creating a callus around my heart. If in order to pass him by, I repeat to myself all the rationalizations—that beggars are addicts, scam artists, who have many sources of support from taxes and institutional programs, that giving to them makes one codependent in their homelessness—do those rationalizations not, over time, harden my heart to all appeals for help? How many times can one turn away and refuse to look at people seeming to suffer without becoming immune to suffering? Calluses grow thicker and thicker over time.

These are the questions of virtue ethics, which forces us to ask: What kind of person do I want to be? And how do I best become that kind of person? One of the most common theological answers to that question of how one acquires virtue comes, among others, from Thomas Aquinas, a medieval philosopher/theologian, whose answer was that virtue is largely habit.[12] One does what virtuous persons do, and eventually one becomes a virtuous person also. Virtue for Thomas is a discipline that must be learned. In the beginning, one might only have the desire to be virtuous, without fully understanding what that means. It is by practicing virtuous acts that we learn virtue, that we take on a virtuous disposition.

Moral Risks in Dealing with Powerless People

Virtue ethics, of course, is not the only important perspective to take, because good intentions do not always protect us from imposing injustice or suffering. Care for others always involves the use of power. This use of power in the name of the needs of the other can easily, often without our realizing it, become an imposition of the care we want to give on the Other who might desire a very different kind of care. The very powerlessness that is often at the root of poverty makes the poor—and children, the elderly, the mentally disabled, and chronically ill—unable to articulate their needs and desires clearly. In the absence of clearly articulated needs by the poor, caretakers initially supply what they see as the relevant needs. This substitution of what I think the poor need for what the poor really need but are unable to articulate can become habitual, so that we become completely deaf to the voices of the poor even when they could speak, if we only would listen. The poor should be at the mercy neither of individuals practicing to achieve personal virtue in the form of compassion, nor of those whose love of the poor does not include the ability to hear their voices.

In some ways institutional approaches to the poor would seem to be more efficient—they can provide not only small sums of daily money, but also housing, education, and medical care, because they involve large-scale organization and planning that most of us are not able to achieve in the distribution of our individual charity. Every society needs collective, institutional approaches to charity. But religious traditions have been correct to teach that collective approaches, while necessary, are not sufficient, for two reasons. One of those reasons is that the very planning that institutions must do in their outreach to the poor approaches the poor as a group of persons with homogenous needs. They ask, "What do the poor need?" even when prior experience has shown that the homeless who are mentally ill have different needs from homeless alcohol and drug addicts, and both of these groups have different needs from families who were doing well until they lost jobs and homes. The circumstances of each poor person or family are different, and require different forms of care. Institutions

offer the poor what the institutions have and are best at doing, but within each category, it is the same. This is inevitable when dealing with large groups of persons.

The other reason why giving our charity to institutions to administer is not enough is that limiting ourselves to institutional charity—writing a check to United Way—protects us from having to deal with our needy neighbor. We Americans are generous with our money in response to tragedy—the 2011 Japanese earthquake/tsunami/nuclear accident, the 2008 Haitian earthquake disaster, the 2005 Asian tsunami, and the 2004 Hurricane Katrina and the breaks in the New Orleans levees. In all of these cases, Americans donated many millions. But some of us bought off our consciences with those donations. We could spare $10, or $100, or even $1000, and still live our lives without being faced with the need to personally look the suffering of others in the eye.

Looking the Needy in the Eyes

We need to periodically look suffering people in the eyes. We need to do it not only so that our own sufferings are relativized and put in perspective. We need to do it so that when the day comes that someone we love dearly is that suffering person in front of us, we can look our loved one in the eye and share his or her suffering without turning away. But beyond that, we need to do it in order to preserve our humanity, to make it possible for us to move to the next steps in the discipline of virtue, to loving our neighbor.

Though the traditional advice of many religious traditions that we should pray for the poor is often ridiculed, it is good to pray for the poor, to pray for all who suffer. Do the suffering benefit from being prayed for? Certainly knowing that someone is praying for one can help suffering persons feel less isolated. Many believe that prayer helps even when persons do not know they are prayed for. But there can be no doubt that prayer benefits the one who prays. Praying for the poor, for those who suffer, can be an early step in the discipline of neighbor love.

We need to look suffering in the eye; we need to pray for those suffering. The alternative—merely pitying the child dying of malnutrition, the uninsured mother's daylong wait to be seen in the ER, the traumatized vet back from Afghanistan or Iraq, or deploring the existence of the homeless beggar, the teen cashier who can't add, the pregnant twelve-year-old—and refusing to look them in the eye, grows a callus on our hearts that not only allows us to set these outside the personal reality for which we accept responsibility, but also allows us to dwell on our own sufferings overlong, to indulge in anger and self-pity.

This does not mean that we should give to every beggar in the street. My drugstore is next to a liquor store, and there are invariably two or three dirty, foul-smelling inebriated homeless men sitting on the sidewalk between the doors of the drugstore and the liquor store, soliciting passersby for change. I probably will never be moved to give money to one of these. Perhaps I just can't see that far down the road of the discipline of becoming charitable. Today it still seems to me that responsible giving means that our institutional giving should go to organizations with low overhead and a maximal proportion of contributions going to the needy, and that our personal giving should strive to be equally effective. It will not always be. Once in Indonesia I was so moved by the skeletal condition of a toddler lying across his mother's lap that I folded up a 50,000-rupiah note

(about five dollars then) and passed it to her. (In Indonesia then and now, this was enough to feed both for a week or more.) My Indonesian graduate student, a native of the city, pulled me away and told me the woman was notorious in the neighborhood for renting sick and dying children from her fellow poor for purposes of raising her begging income and had different children each week. Once I knew that, I probably would choose to give to other beggars around her, not to her. But it would be wrong to pass by all the mothers with skeletal children by telling myself that they were all scam artists. Even in this case, as I learned from my grad student, the beggar woman really was poor, without any source of income other than begging. Faced with her situation, I could not even be sure that I would not have done the same as she. Perhaps she is just a smarter beggar than the others. Here the Jewish tradition, with its insistence that charity to the poor is a form of justice, is most relevant. To deserve justice, it is enough to be human. One need not be virtuous to deserve justice.

The Role of Prudence in Compassion

Compassion is a virtue that has a role in many different parts of our lives. But no virtue stands alone; they are all connected. If our compassion is to be effective, it requires prudence. We all have limited personal and social resources, and an obligation to see that they are used effectively. Prudence helps us distinguish what the best uses of those resources are; it helps us weigh the relative advantages and disadvantages of the options available for compassionate giving, whether of our time or our money. Compassion should be our motivation, but prudence needs to guide that compassion.

To some extent, becoming a prudent person entails learning from our experience, not just from our personal experience, but also from our collective social experience, our history, as well. Just as we know that not every person with a hand stretched out on the street is needy, not every charity we find on the Internet and not every government program that purports to be for the poor is equally worthy of our compassionate support. We can never be totally sure of what uses our dollars will be put to by a homeless person on the corner, or which disaster relief program will make best use of our contributions, or which proposed bills in our legislatures will alleviate the most suffering. We

have to make the most prudent choices we can with our limited knowledge.

But if compassion requires prudence to be effective, prudence also requires compassion, for prudence is only a means to other ends. It is a tool, not an end in itself. It is very easy for prudence not motivated by compassion to become cynical, to use any uncertainty that our gift will be used effectively to justify not giving at all. This misuse of prudence moves us to distrust of others in general, a distrust that can easily lead to anger and isolation. In contrast, the message at the center of all religions has been that it is compassion that ultimately connects us, creating a web of connections that we today might call a kind of safety net.

Case Study: Charity and Beggars

The TV news in the airport was about a new presidential candidate's income tax releases, Alexis noted. It seems that the candidate and his wife made about $1.5 million each year for the last five years and yet listed only $4K in charity, most of that to their church. He was being bashed by liberals as a hypocrite, since he was running as one of the darlings of the Christian right, which was not responding to the attacks on him. For those churches that taught tithing—giving 10 percent to charity—like the candidate's did, he was not a good example.

As Alexis sat and watched, waiting for her plane home, she asked herself: "I wonder how Bob and I would look if we had to make public our income and charity for the last few years? We don't make a million dollars or more, but we have a comfortable life, with a joint income of about $150K. I wonder how much we give to charity?"

Driving home from the airport, she passed a shaggy man with a battered sign that read: HUNGRY. The sign caught her attention and made her remember the broadcast she had seen at the airport. At dinner that night, Alexis recounted the news story to Bob and asked him, "You filled out our tax return last year—do you remember how much we gave to charity?"

"No, not exactly," he replied. "We give a few hundred to National Public Radio, another few hundred to the SPCA and two or three environmental groups, and about $2K to the church. We're probably not far from the $4K level of a presidential candidate, on a much smaller income. Do you want me to look it up?"

After dinner they did look it up. Alexis pointed out that while they were not sure how much if any of what they gave to the church went to persons in need rather than to pay salaries and building repairs, everything else they gave was to nonprofit groups, none of which directly served the hungry or homeless or abused. "We give money to feed and house homeless animals," she said, "but not poor people. All the causes we give to are worthy, but I wonder how well selected they are. I keep remembering that parable of Jesus (Matt. 25:45) that ends: 'Then he will say to them, "I tell you with certainty, since you didn't do it for one of the least important of these, you didn't do it for me."' We aren't doing anything to care for the hungry or sick or any needy human group."

This case could end in a variety of ways. Do you think that any of the following possibilities are better than the others? If so, why?

1. Alexis and Bob decided to talk to a group of their friends at church about starting a project that would participate in the Haiti reconstruction that was dragging on and on. They wanted to put together a crew that would fund and build houses for the still homeless, possibly in conjunction with Habitat for Humanity.

2. Alexis and Bob talked to their pastor about their concerns, who suggested that the way to be more personally involved was to volunteer their service at some local agency so that they might see what needs call out to them. "Being face-to-face with a human need makes us much more inclined to provide for that need—the suffering of others calls to us. Your service doesn't have to be every week, so long as it is regular. Every other Saturday morning, for example, at the Salvation Army soup kitchen on Price Street, would be a beginning," suggested Rev. Koscielski.

3. Alexis and Bob decided to look for a long-term service program to which they could become a regular supporter. They were also considering taking responsibility for either a specific family with unmet needs (specifically a chronically ill child) or a group home for children with HIV/AIDS, that would call on both their time and resources, as well as their hearts.

DISCUSSION QUESTIONS

1. Examine your feelings about beggars. Do you assume that they are shysters? Are you afraid to get near them?

2. If you have ever faced poverty in another culture, did it feel different to you? Why?

3. Do you agree that charity is best given anonymously? Why or why not? What difference does it make to the recipient? To the giver?

4. Do you agree with the argument that public assistance for the poor is not enough, that refusing to give personal charity erodes our capacity for empathy in the face of suffering and need? Why or why not?

5. What kinds of questions would you ask of a charity to which you were considering a donation before making a final decision? Would you consult a watchdog organization such as www.charitywatch

6. Is there really a connection between loving those close to us—our family and friends—and caring for needy strangers? What would it be?

FOR FURTHER READING

Clark, Janine A. *Islam, Charity, and Activism: Middle-Class Networks and Social Welfare in Egypt, Jordan, and Yemen.* Bloomington: Indiana University Press, 2004.

Elizondo, Virgil. *Charity.* Maryknoll, NY: Orbis, 2008.

Johnson, Kelly. *The Fear of Beggars: Stewardship and Poverty in Christian Ethics.* Grand Rapids: Eerdmans, 2007.

Lupton, Robert D. *Toxic Charity: How Churches and Charities Hurt Those They Help (And How to Reverse It).* New York: HarperCollins, 2011.

Sider, Ronald J. *Just Generosity: A New Vision for Overcoming Poverty in America.* Grand Rapids: Baker, 1999.

Smith, David H., ed. *Religious Giving: For Love of God.* Bloomington: Indiana University Press, 2010.

Weeden, Curt. *Smart Giving Is Good Business.* San Francisco: Jossey-Bass, 2011.

FILMS

Freakonomics with Levitt and Dubner. Films for the Humanities, 2006.

Bill Moyers Journal: Economic Justice for All? Films for the Humanities, 2010.

Down . . . but Not Out! A Look at Situational Poverty. Films for the Humanities, 2007.

Bill Moyers Journal: The Business of Poverty/ Facing Up to the Economy. Films for the Humanities, 2008.

Love, Hate, and Everything in Between: A Film on Empathy. Films for the Humanities, 2012.

NOTES

1. In 2011 the capital city of Jakarta banned street begging, which caused a major political controversy, given the numbers of persons dependent upon begging and the shortage of alternative forms of income.

2. Stephen E. Wessley, *Joachim of Fiore and Monastic Reform* (New York: Peter Lang, 1990).

3. John Boswell, *The Kindness of Strangers: The Abandonment of Children in Western Europe from Late Antiquity to the Renaissance* (Chicago: University of Chicago Press, 1988), 256–58.

4. David I. Kertzer, *Sacrificed for Honor: Italian Infant Abandonment and the Politics of Reproductive Control* (Boston: Beacon, 1993).

5. Ibid., 103–22.

6. This was the second to last line of T. S. Eliot's famous poem, *The Waste Land.* New York: Horace Liveright, 1922.

7. Translation by Dr. H. V. S. Shastry, Hindu Council, UK. August 25, 2007, http://www.hinducounciluk.org/newsite/circulardet.asp?rec=49.

8. Anguttara Nikaya VI: 45. Translated from Pali by Thanissaro Bhikkhu, 1998, http://www.accesstoinsight.org/tipitaka/an/an06/an06.045.than.html.

9. Irwin Unger, *The Best of Intentions: The Triumph and Failure of the Great Society under Kennedy, Johnson and Nixon* (New York: Doubleday, 1996).

10. Diana B. Henriques, *The Wizard of Lies: Bernie Madoff and the Death of Trust* (New York: Times/Henry Holt, 2011).

11. "Women Say Some Rape Victims Should Take Blame—Survey," *BBC News*, February 15, 2010, http://news.bbc.co.uk/2/hi/uk_news/8515592.stm.

12. Thomas Aquinas, *Summa Theologiae* I–II, q. 55, a. 1 (Cambridge/New York: Cambridge University Press, 2007).

GLOSSARY

Abrahamic religions. The three religions whose members understand their ancestors as descendants of Abraham: Judaism, Christianity, and Islam.

adiaphora. Things that are morally neutral in moral law, neither commanded nor forbidden.

adultery. Sexual acts or relationships by married persons with persons not their spouses; a violation of marital vows of fidelity.

Advent. For Catholics and some Protestant Christians, the four weeks preceding Christmas, understood as a time of spiritual preparation.

agnosticism. Agnosticism is the position that humans lack the necessary evidence to support either acceptance or denial of specific truth claims. The most common claims of agnosticism have to do with claims about the existence or nonexistence of [a] divine being.

ahimsa. Nonviolent practice toward all sentient or living beings. The concept originated in India, in Jainism, and was later adopted into both Hinduism and Buddhism.

All Saints' Day. November 1 in western Christianity. A holy day that celebrates all those who have attained the beatific vision (heaven). It comes a day after Halloween and the day before All Soul's Day, which commemorates the dead who have not yet attained heaven but are in purgatory.

Amish. Subgroup of Christian Mennonites begun in the late seventeenth century that practice nonresistance, separatism, and a ban on the use of modern machines/technology, and known for their distinctive, plain, and modest dress.

anencephaly. A condition that develops in the fetus at the end of the first month of pregnancy, resulting in the absence of the forebrain and skull. If born live, the fetus is permanently blind, deaf, unconscious, and unable to feel pain. The usual prognosis for those who survive to birth is death within hours to days.

Anglican Church. The churches that developed from and are in communion with the Church of England. In the United States the Anglican Church has been known as the Episcopal Church. Recently, following a schism, part of this church became the Anglican Church of the United States. The titular head of the Anglican Church is the Archbishop of Canterbury.

antibiotic resistance. Overuse of antibiotics has been linked to the emergence of antibiotic resistance when the bacteria are able to adapt to the presence of these medicines by altering their genetic makeup. The resistant bacteria can eventually multiply and become more common in the environment.

Ascension. In Christianity, the movement of the risen Jesus Christ from earth to heaven forty days after his resurrection.

asramas. Four stages in the life of a Hindu male (student, householder, retiree, renunciant) as laid out in the Manu Smriti.

Assumption. In Christianity, the movement of the deceased Mary, body and soul, from earth to heaven.

avatar. The earthly manifestation of a Hindu deity. Avatars of Vishnu are most common, but the term is not limited to Vaishnavism.

baptism. A Christian ritual signifying entrance into the church and forgiveness of original sin based on the saving actions of Jesus Christ. Some denominations practice adult baptism, but most practice infant baptism, with renewal of vows occurring on special occasions.

bestiality. Sexual activity of humans with nonhuman animals, or the desire to do so.

bhikkhu. Male monk, member of the Buddhist *sangha*, founded by Buddha himself. Monks are celibate, live in community, and obey the 227 rules of the Patimokkha. The goal of *bhikkhus* is attaining *nirvana*; monastic life is generally regarded as the swiftest and most likely path to *nirvana*.

bhikkhuni. Female monk, member of the Buddhist *sangha*. Buddha admitted *bhikkhunis* later than he founded the *bhikkhus*, after repeated appeals. *Bhikkhunis* follow additional rules (331 total vows) that subordinate them in some ways to the *bhikkhus*. Some nations have never had *bhikkhunis*, and in others, *bhikkhuni* orders died out. In the twentieth to twenty-first centuries, there are movements to restore *bhikkhuni* orders in Sri Lanka (completed), in Thailand, Indonesia, and other nations with Theravada Buddhism. *Bhikkhunis* largely survived in Mahayana traditions.

bindi (tilaka). A *bindi* is a forehead decoration worn in India, Bangladesh, Nepal, Sri Lanka, and Southeast Asia, usually by women. The most common *bindi* is a red dot, but followers of specific Hindu deities can have more elaborate *bindi*. Wearing of the *bindi* was originally common to both men and women, but now is only common for women, usually married women, though in southern India unmarried women now wear *bindi* also.

bodhisattva. In Buddhism, a *bodhisattva* is one who is motivated by great compassion to become a buddha, for the benefit of all living beings.

bracketing. Bracketing is the practice of setting aside—in philosophy and religion, of setting aside previous understandings and definitions in order to be open to all the characteristics of a new encounter, event, or thing.

Brahmachari. The student stage, or *asrama*, in Hinduism, which generally lasts for the first twenty-four years of male lives. It is also a term for celibacy in Hinduism, essentially for achieving the absence of sexual desire, which is advocated at specific times in the life of householders, and for *sannyasi*, or renunciants, in the final *asrama*.

bride price. In most traditional societies, in order for a marriage to take place, some form of wealth passed from one spouse or family to the other spouse or family. Bride price is that wealth that passes from the groom or groom's family to the bride or (more commonly) the bride's family. The usual explanation was that brides were valuable in that they were producers not only of children, but of household goods such as gardens or herds.

buddha. In Buddhism, a *buddha* is someone who has reached *nirvana* (is enlightened). Normally this is understood to be the climax of a long series of rebirths as a *bodhisattva*, during which one acquires all the moral and spiritual qualities that reach their climax in a *buddha*. These qualities are called *paramis* or *paramitas*, transcendent virtues or perfections. The original Buddha, who laid out the Middle Way for others to follow, was Siddhartha Gautama.

burka (burqa). A full body cloak worn by some Muslim women in public. A *burka* covers all parts of a woman except her eyes, and is usually black.

canon law. The body of laws and regulations made or adopted by ecclesiastical authority in Christianity. The Roman Catholic, Orthodox, and Anglican churches all have different systems of canon law.

casuistry. Determining right and wrong in questions of conduct or conscience by analyzing cases that reveal relevant general ethical rules.

Christmas. December 25, the date on which Christians celebrate the birth of Christ. The actual date of Christ's birth is not known. Christian missionaries to Europe in the early centuries of the common era began celebrating Christ's birth in late December to entice pagan tribes who were reluctant to abandon elaborate pagan celebrations of the winter solstice. Many of the solstice practices were gradually incorporated into the celebration of Christmas.

colonialism. The subjugation of one people to another. The classic case is European colonization of Asia, Africa, and the Americas militarily, politically, and economically beginning in the late fifteenth through the midtwentieth centuries.

compadrazgo. The social institution of co-parenting, in which birth parents ask a person with sociopolitical and economic resources to be the godparent of the child at baptism. A prominent institution in Catholic Mediterranean and Latin American countries, *compadrazgo* is a way of securing for a child a patron who sometimes pays school fees or arranges work.

Congregation for the Doctrine of the Faith. A Roman Catholic curial office in the Vatican that oversees matters of doctrine, including disciplining theologians and church officials.

consequentialism. (See teleological ethics.)

Conservative Jews. Less traditional than Orthodox Jews but more so than Reform Jews, Conservative Jews accept the binding nature of Jewish law but believe that it changes with new contexts and historical periods.

couvade. A custom in certain cultures in which the husband of a pregnant woman is treated as if he, too, is pregnant with the child and must obey certain taboos to ensure the welfare of the child.

covenant. A solemn agreement between two parties—a treaty—to engage in or refrain from certain specified actions. A frequent term in religion for agreements between a people and a god.

Dalits. In the Indian caste system, *dalits* are the "untouchables," persons without caste, who are at the bottom of the social status ladder; most suffer serious discrimination.

demographic transition. Demographic transition begins when a society previously at equilibrium experiences a drop in the death rate, and ends when the birthrate drops sufficiently to reestablish equilibrium with the death rate. During this period, population levels rise rapidly.

deontological ethics (rule-based ethics). Deontological ethics is a normative system of deciding what ought and ought not to be done based on duty to established rules or laws. It is most often opposed to teleological, or consequentialist, ethics.

diaspora. A movement, migration, or scattering of people away from an established homeland. Common examples are the first-century diaspora of Jews under the Romans and the sixteenth- to nineteenth-century diaspora of Africans under slavery.

Divali. Indian Festival of Lights, celebrated in South Asia by more than one religion. It is a five-day festival of family, for which houses are cleaned, new clothes are worn, and extended families visit and entertain. Rows of lights are lit outside to welcome Lakshmi, the goddess of wealth and prosperity, and firecrackers are lit to scare off demons. For Jains, Divali is the birthday of Mahāvīra.

donation. A gift. In Christianity, one form of donation was that of children by their families to monasteries and convents, with the understanding that the child would become a member of the order upon adulthood.

double burden. In North America, a term referring to the fact that even when married women have full-time jobs outside the home, they still perform the bulk of housework and childcare in the home, and hence carry a "double burden" compared to that of their husbands.

dowry. A payment, often in household or farm goods (ranging from a herd of animals to a set of bed linens, depending upon class and culture) that a bride takes with her into marriage. In some cultural religious systems the dowry is the property of the husband, in others his extended family, and in yet others it becomes part of the household goods of the couple.

Easter. Christian celebration of the resurrection of Jesus Christ from the dead following crucifixion. Understood as the highest feast of the church year.

Eid-al-Fitr. The holiday that celebrates the end of the month-long fast of Ramadan for Muslims. It is the major annual holiday with great feasts and gatherings of families and friends. (Spelled differently in some settings: e.g., *Idul Fitri* in Indonesian.)

ethical egoism. It is necessary and sufficient in ethical egoism for an action to be morally right if it maximizes one's own self-interest.

exogamy. Marriage system in which persons may only marry those from outside their clan or village.

extended family. An extended family consists either of grandparents, parents, and children, or of adult siblings and their spouses and children, or some blend of the two, usually living in a single household/compound or in close proximity.

Feast of Mary, Mother of God. Catholic holy day, celebrated on January 1, replacing the holy day of the Circumcision of Jesus.

female circumcision. This practice has at least three very different types, the most common involving removal of the clitoris. But a less mutilating form, more analogous to male circumcision, involves removal of only the clitoral hood. The most radical, mutilating, and dangerous form is genital infibulation, which involves removal of the clitoris, the labia minora, and much of the labia majora, and the tight stitching of the remaining parts of the labia majora, leaving small openings for urine and menstrual flow. Female circumcision is practiced in some parts of Africa as part of adolescent females' rite of passage, both within Islam and native African religions, though there are many national and international attempts at eradicating it.

feminism. Feminism is a movement for the equality of men and women; a person's commitment to the equal dignity and welfare of women with men.

fertility rate (total fertility rate). The fertility rate of a society is the number of children born to the average woman in that society.

fictive kinship. Custom of recognizing some persons who are not kin as if they were, as in godparents, honorary aunts and uncles, and in some cultural systems, adoption.

First Communion. Catholic celebration at which whole groups of children, usually seven to nine years old, receive Eucharist (Holy Communion) for the first time. Traditionally those making first communion wear white.

Five Daily Prayers (Islam). One of the Five Pillars of Islam is *salat*, prayer. Muslim prayer occurs five times a day for all those who have reached puberty. Prayer times are at dawn, noon, late afternoon, sunset, and before retiring.

Five Major Vows (Jainism). The five major vows of Jain monastics, adapted for laity, are those of *ahimsa* (nonviolence); *satya* (truth); *acharya* (nonstealing); *brahmacharya* (celibacy/chastity); *aparigraha* (nonattachment).

Five Moral Precepts (Buddhism). The Five Moral Precepts are prohibitions against (1) killing, (2) stealing, (3) sexual misconduct, (4) lying, and (5) taking intoxicants.

Five Pillars of Islam. The Five Pillars of Islam, required of every Muslim, are *shahadah* (profession of faith); *salat* (five daily prayers); *zakat* (alms tax); *sawm* (Ramadan fasting); and *hadj* (pilgrimage to Mecca if possible).

fornication. Negative term for sex between unmarried persons.

Genesis. First book of the Hebrew Scriptures and the Christian Old Testament.

GLBTQ. An acronym standing for gay, lesbian, bisexual, transgender, and queer. Used as an adjective.

Golden Rule. Perhaps the most basic rule of morality: Do unto others as you would have them do unto you.

Goths. Followers of a contemporary dress style for male and female youth, involving black dress, often leather, and black body adornments (nail polish, lipstick) and distinctive hairstyles (mohawks, shaved heads, scalp designs, streaked hair), often with jewelry featuring chains and crosses.

Grihasta. A householder in the second stage of the Hindu *asrama*; one who raises a family and supports them in the second stage of life following the student stage.

hadith. Accounts of the sayings and deeds of the Prophet Mohammed; the most reliable can be traced back to contemporaries of his.

hadj. The fifth of the Five Pillars of Islam, *hadj* is a pilgrimage to Mecca, which all Muslims are obliged to make at least once in their lives if they are at all able.

Hasidim. Members of Orthodox Judaism who belong to the various branches of the Hasidic movement, which developed in the eighteenth century in Eastern Europe in opposition to excessive legalism in the mainstream Judaic tradition. The Hasidic movement advocates a spirituality of joy and celebration through mysticism. Hasidic male dress is distinctive: men wear black suits and black hats (often fur hats for holy days). They discourage shaving beards and usually wear long side-curls called *peyot*.

HD. Abbreviation for high-definition television, introduced in the first decade of the twenty-first century.

hermeneutics of suspicion. Originally proposed in relation to biblical interpretation in the late nineteenth century, the term *hermeneutics of suspicion* has now been adopted as an approach not only to biblical texts, but to texts and authoritative systems of pronouncements. The meaning and authority of the text are interrogated rather than being accepted at face value.

High Holy Days. In Judaism, the ten days that begin on the first day of the Jewish month of Tishri, Rosh Hashanah, and extend through Yom Kippur, the Day of Atonement.

honor killings. The term used for the North African practice of family members killing women, understood as carriers of the family honor, who are thought to have violated modesty and chastity standards. Legal treatment of honor killings varies from nation to nation in the region.

hospitality. The practice of welcoming and entertaining guests. Enshrined in many religions as a virtue, even mandated, hospitality was one support for survival in the ancient world due to the dangers of travel. Today it continues to be a virtue, newly stressed in postmodernity as an antidote to the anonymity and potential isolation that prevail in much of society.

Immaculate Conception. The Catholic holy day celebrating the sinless conception of Mary the mother of Jesus by her parents, Anna and Joachim.

incest. Forbidden sex between close relatives. Different religious cultures define the relationships that constitute incest differently, though most forbid parent-child sexual relationships, and almost all intersibling sexual relationships (though ancient Egypt often married royal brother and sister to reduce warring over the throne). Some cultures allow marriages between cousins, while for many this would be incestuous. Similarly, some cultures prefer marriages between uncles and nieces, while in most cultures this would be incest. Regardless of the differences in the kinds of relationships that fall under incest rules, all societies view incest as a heinous moral transgression.

invincible ignorance. Ignorance that is beyond the individual's control, for which one has no responsibility, and therefore for which one cannot be held accountable.

in vitro fertilization. Common treatment for infertility when other methods of assisted reproduction have failed. It involves obtaining female ova and male semen and fertilizing the ova outside the womb, and then implanting the fertilized ova in the womb.

Jägerstätter, Franz. World War II Austrian conscientious objector whose religious conscience led to his beheading.

jilbab. In Indonesia, the headscarf worn outside the home by Muslim women to satisfy Qur'an 33:59. In Indonesia, the headscarf has been deemed sufficient to announce the virtue of Muslim women and protect them from molestation when in public.

justification by faith. The Lutheran insistence that justification (salvation) cannot be earned by good works, but comes only through developing a relationship of faith with God.

Krishna. One of the avatars of Vishnu, Krishna is perhaps the most beloved of Hindu gods, known for compassionate love of humans.

Lent. For Christians, the forty-day period before Easter during which persons prepare for the feast of the Resurrection. It is normally a period of sacrifice and repentance.

levirate marriage. Custom of the biblical Hebrews and some African groups today that when a married man dies without an heir, one of his closest male relatives take his wife in order to raise up children for the dead man. The child inherits from the dead man, and is regarded as his lineage. The union with the widow can be short term, only until the child is born, but is more often long term.

Māhavīra. The twenty-fourth Jain *tirthankara*, Māhavīra, also known as Vardham na, was the founder of many of the enduring tenets of Jainism.

masturbation. Sexual self-stimulation.

matrilineal. A society is matrilineal when it calculates lineage through the mother rather than the father, and when children inherit not from fathers, but from the brothers of their mother.

matrilocal. A society is matrilocal when a married couple lives in the village, and sometimes the extended household, of the wife's family, rather than with the family of the husband.

meat abstinence. Meat abstinence takes various forms. Sometimes it means complete abstinence from all meat products that require the death of the animal, as in Hinduism. Sometimes meat abstinence includes not only the meat itself, but the products of the meat animal, as with vegans who do not eat milk or eggs. Sometimes meat abstinence is not quotidian, but only for special days, as in Catholic meat abstinence, and in this, while the flesh of the animal is forbidden, meat juices, gravies, and flavorings are not.

menarche. The first menstrual flow in an adolescent female.

men's house. In some tribal cultures, there is a central men's house, in which adolescents and young men live until they marry. The men's house is usually in the center of the village and is the site of ceremonies. Young boys who no longer need the daily care of their mothers move to the men's house.

mikvah. In Judaism, a ritual bath required for women after menstruation and childbirth, and sometimes used by men as purification before major religious events. *Mikvahs* were historically built and maintained by Jewish communities, now often by synagogues. It is both place and personal ritual.

modesty. A virtue that involves behavior, manner, and appearance that avoid impropriety or indecency. Standards of modesty usually discourage nonessential exposure of the body. Standards of modesty are often more rigorous for, and more aimed at, women than men.

moksha. In Hinduism, release from the cycle of *samsara* (the wheel of rebirth), the final goal of life, which demands achieving the state of no-self.

nirvana. The Buddhist equivalent of *moksha*, though Buddha taught that unlike in Hinduism, *nirvana* was possible in one lifetime by following his middle way, that it did not require successive rebirths until one was reborn as a male Brahmin.

nuclear family. Family consisting of parents and their children. Can include single parent with children also, but not grandparents or grandchildren.

one-child policy. China's 1979 policy that limited couples to one child, unless they were members of racial minorities or rural dwellers, in which case two children were allowed. The policy now allows couples with no siblings to have two children. Between 1979 and 2011 it prevented the births of at least 400 million by levying fines and restricting work to those who were compliant.

open adoption. In contrast with traditional adoption policies in the United States in which the biological parents gave up all rights and contact with the child, open adoption allows for a continued relationship between a biological parent and the child in the adoptive family.

organic food movement. Organic food is food that has been raised without chemicals, antibiotics, or hormones, with a concern for both human health and the health of the soil and environment. Between the 1970s and the early twenty-first century, the organic food movement grew rapidly in North America and Europe.

Orthodox Jews. Following Jewish emancipation in Europe (c. 1848), traditional Judaism gave way to new divisions. The bulk of European Jewry, including most rabbis, did not embrace the new Reform movement, but organized as Orthodox Judaism and preserved as many of the practices of traditional Judaism as was possible in the new political situation, including dress and dietary regulations.

Passover. The Jewish spring holiday that celebrates God warning the Hebrews in Egypt to mark their homes so that the angel of death sent to kill the firstborn in all other Egyptian households would pass over their homes. This final plague convinced the Pharaoh to free the Hebrew slaves and allow their exodus from Egypt to Canaan. Passover is celebrated with a ritual *seder* meal.

patrilineal. In a patrilineal society, lineage and inheritance descend through the father's line.

patrilocal. In a patrilocal society, married couples live in the village or household of the husband's kin.

Peter the Great. Czar of Russia (1672–1725) who attempted to modernize Russia.

Pillars of Islam. The Five Pillars of Islam are *shahadah* (creed), *salat* (daily prayer), *sawm* (fasting during Ramadan), *zakat* (almsgiving), and *hadj* (pilgrimage to Mecca).

postmodernity. The period of history, generally thought to have begun between the 1960s and 1980s, marked by the shift from national to global capital, decreased power of states, digital communication, the explosion of diverse voices in the public square (racial, religious, and class), and a general hermeneutics of suspicion regarding the claims of traditional authorities.

private religion. A term that can either refer to the modern movement to shift religion from the public to the private sphere (as in separation of church and state), or to the attempt of individuals to disassociate from organized religion but still practice a faith.

pronatalism. An attitude or belief that supports raising birthrates, and encourages couples to procreate.

purdah. Practice of concealing women from unrelated men. Practiced by both Muslims and Hindus in North India, purdah is enforced by high walls around compounds, screens in the home, and female clothing that conceals virtually the entire body when in public.

Qur'an. The scripture of Islam, understood as the word of Allah as recited to the Prophet Mohammed and by him to the Muslim community, later written down.

rabbis. Literally "teachers," rabbis have been trained in the sacred texts and history of Judaism. When the Temple in Jerusalem was destroyed by the Romans in 70 CE and many of the Temple priests killed, the teachers in the Pharisaic reform movement became the new center of the Jewish community that kept the tradition alive. Since then, Judaism is known as rabbinic Judaism. While not predominantly liturgical leaders, rabbis in each congregation are the scholars, counselors, and judges.

Ramadan. The month in which Muslims fast from all food and liquid from dawn until dusk. Because Ramadan is a lunar month, it moves around the calendar and can fall in any month of modern calendars.

Rastafari dreadlocks. Dreadlocks are thick, often braided locks of uncut hair covering the head. Often identified with Rastafari members, though some Rastas do not wear dreadlocks and some non-Rastas do. Rastas believe that razor and scissors are alien and to be avoided. The Rastafari religion began in the 1930s in Jamaica among the descendants of African slaves; it centered on the worship of Haile Selassie I, king of Ethiopia, as the second coming of Jesus Christ.

reincarnation. The rebirth of a spirit/soul in a new body following death of the former body. A number of religions, including Hinduism and Buddhism, believe that all souls are recycled following death and born into other bodies. Most religions that believe in reincarnation understand it as both governed by *karma* and as opportunity to earn merit toward eventually escaping the cycle of reincarnation, which is understood as oppressive.

Reform Jews. In Europe following Jewish emancipation (an unintended result of the shift from Christian monarchies to secular republics), the Jews who spoke the vernacular and had interacted most with the Christian community desired to utilize emancipation to integrate into European society, and reformed Jewish practices to enable that integration, discarding the dietary law, dress regulations, segregation of the sexes in worship, and the use of Hebrew in worship.

Reformation. In Christianity, the sixteenth-century revolt of many areas of Europe from Roman Catholic authority. The Reform groups enacted a number of reforms in belief and practice, focusing on corruption in the Catholic Church. In the course of the Reformation, the Protestant churches separated from the Catholic Church.

religious. (noun) *Religious* is a term used for members of religious orders in Christianity; they are monks (male) and nuns (female). Monks may be either priests or brothers. Ordinarily, religious live communally, and their communities are governed by the rule adopted by their order. Most religious are Catholic or Orthodox, though there are also Anglican religious.

replacement rate. The human replacement rate in late modernity is 2.1. This is the total fertility rate that generally (given food sufficiency and adequate healthcare) results in a stable population level, neither increasing nor decreasing. (Total fertility is the number of children born to the average woman in a population.)

road-rage. Anger aimed by one "driver" at another. Road-rage is not a modern phenomenon, but is known to have existed in ancient Rome. Yet the combination of larger urban populations with vehicles, civilians with deadly arms, and the growth of traffic jams has increased the frequency of, and the violence level in, angry confrontations between drivers, and sometimes between drivers and police. Road-rage is the result.

Rosh Hashanah. The Jewish New Year, Rosh Hashanah is the first of the ten days called the High Holy Days, and is understood as the day of judgment, on which the righteous are written into the Book of Life, the wicked are blotted out, and those in the middle are given ten days until Yom Kippur, the Day of Atonement, to repent.

rumspringa. A period when Amish youth between sixteen and eighteen are to decide whether they will accept baptism as adults in the sect. During this time they are allowed some experimentation with the wider world whose ways they will permanently reject if they accept baptism, as most do.

sacrament (sacramentalism). In Christianity, a sacrament is a sign instituted by Jesus Christ to give grace to the recipient. Catholics and Orthodox have seven sacraments, but in the Reformation various Protestant groups reduced the number to at least two (Baptism and Eucharist), and in some Protestant churches there is no stress on sacramentality (grace-giving rituals).

sacred thread. In Hinduism and Buddhism, the sacred thread is bestowed on youngsters—males in Hinduism, but both sexes in Buddhism—in a rite of passage marking the beginning of the student *asrama*. Restricted in the past to members of the upper three castes among Hindus, the sacred thread ceremony inducted members into the twice-born castes, but today it is practiced more widely.

sadaqah. Voluntary charity in Islam. *Zakat* is obligatory charity often collected through taxes, while individuals decide *sadaqah* for themselves voluntarily.

samsara. The wheel of birth, death, and rebirth on which all beings exist until liberated through enlightenment (*nirvana* or *moksha*).

sangha. The Buddhist community. In some parts of Buddhism, generally Theravada, the *sangha* consists only of *bhikkhus* or *bhikkhus* and *bhikkhunis* (monks and nuns), while in Mahayana Buddhism, the Buddhist laity is also considered part of the *sangha*.

Sannyasi. In Hinduism, a *sannyasi* is a renunciant, one who, usually in the fourth and final stage of life, has left behind all family and possessions and begs for his or her food; a *sannyasi* is devoted to prayer and meditation.

secular priests. In Christian history and still today in Catholic and Orthodox traditions, a secular priest is one who is not a member of a religious order (like Jesuits, Franciscans, and Benedictines), but who was ordained specifically to work in the world, usually as a parish pastor. Secular priests work under the supervision of bishops, while religious priests live under the supervision of the head of their religious order.

secularism. Secularism can mean the exclusion of religion or religious beliefs from public space, law, or philosophy. It can also refer to dismissive attitudes toward religion in general.

secularization theory. Secularization theory exists today in several forms. Originally it maintained that modernity causes religion to be less and less important, and to gradually disappear. Later versions of secularization theory focus on the change modernity has made in religion: religion has been pushed out of the public realm and into the private realm, making it an individual matter.

serial marriage. In some, especially modern, cultures where monogamy is the rule, many people may be married to a series of persons, one at a time, with divorce ending old marriages before new ones begin.

Shabbat. For Jews, the seventh day of the week on which God rested after creating the world. Shabbat begins at sunset on Friday and ends at sunset on Saturday.

Shakers. A religious group begun by Ann Lee, which broke off from the English and American Quaker movement in the late seventeenth century. Shakers formed celibate agricultural collectives and successfully attracted new members for over two hundred years, dying out in the twentieth century.

Shakti. In Hinduism, *shakti* is the primordial cosmic energy that moves through the universe. Particularly associated with women, *shakti* is personified as the Great Mother goddess.

Shavu'ot. Jewish holy day that commemorates God's gift of the Torah, which allowed Jews to know how to keep the covenant. Also a harvest celebration.

Shemini Atzeret. Jewish holy day that occurs the day before Simchat Torah, sometimes referred to as the eighth day of the Sukkot holy day, the festival of booths.

Shiva. One of the three major gods in Hinduism, whose role in the cycle of life is destruction/death.

Shudras. The lowest of the four Hindu castes; peasants, not of the twice-born.

Simchat Torah. Jewish holy day celebrating the end of the annual Torah reading cycle.

Socially Engaged Buddhism. A late-modern movement within Buddhism to actively engage in movements for peace, justice, and environmental protection. Though a new movement, more popular in the West than the East, Socially Engaged Buddhism is based upon the traditional understanding that true enlightenment involves concern not only for one's own enlightenment, but also compassionate caring for the ultimate welfare of all.

sodomy. Anal intercourse. In the Christian Bible, often used to translate the Greek *porneia*, a term better translated as sexual "perversion."

specialization. Division into a variety of kinds of labor, or one kind of labor among many others.

street children. Children who have been abandoned to live on the streets. Street children are found among virtually all cultures and societies, though in richer societies, street children are generally older. Street children generally survive by a combination of low-paid work, theft, and begging.

Sufi. Muslim mystic. There are a number of Sufi schools/traditions.

Sukkot. Jewish festival of booths, a holy day that was originally a harvest festival.

sumptuary laws. Laws in various cultures that limited consumption and/or ostentation.

supererogatory. Actions that are above and beyond that which is required or expected.

sweat lodge. A ceremonial sauna utilized by many different cultures, including some North American native cultures, for purposes of purification, sometimes before other ceremonies.

taboo. A strong social ban on a specific activity, sometimes permanent and sometimes for temporary periods.

Talmud. Consisting of two parts, the Mishnah and the Gemara, the Jewish Talmud is a central text for Jews. It records rabbinic discussions from the early common era involving verses from the Torah, often using relevant case applications.

teleological ethics. A normative ethical theory holding that the ultimate basis for any judgment about the rightness of conduct is the consequences of the action. Thus, from a consequentialist (teleological) standpoint, morally right acts (or omissions) produce a good outcome.

temporary food taboos. Foods that are forbidden not generally, but only on special days, as in Catholic days of meat abstinence, or in special circumstances, such as pregnancy, or before certain rituals.

Ten Commandments. The ten rules given to Moses on Mount Sinai for the Hebrew people to observe as their part of the covenant with Yhwh, their god.

tilaka (See *bindi.*)

Torah. The Jewish law; the first five books of the Hebrew Scriptures originally believed to have been written by Moses.

trafficking. Illegal movement of persons across international borders for purposes of work. Trafficked persons sometimes volunteer, are sometimes coerced, but often are seduced by lies of ideal work conditions and pay and later coerced.

Umbanda. Originating in Brazil, Umbanda is a religion that blends African tribal religion, Catholicism, spiritism, and some native Brazilian lore. Basic beliefs involve a creator god, spirits of the dead who send messages to the living through mediums, and reincarnation.

umma. The Muslim community, historically understood as both a religious and political community (a state). Mohammed attempted to unify the Arabian tribes by stressing membership in the *umma* over that of the tribes.

Vanaprastha. In the third of the four stages of the Hindu *ashramas*, the Hindu becomes a "forest dweller"—one who has retreated from the world to reflect and meditate. In this stage the individual may decide to proceed to the fourth and final stage of *sannyasi*, renunciant.

vegan. The strictest form of vegetarian. A vegan does not use any animal products, including milk, eggs, fur, leather, wool, or down.

vegetarianism. The practice of not eating animals. Some vegetarians eat fish, and some do not. The strictest vegetarians (vegans) do not use any animal products.

virtue ethics. Also known as aretaic ethics, virtue ethics is focused on the character and virtue of the agent, rather than on either rules of action or material consequences.

Vishnu. Hindu god, preserver of the universe. One of the three most important Hindu gods along with Shiva (the destroyer) and Brahma (the creator).

women's movement. The modern movement of women for equal dignity, participation, and welfare that began in the West in the midnineteenth century and has spread over the world, its goals now enshrined in international law.

Yom Kippur. Jewish Day of Atonement, the holiest day of the year, on which Jews practice repentance and atonement.

zakat. One of the Five Pillars of Islam, *zakat* is charity. In Muslim nations, *zakat* is often collected in the form of taxes that are used for the poor.

INDEX